The Kibbutz

The Kibbutz

Awakening from Utopia

DANIEL GAVRON

ROWMAN & LITTLEFIELD PUBLISHERS, INC.
Lanham • Boulder • New York • Oxford

ROWMAN & LITTLEFIELD PUBLISHERS, INC.

Published in the United States of America
by Rowman & Littlefield Publishers, Inc.
4720 Boston Way, Lanham, Maryland 20706
http://www.rowmanlittlefield.com

12 Hid's Copse Road
Cumnor Hill, Oxford OX2 9JJ, England

British Library Cataloguing in Publication Information Available

Library of Congress Cataloging-in-Publication Data

Gavron, Daniel.
  The kibbutz : awakening from Utopia / Daniel Gavron.
    p. cm.
  Includes index.
  ISBN 0-8476-9526-3 (alk. paper)
  1. Kibbutzim. 2. Kibbutzim—History. I. Title.

HX742.2.A3 G39 2000
307.77′6′09—dc21

99-058411

Printed in the United States of America

♾ ™ The paper used in this publication meets the minimum requirements of American
National Standard for Information Sciences—Permanence of Paper for Printed Library
Materials, ANSI/NISO Z39.48–1992.

For the kibbutznik, of whom too much was always expected.

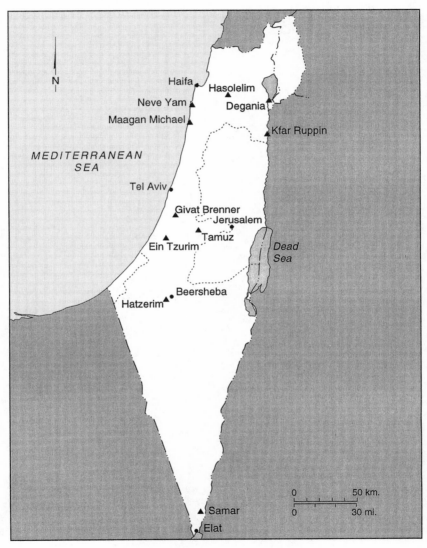

Haifa
Hasolelim
Neve Yam
Degania
Maagan Michael
Kfar Ruppin

MEDITERRANEAN
SEA

Tel Aviv
Givat Brenner
Jerusalem
Tamuz
Ein Tzurim
Dead
Sea
Beersheba
Hatzerim

Samar
Elat

50 km.
0   30 mi.

▲ = kibbutz   ● = town

CONTENTS

Foreword   *Howard Fast*   *ix*

Acknowledgments   *xi*

Chronology   *xiii*

Introduction: Uncertain Future   *1*

PART I. WHAT HAPPENED?

  1 Degania: Starting Out   *15*

  2 Givat Brenner: Flagship in Stormy Seas   *43*

  3 Hasolelim: Repairs in Midflight   *89*

  4 Neve Yam: Surviving Collapse   *107*

  5 Hatzerim: Proving It Can Work   *119*

PART II. WHAT WENT WRONG?

  6 The Collapse of 1985   *143*

  7 The Limits of Education   *159*

PART III. FACES OF THE FUTURE

  8 Maagan Michael: Divorce Settlement   *191*

  9 Kfar Ruppin: Capitalist Kibbutz   *209*

  10 Ein Tzurim: No Immunity   *229*

  11 Tamuz: Urban Commune   *245*

  12 Samar: Touching Utopia   *259*

Conclusion   *275*

Glossary	*285*
Selected Bibliography	*287*
Index	*289*
About the Author	*295*

FOREWORD

Howard Fast

I read Daniel Gavron's book with great pleasure—and always with the feeling that I was reading an important historical study of my time, a book that will be read and reread for years to come. I know of no book that equals it as a study of the kibbutz movement. I spent a month in Israel some years ago, part of the time at Kibbutz Kinneret; reading Gavron's book focused my memories. Thus, I can make some observations of my own about the kibbutz movement—at least sufficient to whet your mind for what follows.

Of all the sociological experiments of the twentieth century, I consider the kibbutz movement in Israel the most important and believe that some day it will become the way of life for a goodly part of the human race. At this moment of outrageous consumption and greed in the wealthiest sections of the earth, and hunger, misery, and poverty in the poorer sections, the kibbutz way of life appears as a dream; and I'm afraid that it will remain a dream for many years to come. Gavron sets before us the coincidental set of circumstances that brought it into being, the Zionist passion, the cruel anti-Semitism of nineteenth- and twentieth-century Europe, the two world wars, and of course the Holocaust. That, together with the tribal sense of Judaism and the desperation, wit, and inventiveness of the Jews, combined at an instant in history to create the boldest experiment in communal and collective living and creativity that the world had seen. This must never be underestimated. There had been many attempts at such efforts before, but never with the scope, ideological commitment, and success that marked the kibbutz movement.

Gavron's analysis of this movement and his intimate investigation of selected kibbutzim is a worthy journalistic and historical achievement. He does not idealize or spare the failures or lessen the difficulties.

The kibbutzim are part of the world, islands in the ruthless capitalistic culture—in Israel as elsewhere.

Gavron shows how the very economic success of Israel created a technology that undermined the kibbutz and describes the desperate struggle of the kibbutz to exist within that world of superior technology. He raises the question of whether the kibbutz can continue in the new society that is modern Israel, and he delves into the problems that the kibbutzim face.

As I write this, in December of 1999, I live in a world where the worship of greed and money has reached heights I never knew in eighty-five years of living. Gavron's history of the kibbutz movement over the past century comes as a breath of clean fresh air, a hope and dream for the future of mankind. No student of Israel should be without this book. It is inspiring and quite wonderful.

ACKNOWLEDGMENTS

I would like to thank the more than a hundred kibbutz members, former members, scholars, consultants, and others who generously gave me their confidence, time, and expertise. Most of them are directly quoted, but those who are not mentioned also contributed to the writing of this book.

Three good friends deserve my particular gratitude for reading my manuscript, correcting my mistakes, and making valuable comments. They must not be blamed for any remaining errors, nor must they be in any way associated with my opinions or conclusions: Yaacov Oved of Kibbutz Palmahim, professor of history at Tel Aviv University and Yad Tabenkin and author of *Two Hundred Years of American Communes* and many other studies of communal life, who supported and encouraged me throughout the project; Zeev Hirsh, formerly a member of Kibbutz Maagan Michael, later professor of International Business at Tel Aviv University, and currently head of the MBA program at the Rishon Lezion College of Management, who gave me the benefit of his considerable knowledge, particularly (but not exclusively) with regard to economic matters; and Colin Primost, general manager of Kibbutz Kfar Hanassi, who is directly involved in carrying out the current process of change in his community and whose friendship, wisdom, and insight have been important to me for nearly half a century.

The core of the book is based on interviews with kibbutz members and others, conducted in the years 1998–1999 in kibbutz homes, gardens, dining halls, and offices. Except in those few cases in which the interviewees were native English speakers, the interviews were in Hebrew and later transcribed by me into English. All the interviews took the form of informal, unstructured conversations, starting with the interviewees' personal history, moving on to their experiences at the kibbutz, the general history of their kibbutzim, and finally their attitudes to the current changes and the role they were playing (or not playing) in the process.

Although these conversations are the main source for what I have written here, brief membership of a kibbutz, followed by forty years of close contact with kibbutz members all over Israel, have also made their contribution. At the same time, dozens of books, journals, and other documents (many of them from kibbutz archives) have contributed to my understanding of the subject. Specifically, I would like to thank the archivists of Degania, Givat Brenner, Hasolelim, Neve Yam, Hatzerim, Kfar Ruppin, and Yad Tabenkin for their assistance.

CHRONOLOGY

1870   Establishment of Mikveh Yisrael, first Jewish Agricultural School in Palestine.

1880   Start of huge Jewish migration from Russia and Eastern Europe, mostly to the United States.

1882   Start of first *aliya* (immigration) of Jews to Palestine.
First three modern Jewish villages established in coastal plan and Galilee.

1896   *The Jewish State* published by Theodor Herzl.

1897   Herzl convenes first Zionist Congress in Basel, Switzerland; establishes Zionist Organization.

1898   Herzl meets Kaiser Wilhelm II of Germany in Jerusalem.

1904   Start of second *aliya* (immigration) of Jewish pioneers to Palestine.

1909   Establishment of *Hashomer,* Jewish guards for new settlements, organized in mobile communes.

1910   Degania, first *kvutza* (permanent commune) established.

1914   World War I starts.

1917   Bolsheviks seize power in Russia.
Balfour Declaration issued by Britain.
British Army conquers Palestine from Ottoman Turks.

1918   World War I ends.

1920   League of Nations founded in Paris.
Labor Battalion established.
Start of Third *Aliya* (immigration) of pioneering socialist Jews.
First severe Arab attacks against Jews in Jerusalem.
Histadrut Labor Federation established.
Hagana Jewish defense force established.

1921   Britain awarded mandate for Palestine by League of Nations.
Ein Harod, first large kibbutz, established.

1923   Members of Our Community establish Beit Alpha.

1926   Kibbutz Artzi, federation of left-wing kibbutzim, established.
1927   Kibbutz Meuhad, federation of large kibbutzim, established.
1928   Givat Brenner established.
1929   Arab attacks on Jews throughout Palestine.
1933   Adolf Hitler becomes German chancellor.
       First Nazi concentration camps established in Germany.
       Increased Jewish immigration from Germany and Eastern
       Europe.
       Hever Hakvutzot, federation of small kibbutzim, established.
1934   Kibbutz Dati, federation of religious kibbutzim, founded.
1936   Arab general strike.
       British Royal Commission, headed by Lord Peel, visits
       Palestine.
1937   Arab revolt against the British administration and the Zionist
       enterprise.
       Peel Commission recommends partition of Palestine between
       Jews and Arabs.
       Jewish field squads mobilized to counter Arab attacks.
1938   Kfar Ruppin established.
       Kristallnacht anti-Jewish pogrom in Germany.
1939   Start of World War II.
       Germany invades Poland: anti-Jewish persecution escalates.
       British White Paper limits Jewish immigration to Palestine.
       Jews (many of them kibbutz members) organize "illegal"
       immigration.
       Neve Yam established.
1940   Jews of countries occupied by German Forces sent to
       concentration camps.
1941   Establishment of Palmah striking force of Hagana, based in
       the kibbutzim.
1942   Wannsee Conference in Germany discusses "Final Solution"
       of Jewish problem,
1943   First reports of Holocaust, mass murder of European Jews,
       reach the West.
1945   End of World War II.
       Dimensions of Holocaust become generally known.
1946   Hatzerim established.
       Ein Tzurim established in Hebron hills.
1947   United Nations votes to partition Palestine: Jewish-Arab
       clashes escalate.

1948   British Mandate ends.
State of Israel declared: war with Palestinian Arabs.
Attempted invasion by armies of five Arab states.
Borders of new state determined and defended largely by the kibbutzim.
Ein Tzurim surrenders; members imprisoned in Transjordan.
Start of mass immigration that doubles Jewish population in four years.

1949   Israel and Arab states sign armistice accords.
Maagan Michael and Hasolelim established; Ein Tzurim reestablished.

1951   Split in Kibbutz Meuhad; minority joins Hever Hakvutzot to form Ihud Hakibbutzim Vehakvutzot, the Ihud.

1952   German restitution payments to victims of Nazi crimes bring large sums of private money into many kibbutzim.

1956   Sinai Campaign: Israel takes Sinai Peninsula from Egypt.

1957   Israel forced to withdraw from Sinai.

1960s   Industries established in most kibbutzim.

1967   Six Day War: Israel takes West Bank, Golan, Gaza, and Sinai.

1970s   Kibbutz children start sleeping in parental homes instead of children's houses.
Kibbutz schools exempted from government integration program.

1976   Samar established.

1977   Likud government elected in Israel, the first not led by the Labor Movement.

1979   Israeli-Egyptian peace treaty.

1980   Kibbutz Meuhad and the Ihud unite in the United Kibbutz Movement (UKM).

1982   Israel completes evacuation of Sinai; invades Lebanon.

1984   National Unity Government formed in Israel.

1985   Inflation in Israel tops 400 percent: Israel Government introduces emergency economic plan.
Debt crisis rocks the kibbutzim.

1986   Ravid Plan for recovery of Israeli agricultural sector presented.
Yehuda Harel publishes series of articles in weekly journal *Kibbutz* on the need for radical change in the kibbutz system.

1987   Ravid Plan torpedoed in Knesset (parliamentary) Finance Committee.

Kibbutz Beit Oren abandoned by younger members; taken over by new group.

Tamuz established.

1988   Collective kibbutz debt escalates to between $5 and $6 billion.

1989   Kibbutz Arrangement (debt settlement and recovery plan) agreed with government and banks.

1993   Kibbutz Ein Zivan introduces differential incomes; threatened with expulsion from UKM; *The New Kibbutz* published by Yehuda Harel.

1996   Supplementary Kibbutz Arrangement signed.

1997   Some 20 percent of kibbutzim introduce various forms of differential incomes.

1998   Process of change gathers pace in the kibbutzim.

1999   Amendment to Supplementary Kibbutz Arrangement signed. Kfar Ruppin becomes Israel's first capitalist kibbutz, allocating shares in its assets to its members.

Founding convention of the "Communal Trend," association of kibbutzim aiming to preserve traditional values.

UKM and Kibbutzim Artzi agree to unite in one movement.

INTRODUCTION
UNCERTAIN FUTURE

The Israeli kibbutz movement is in a state of turmoil. The dream that began in the first decade of the twentieth century, with the establishment of the first kibbutz on the banks of the River Jordan, is disintegrating, and the dreamers are waking up to a harsh reality. The world's most successful commune movement is in disarray, with less than half of its 120,000 members believing that the kibbutz has a future. The vision of a new human being, a just society, a better world, as proclaimed by the prophets of Israel, has gone the way of previous utopian visions. Human nature has triumphed over idealism; ambition has proved stronger than altruism; individuality has vanquished communal responsibility.

Of course, "the end of the kibbutz" has been forecast with confident regularity since the earliest days of the communes in Palestine. The first time that a kibbutz member made a cup of coffee in his private room instead of drinking with his comrades in the communal dining hall, he was accused of destroying the communal way of life. Similar portentous pronouncements greeted every move toward a more private life for the individual kibbutz member. Personal showers and lavatories, private radio sets, meals taken in the family circle, children sleeping in the parental home, and even the replacing of benches in the dining hall with "individual" chairs—all these were seen at various times as the final betrayal.

It was the success of the kibbutz movement that it defied these gloomy predictions and managed to reinvent itself several times in the nine decades of its existence as a voluntary democratic society, based on common ownership, collective responsibility, and a genuine degree of equality. Having made this point, it has to be said that this time it may be different: the kibbutz is facing its most serious challenge to date, and there is no guarantee that it will survive.

The 267 kibbutzim in Israel vary in size from less than a hundred members to over a thousand. They are situated all over the country from

Galilee in the north to the southern Negev desert. Most of them are within the boundaries of the State of Israel, but some exist in the occupied territories. They are religious and secular, atheist and agnostic, Marxist, liberal, and social democratic. They are populated by immigrants and native-born Israelis, people of European origin, Americans, and those who hail from Asia and Africa. The youngest inhabitants are newborn babies; the oldest, great-grandparents. There are rich kibbutzim and poor kibbutzim. Some are still based on farming, many have tourism and recreational facilities, most have some sort of factory, and a few boast sophisticated high-tech industries. Nevertheless, despite the differences, until the early 1990s it was still true to say that all kibbutzim were essentially the same.

Until then, every kibbutz espoused the principle "from each according to his ability, to each according to his needs." Every kibbutz was governed by decisions of the general meeting of the entire membership, which took place every week or every two weeks. The general meeting elected a secretariat, with a secretary, treasurer, work organizer, farm manager, and other officials, who held office for two or three years. It also elected a number of committees for planning, work, housing, security, education, culture, vacations, and personal problems. The officials ran the kibbutz on a day-to-day basis. Longer-term problems were worked out in the committees, and decisions were brought to the general meeting for approval.

The kibbutz belonged to all its members, and each member was personally responsible to the collective. The community, its services, and the productive branches made up a single unit. All members were entitled to housing, furniture, food, clothing, medical services, cultural activities, and education for their children. In return, they were expected to work in the kibbutz at the task assigned to them by the work organizer.

Every kibbutz had a communal dining hall, cultural center, library, offices, and children's houses. Most kibbutzim had basketball courts and swimming pools. A number possessed tennis courts, concert halls, and ball fields. The buildings were always set in beautifully landscaped public gardens, and the living area was traffic-free. The workshops, garages, and factories (if they had them) were positioned to the side.

Although anyone familiar with a kibbutz can still arrive at one and quickly find his or her way around, today's uniformity is superficial. Until recently, one could say that every kibbutz was basically the same. In the past few years kibbutzim have become increasingly different.

This upheaval is deeply disturbing for a majority of kibbutz members. For, although it started out as a revolutionary society aiming to change traditional ways of life and to create new human relationships, the kibbutz became in the ninety years of its existence an extremely conservative society. Radically different from the surrounding society, it was nevertheless set in its ways, conventions, and basic assumptions. Life was an almost iron-clad routine. Kibbutz members, more than almost any other people on the planet, knew what they were going to do when they got up in the morning, how they would spend their afternoons and evenings, and how they would observe Friday night and the Sabbath. They knew how their kibbutz would celebrate the Jewish festivals throughout the year: the tradition of Passover, the joy of Independence Day, the solemnity of Memorial Day, the fun of a class bar mitzvah, and the self-conscious drollery of a kibbutz wedding.

Above all the members knew that, whatever its faults, the kibbutz system worked. They could also be confident that their families were secure and that, provided they abided by the rules, the kibbutz would always look after their welfare.

This is no longer the case: the identity between the kibbutz and its members has been fractured. Individual kibbutz members, used to relying on their community, are becoming increasingly responsible for their own future, and in many cases they are ill equipped for the task. The fact that tens of thousands of people who have devoted their lives to a cause are now facing an entirely new situation makes this a moving human story. Some will see it as tragic, others as inevitable; everyone has something to learn from it.

What has happened, how it happened, and what the future probably holds are the subjects of this book. In this brief introduction my purpose is to review the history, set the scene, and report on general current developments.

Since the dawn of history, people have aspired to improve their societies. The "Sun State" of Spartacus and the Essene community in the ancient world, the medieval Hutterite communities in Transylvania, and the mostly Christian eighteenth- and nineteenth-century communes in America have been succeeded in our time by alternative societies and communes in Europe and the United States. What has made the kibbutz movement unique is its size and its centrality to the national life of the Jewish community in Palestine and then of Israel. Where other communes rejected society and retreated from it, the kibbutz embraced society and sought to lead it. The symbiosis between the kibbutz and the surrounding community is what gave it its strength and influence; it also contained the seeds of its destruction. As a vital, organic part of the community, it was not immune from its diseases. It strongly influenced society, but it was influenced in its turn.

For the first forty years of its existence, from 1910 to about 1950, the kibbutz was respected as an institution and in some measure set the national tone. In addition to being an experimental society, the kibbutz was a vital tool in the implementation of the Zionist dream. It not only settled Jews in Palestine and restored the country's agriculture, but it also aimed to transform the social structure of the Jewish people and to revive Judaism as a way of life rooted in the soil. At its zenith, the kibbutz was home to about 7 percent of the Israeli population; most of the time it was nearer 3 percent, but those 3 percent played a role in the nation's life out of all proportion to their numbers.

The kibbutz always saw itself as a synthesis of Zionism and socialism, but as the political clash between Jews and Arabs in Palestine escalated in the 1920s and 1930s, the Zionist task of the kibbutz tended to overshadow its role as a social experiment. With its tight communal framework, the kibbutz was ideal for establishing settlements. The kibbutz movement embarked on a period of establishing "tower and stockade" settlements. The new kibbutzim were subject to determined Arab attacks. They were therefore secretly mobilized and established in a single day, during which a perimeter fence and a watchtower with a searchlight were constructed. The Arab attacks usually came at nighttime during the first weeks and in most cases were successfully repulsed.

In the late 1930s, the ambivalent relationship between the kibbutzim and the Arabs of Palestine, which had always existed, became more extreme. On the one hand, the kibbutznik pioneers were socialists, devoted to the ideals of human fellowship and equality, who saw the Arabs as fellow workers. At the same time, they were the vanguard of Zionist colonization, settling on land where Arabs had been living. The land farmed by the Arabs was often owned by citizens of Damascus or Beirut, and the Jews bought it legally, but the Arab peasants who were turned off their land naturally smarted from the injustice. There were examples of coexistence, but there were also frequent clashes. This ambivalence continues in Israel today, with kibbutzim supplying both much of the manpower for the army's best combat units and many of the nation's leading peace activists.

When the United Nations voted in 1947 to partition Palestine between the Jews and the Arabs, it was largely the geographic positions of the various kibbutzim that determined the borders of the Jewish state, and the settlements played a notable part in defending those borders when war broke out. By the time of the establishment of the State of Israel in 1948, the kibbutz movement held a unique position of prestige, providing many of the nation's best military commanders, as well as a third of its government and 26 of the 120 members of its parliament, the Knesset.

As new immigrants poured into the country, both survivors of the Nazi Holocaust from Europe and immigrants from the Arab and Muslim nations of the Middle East, the kibbutzim faced a renewed challenge to their social aspirations. The new immigrants were not attracted to communal life; less than 4 percent of this immigration joined kibbutzim. However, the government located them in transition camps, moshav cooperative farms, and new towns in the vicinity of the kibbutzim. The newcomers were desperate for work, just when the kibbutzim needed manpower for their expanding agriculture. David Ben-Gurion, Israel's first prime minister, demanded that the kibbutzim give employment to the new immigrants. A number of kibbutzim resisted the idea of "exploiting" outside labor and creating a "master-servant" relationship, but the majority bowed to the national imperative. The result was beneficial both to the immigrants, who found employment, and to the kibbutzim, which solidified their economic base and increased their standard of living, but the ideological wall was breached and the seeds of future resentments were sown.

Over the next decade, a large population of new immigrants increasingly resented the kibbutzim and regarded their members as hypocrites and snobs. "We are welcome in the kibbutz fields but not in its swimming pool," they said. "We are welcome in their factories, but our children are not welcome in their schools." There was a strong element of truth in their accusations. Most kibbutzim prospered in the 1950s, but their reputation declined.

Two other developments in those years failed to improve the situation. The largest kibbutz movement, Kibbutz Meuhad, broke up over the issue of support for Marxist socialism. This ideological quarrel, which had no practical relevance to the way the kibbutzim were run—although it did affect the schools and youth movements—split dozens of kibbutzim asunder. Members who had labored together for decades were not on speaking terms, veterans were uprooted from their homes, school classes were divided along political lines, and in some cases violence even erupted, necessitating police intervention. Many kibbutzim were damaged by splits and almost destroyed. As most of the Israeli population failed to understand the reasons for the bitter quarrel, the reputation of the kibbutz suffered further damage.

᾽   The second occurrence was the receipt of German reparations for victims of the Nazis. This fueled significant development in some kibbutzim. At the same time, though, large amounts of private money were brought into the kibbutzim for the first time, causing potential problems of inequality. On the whole, humane solutions were found, but some newly wealthy members left, and dangerous precedents were set.

In the 1960s, Israel experienced a spurt of industrial development. The public sector of the economy, dominated by the Histadrut Labor Federation and its economic organizations, played an important role, and the private sector of the economy expanded considerably. Kibbutz Meuhad, the largest movement, had always favored the development of industry alongside farming, but by the end of World War II there were only fifteen kibbutz factories. In the 1960s, the kibbutzim found themselves falling behind the rest of the country economically, while the increased efficiency of their farming freed manpower for other purposes. Consequently, they resolved to participate in the industrialization process.

Although they had some excess manpower, it was not sufficient for staffing the newly established factories, which necessitated increased employment of outside labor. By now, though, ideology was declining and hiring workers met with less resistance. Although the kibbutzim were continuing to maintain their way of life and even to attract new members, it was increasingly the quality of life that appealed, rather than ideological conviction. In a way it was a vindication of the communal idea, a proof that the system worked. But the spark had been lost, particularly among the young generation: conformism rather than conviction became the quality required of the average kibbutz member.

Increasing numbers of those born and raised in kibbutzim started to have doubts. Almost all kibbutz children took a long trip abroad after their military service, and some of them did not come back. There had always been those who rejected the kibbutz framework for life in the towns, but now increasing numbers, including the kibbutz born, were leaving, and many were abandoning the country altogether.

Together with this, the status of the kibbutz in Israeli society suffered a further decline. New elites became national role models. After the Six Day War of 1967, the army gained in importance and prestige, and as new universities were established and the economy developed, the academic and business worlds became increasingly admired. The leadership role of the kibbutz declined, and the self-confidence of the kibbutz members was seriously eroded.

There was an awareness of the need for change, and changes were indeed implemented, such as the "privatization" of allowances. Privatization in the kibbutz does not mean the same as privatization in a Western economy. There is no selling of public assets to private owners. What it means is the transfer of a number of items from communal to private responsibility. Instead of the community allocating clothing, furniture, home equipment, cultural activities, and vacation and travel expenses, all these things were lumped together in a personal cash allowance, which members could spend any way they wanted. The purists saw this as an infringement of equality according to need; the reformers said that members were gaining personal freedom and autonomy at the expense of the traditional concept of equality; most kibbutz members saw it as simple common sense. Over the years, more and more items were transferred from the communal budget to private allowances.

A more revolutionary decision that occurred during the 1970s was to permit kibbutz children to sleep in their parents' homes. The children's houses of the kibbutzim were for many years regarded as embodying a cardinal principle of kibbutz life. Trained child care supervisors were far more suitable than parents to bring up children, it was postulated. The children were said to be liberated from the "traditional, bourgeois, authoritarian family," to grow up free and equal in a "Society of Children." In fact, every kibbutz member was well aware that the system was seriously flawed. For the most part, it was the children who themselves grew up in children's houses who demanded the change.

Despite the dire predictions of the kibbutz purists, these changes did not destroy the kibbutz as an institution. They probably strengthened it, but they did not address a very basic problem of which most kibbutz members were unaware: the fact that a majority of kibbutzim were living beyond their means and were borrowing to make up the difference. Bringing the children home, which necessitated considerable investment in enlarging kibbutz homes, contributed to the spending spree. At a time of escalating inflation, unlinked (or partially linked) loans were easy to pay back. Although the kibbutzim were not the only institutions in Israel taking advantage of the situation, they certainly joined in. However, when in 1985 inflation reached an annual rate of over 400 percent, the government of Israel was forced to take action to curb it. The remedy was drastic: a sharp devaluation of the currency, the freezing of wages and prices, the maintenance of high interest rates. All over the country businesses went bankrupt. The kibbutzim found themselves with a collective debt that quickly escalated to between $5 and $6 billion. It was a debt that they could not possibly repay.

In time, the kibbutzim, the banks, and the government worked out a recovery program. Some of the debt was written off, some was rescheduled, but the subsequent painful cut in living standards was accompanied by a crippling loss of self-confidence. The number of people leaving kibbutzim, estimated at around four hundred a year before 1985, increased to more than a thousand annually. The overall kibbutz population, which had been on a steady growth curve since 1910, started to decline. Many of those who remained, particularly among the younger generation, started to question the basic principles by which they had always lived.

That the kibbutzim were living beyond their means was an acknowledged fact, but there were also several endemic weaknesses in communal life, one of which was wastage. Food was "free," so members took more than they needed. Huge quantities were thrown away, and expensive items were fed to domestic animals. Electricity was paid for by the collective, so members left their air conditioners on all day in the summer and their heaters on all day in winter.

This wastage was reduced by extending the "privatization" of allowances. Meters were installed, and members paid for electricity consumption out of their (enlarged) personal allowances. With food, the problem was more difficult, because it touched on the communal dining hall, one of the central institutions of kibbutz life. Even here, though, most kibbutz members went along. One kibbutz closed down its dining hall altogether; many others converted their dining halls into "restaurants" in which members paid for their meals. Some were closed in the evenings and on weekends. Although a historical communal institution was downgraded, significant savings were achieved, and the principle of equality was not really harmed.

The "Beit Oren Affair" of 1987 increased the sense of crisis in the movement. Beit Oren, a kibbutz founded in 1939 on Mount Carmel, had never been economically successful. Deeply in debt and refused further credit by the banks, the kibbutz faced the prospect of collapse. A majority of the younger members abandoned the kibbutz, leaving some twenty-five founding members on their own. The United Kibbutz Movement, which by now lacked the resources to provide the necessary economic assistance, undertook to assist the veterans on an individual basis. In due course, Beit Oren was taken over by a group of members from other kibbutzim, who wanted to try out some new ideas that were being discussed. Most of the veterans remained; some were relocated in other kibbutzim; others ended up in old age homes. One bitter old-timer compared his status to that of "an Eskimo elder abandoned on the ice."

The events at Beit Oren still constitute a searing trauma for all kibbutz members. Until then, it had never occurred to kibbutzniks that they could be abandoned in old age. The debt crisis had already planted serious doubts about the viability of the communal way of life in the minds of many kibbutz members. What happened at Beit Oren only served to increase those doubts. Questions began to be asked that for the first time challenged the basic kibbutz principles of communal partnership and equality.

From the earliest days of the kibbutzim, it was recognized that some members worked harder than others. Every kibbutz had a core of leaders who rotated the main tasks among themselves; every kibbutz had its "parasites," who did not contribute their full efforts to the community. The problem was traditionally solved by the pressure of public opinion. A famous story about the early days of Degania, the first kibbutz, told how a new member joined the plowing team and took a break every few hours for a smoke. "Nothing was said," recalled a veteran, "but the atmosphere was such that, at the end of the day's work, the newcomer left us and never returned." The other side of the coin was public approbation: the kibbutz secretary, treasurer, and farm manager enjoyed the esteem and prestige (and power) of their positions, and this benefit was sufficient compensation.

However, for many years it had not been enough, and now the members faced the unthinkable question: should there not be some relationship between effort and reward? This was indeed a blow against the very essence of the kibbutz. No less fundamental was the charge that the celebrated system of kibbutz education was basically flawed. In the 1960s, studies by outsiders had sharply criticized the system of kibbutz education, and their strictures were now partly confirmed by local studies, including those carried out by kibbutz members themselves.

This thesis did not go unchallenged, and the criticism of kibbutz education appeared to be overly severe. The kibbutzim continue to produce constructive, highly motivated, law-abiding young people. They volunteer for national service in addition to their military service and continue to supply a remarkable proportion of volunteers for the elite army units. The critics retorted that kibbutz education had failed to pass on kibbutz values, or even Zionist values. They pointed out that it was not only the elite army units that contained a disproportionate number of kibbutz born but also the Israeli emigrant community of Los Angeles.

The questions were coming thick and fast, but it took a little time before some members started coming up with answers. One group started to discuss the idea of separating the kibbutz economy from the community. The idea was developed further in *The New Kibbutz,* published by Yehuda Harel of Kibbutz Merom Gollan in 1993. Harel asserted that the kibbutz had failed to adapt to the reality of the modern era. All over the world socialism had failed in production, he argued, whereas capitalism had failed in distribution. He suggested a model for capitalist production combined with socialist distribution.

The factories and farming branches of the kibbutz should be organized to make a profit, with boards of directors exercising economic control, proper accounting procedures, professional managers, and payment according to expertise and effort. The wealth thus acquired should be distributed according to kibbutz principles, but with the emphasis on autonomy and independence at the expense of the traditional concept of equality. Another aspect of the "new" kibbutz was the transfer of responsibility for work from the community to the individual. Kibbutz members would be free to seek their own employment, either in the kibbutz or outside it. The kibbutz would recruit suitable outsiders to do anything from managing the kibbutz factory to cooking in the dining hall or caring for the children.

Harel's ideas sparked off a huge debate. There were those who admitted his point about the need to adapt to the modern world but urged new communal concepts and forms. They called for a "renewed" kibbutz rather than a "new" one. Meanwhile, most kibbutzim instituted serious discussions, and a number began introducing changes. For the most part, the movement for change began cautiously, but it has recently gathered pace. Harel's new kibbutz, which seemed so revolutionary when he proposed it, seems almost conservative today in the light of what is happening.

A majority of kibbutzim are engaged in carrying out basic changes in their traditional social frameworks. An ongoing survey conducted by

Haifa University's Institute for the Research of the Kibbutz and the Cooperative Idea shows that over 70 percent of kibbutz factories and 40 percent of their agricultural branches are now run by boards of directors. Forty percent of kibbutzim have taken on private partners for their factories, and no less than 60 percent have hired top managers to run their businesses. Half have turned their branches into "profit centers."

Seventy-four percent of kibbutz members now pay for their own electricity, and 60 percent pay for their dining hall meals. In a radical social change, almost 60 percent of dining halls have stopped serving evening meals, and nearly 30 percent now do not offer breakfast. Seventy-five percent of kibbutzim now have pension plans for their members. Three-quarters of the kibbutzim are encouraging their members to work outside the kibbutz, and they often have to be replaced by outsiders.

Although fundamental changes are proceeding more slowly, a serious erosion of the egalitarian principle is taking place. Almost a third of the kibbutzim now have some sort of differential in their members' incomes, although only 6 percent are actually paying salaries. In half of the country's kibbutzim the members are now permitted to purchase private cars, and a third allow members to extend their rooms at their own expense. About half charge their members for recreational activities that used to be "free." The distribution of shares of the kibbutz assets to the members has been widely discussed, but so far it has been implemented in only one kibbutz.

That, in general terms, is where the kibbutz stands today. To illustrate the changes more fully and to demonstrate how they affect the individual members, we will now focus on a number of specific kibbutzim. Other chapters will take a closer look at the financial crisis of 1985 and at the kibbutz educational system that largely failed to pass on communal and egalitarian values.

Let us begin, then, where the kibbutz saga itself began—with Degania, the first kibbutz.

PART I

WHAT HAPPENED?

1

דגניה

DEGANIA
STARTING OUT

Descending from the hills of Lower Galilee to the shores of Lake Kinneret is an exercise in time travel. The narrow road winds down through a lush green countryside to the azure lake, past villages established by the early pioneers and red-roofed houses, most of them plastered cream, but with an occasional building of the local black basalt rock. There are horses here and donkeys, cows, and poultry. The wells, no longer in use, are still walled round and covered with small tiled roofs. Old plows and harrows rust in quiet courtyards. The birds sing; the bees hum; the old men sit in the shade, talking quietly, or just sitting.

Known in the New Testament as the Sea of Galilee, its Hebrew name, Kinneret, comes from *kinor* (harp or lyre), because the lapping of its water is said to sound as sweet as the music of those instruments. To the east and south, the hills of Golan and Gilad are pale mauve in the afternoon sun, their valleys and canyons etched in charcoal gray. Around the lake the tall eucalyptus cast their shade. Farther back are citrus orchards, fields of pale green peppers, and avocado plantations, their leaves a dark shiny green.

Degania is situated on the east bank of the River Jordan, where it emerges from the Kinneret. At the entrance is a sign in English and Hebrew: "Degania, the First Kibbutz." Inside the gate, the description is in Hebrew: "The Mother of the Kvutzot." Rightly, the members of Degania do not want to confuse the visiting tourists by using the less-known term in English; but, in fact, Degania was and remains a *kvutza* rather than a kibbutz, a small, intimate commune, albeit considerably

Figure 1.1.   Degania in the 1950s, with Lake Kinneret in the background.

Source: (Israel Government Press Office)

larger than the optimal size envisaged by the founders. The distinction between kibbutz and *kvutza* has become meaningless, but it was not always so. Degania saw itself as an enlarged family, run by consensus. When the group became too unwieldy to manage in this way and too large for intimacy, it split like an amoeba, forming Degania A and Degania B. There was also a third Degania, but its members migrated twenty-five miles westward and took a new name. Subsequently, settlements were established that shared Degania's communal ideals but disagreed with its concept of the intimate *kvutza*. Aspiring to expand and grow, they took the name *kibbutz.*

Degania today has a population of over five hundred, and its economic existence is guaranteed by a sophisticated factory for the manufacture of diamond-cutting tools, but it remains a relaxed backwater, at odds with the bustle and rush of modern Israel, its sleepy, bucolic ambiance appropriate to the "Mother of the Kvutzot."

It is an attractive village, set in lush, verdant gardens, extensive well-kept lawns, flower beds, tall palms, and poplars. The houses of black basalt where the early settlers lived, built around a courtyard, have been preserved, and there are museums devoted to the natural environment and the early days. The private homes remain modest. The communal dining hall is airy and spacious but not extravagant. Tall trees shade the swimming pool and the basketball courts from the summer sun. Striking a jarring note, a destroyed tank stands in the peaceful gardens, marking a dramatic event in Degania's history.

At more than six hundred feet below sea level, Degania is burning hot in the summer months; but the heat is alleviated by air conditioning in the private homes, offices, factory, and dining hall. It is a pleasant environment, offering a splendid quality of life, but ninety years ago it was very different.

When the founders of Degania, ten young men and two young women, some of them teenagers, arrived there in 1910, it was a forlorn spot. The hamlet of Umm Juni was previously owned by a Persian family, and the land was worked by twenty families of Arab tenant farmers who lived in mud huts and dug channels from the Jordan for irrigation. From a distance the village was invisible, as the dwellings were the same color as the surrounding soil. Apart from the rushes and some palm trees, there was little vegetation.

The founders of Degania were Jewish immigrants from Russia and Eastern Europe who arrived in Palestine in response to the Zionist challenge. The idea of a Jewish nationalist movement, a return to Zion, had been in Jewish minds since the exile from Judaea in the second century of the common era. Wherever they lived Jews would utter the prayer "Next year in Jerusalem." From time to time revivalist movements emerged, the most successful of which was that of Shabbetai Zvi in Turkey in the middle of the seventeenth century. Thousands of Jews sold their belongings and prepared to return to the Holy Land. Even when Shabbetai Zvi turned out to be a "false Messiah," accepting conversion to Islam, and his movement collapsed, the spirit among the Jews was only temporarily dampened.

In the nineteenth century, under the influence of movements for national independence in Europe, the idea of reviving a Jewish nation began to take on a political connotation, and in 1881 events triggered a practical response. That year there were serious *pogroms,* anti-Jewish outbreaks, all over Russia, in which hundreds of Jews lost life and property. Far from putting down the attacks, the czarist authorities ignored, and sometimes even encouraged them. The shock prompted many Jews to join revolutionary movements for the overthrow of the czar and his

Figure 1.2.   Degania in the 1990s.

Source: (Israel Government Press Office)

regime. Many more participated in the vast migration that was to carry more than two million Russian and Eastern European Jews westward in three decades, most of them to North America.

However, among those wishing to leave Russia, there was a minority who demanded more than just another refuge. They sought to create a modern Jewish nation in the ancient homeland of the Jewish people. They formed groups of Lovers of Zion, and a trickle of immigration to Palestine, then part of the Turkish Ottoman Empire, began. The first settlers founded the villages of Rishon Lezion, near today's Tel Aviv, and Rosh Pina in Galilee. They were joined in their endeavors by young Jews from the religious community of Jerusalem, who rejected the way of life of their parents, which was based on prayer and study, supported by charitable contributions from Jews all over the world. Like the new immigrants, they aspired to establish a self-supporting community. They founded Petah-Tikva. Both types of village, those of the immigrants and those of the indigenous Jews, struggled to survive in the harsh conditions in Palestine and were rescued from collapse by two French Jewish philanthropists, Baron Edmond Rothschild and Baron Maurice Hirsch.

In 1895, Theodor Herzl, a Viennese journalist appalled by the virulent anti-Semitism unleashed in ostensibly liberal France when a Jewish officer, Captain Alfred Dreyfus, was unjustly found guilty of treason, wrote a pamphlet entitled *The Jewish State,* in which he argued the case for reviving a Jewish national entity. In 1898, he convened a Zionist congress in Basel, Switzerland, where the Zionist Organization was established. Herzl advocated a political deal with the Ottoman sultan and an organized mass return of Jews to Palestine, but he died in 1904, and his movement came under the control of leaders who called themselves "practical Zionists." They supported gradual settlement, and to this end they established a Zionist Settlement Office in Palestine and began purchasing land, sometimes in cooperation with Rothschild and Hirsch.

The Jewish immigrants arriving in Palestine from Russia and Eastern Europe after the turn of the century were not merely nationalists. They were also influenced by revolutionary and socialist ideas in their countries of origin. They were disgusted by the recently established villages, with their Jewish overseers, Arab peasant laborers, and Bedouin guards. They aspired to what they called the "conquest of labor," believing that only by Jewish physical work could the land be redeemed and a Jewish nation reestablished. They also insisted that the Jews must undertake their own self-defense.

They looked for work in the older villages, but the Arab laborers were more experienced and prepared to work for lower wages. In one famous incident, Jewish workers uprooted and replanted a forest in memory of Theodor Herzl because it had originally been planted by Arabs. The struggle for Jewish Labor was bitter, and in a move to assist the newcomers, the Zionist Settlement Office established several agricultural training farms, one of them at Kinneret, on the shore of the lake. It was not long before the young Jewish pioneers who worked there quarreled with the Russian agronomist appointed to run the farm and went on strike to demand his dismissal.

It was their good fortune that the settlement office was run by Dr. Arthur Ruppin, a German Jewish sociologist of faith and vision. Ruppin did not accede to their demands for the agronomist to be fired, but he did give a carefully selected group the chance to work the land of nearby Umm Juni on their own. Another group of workers left the training farm and worked around the village of Hadera in the coastal plain. They lived as a commune, pooling their wages and eating their meals together. The first group left Umm Juni after less than a year, and the Hadera Com-

mune was invited to take up the challenge of working there independently.

The ten men and two women of the commune knew how to work—
they had proved that in the farms around Hadera—but they had no capital. Consequently, they signed an agreement with the settlement office,
undertaking to work the land at Umm Juni "until after the grain harvest."
In return they would each receive fifty francs per month wages and half
of any profits accruing at the end of the period. The Office supplied them
with mules, horses, and plows and advanced them the money to buy
seeds and other requirements.

They were soon writing to Ruppin about their problems. Temporary huts erected for the earlier group were in a state of disrepair, and
they could not find a carpenter. They carried out what repairs they could,
but the rains caught them before they had transferred all the fodder into
the barn, and the food for the livestock might not last for the full year.
When going to Tiberias to buy wood to complete the repairs, two of their
members, a man and a woman, were attacked by armed Arabs. They
managed to fight them off with a pistol, but their mule was wounded. At
the same time they described their relations with their Arab neighbors
as "friendly." The Arabs, who had stayed on in the part of Umm Juni
not purchased by the settlement office, taught them about farming; they
supplied the Arabs with medicines. They exulted in the freedom of managing their own work after working for others, and, although they admitted their lack of knowledge and experience, they proclaimed that they
possessed "the ability to work, self-confidence, and faith."

Despite the strict equality among its members, the small group contained several prominent personalities who assumed positions of leadership: Yosef Baratz and Miriam Ostrovsky, the only regular couple;
Tanhum Tanpilov, the strongest worker; and Yosef Bussel, at nineteen
the youngest member, who was also the acknowledged intellectual
leader. Yosef Baratz from the Ukraine was stocky and sunburned, an
experienced worker who had already learned the building trade as well
as farming. He had lived and worked in several different locations,
including Jerusalem. An early account describes Miriam, his companion, as "cheerful, healthy and capable of any work that the men could
do. Her joy affected her environment. In the difficult days, the days of
hunger, when you heard singing and dancing, you knew that she was
leading it." Tanhum Tanpilov was of medium height, broad shouldered,
with a measured step, "the rock on which the *kvutza* was built. He set an
example in his daily life that all tried to follow. He always arrived at
work first and left last." Tanpilov was taciturn and spoke little. Bussel

was "taller than average, with a thin stringy build and long curly hair. He didn't look capable of physical labor, but he became one of the best workers. His eyes blazed with conviction. His movements were determined, his self-confidence and decisiveness overwhelming."

They had no ideology at the outset, except a desire to create a new Jewish society and a determination to work the land independently, without supervisors or bosses. Tanpilov declared, "On the basis of my own experience, a Jewish worker can make a living in Palestine from the fruits of his own labors." Bussel aspired to create "a system that will truly give the worker individual freedom, without his having to exploit the work of others." Baratz recalled, "We wanted to work for ourselves and to do it not for wages but for the satisfaction of helping each other and of tilling the soil."

Shmuel Dayan, who joined the *kvutza* early on, wrote, "Everyone tells about his working day, one tells of his mule's intelligence, another of his mule's stupidity, a third of his mule's obstinacy, and everyone relates how he felt during the day. You feel the partnership. You are not alone! The new family, the family of the *kvutza,* is very strong and powerful." But he also recalled, "Not everyone was equally conscientious, skilled, and energetic. Some were careless and even lost their tools. There were crises and arguments."

Dayan's memoir of his life in Degania was published in 1935 and contains many vivid cameos of the early days of the *kvutza* and its members. Years later Baratz narrated a memoir to a journalist, which was published in English in 1956. It presents an idealized picture of the early days.

The work was backbreaking; the living conditions were harsh. In the summer the heat was unbearable; in the winter the youngsters were up to their thighs in mud. Several of the group were already suffering from malaria, and now the others also caught it. In the words of an early pioneer, "the body is crushed, the legs fail, the head hurts, the sun burns and weakens." In the summer usually 20 percent were sick in those early days, and sometimes as many as half the members couldn't report for work. Nevertheless, at the end of the first year, the group renewed its contract with the settlement office and continued to do so every year.

Not that the decision passed smoothly. Some members felt that, having cultivated the land at Umm Juni and grown crops there successfully, they should leave it to others to carry on the work and seek new challenges elsewhere. One location that attracted them was the moun-

Figure 1.3.   Degania in 1911.

Source: (Yad Tabenkin Archives)

tainous area across the Jordan, but Tanpilov rebuked his comrades, noting that the Jews were always the first in any revolution but lacked the ability to preserve their achievements. He called on them to root themselves in the soil of a specific location and "make the desert bloom." His argument was accepted; the group remained at Umm Juni, justifying its claim to be the "First Kibbutz."

It was not the only workers' commune in the Palestine of those years. Others formed communal groups of laborers, but they were mobile gangs that moved from one location to another, where there was work available or laborers required. Although there was no real Arab nationalist movement in Palestine in the early years of the century, the Arab peasants resented the Jewish pioneers, who settled on land previously worked by them. Apart from any specific hostility to newcomers, Ottoman Palestine was a lawless land, and Bedouin raiders, some of them from across the Jordan, would often plunder settled villages. (The attack on the Degania settlers, described earlier, was probably by Bedouin.) For that reason the early Jewish settlers founded the Hashomer defense force in 1907. Hashomer was organized in communes, but its members moved around the country to wherever guards

Figure 1.4.   Photostat of a note from founder-member Yosef Bussel to Dr. Arthur Ruppin, head of the Zionist Settlement Office 1911: "We hereby inform you that we have decided to call our new settlement 'Degania,' after the five types of cereals grown here. On behalf of the kvutza, Y. Bussel."

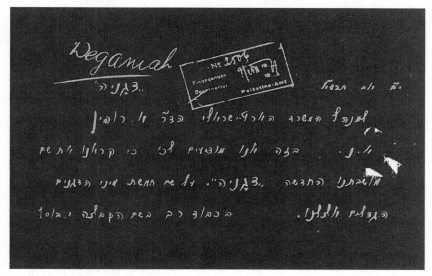

Source: (Yad Tabenkin Archives)

were needed. The Umm Juni group was the first to stay in one place and establish a permanent settlement.

The settlement office financed the construction of barns, stables, and storerooms from the black basalt stone of the area. These were built around a courtyard, next to which was erected a two-story wooden building for the living quarters and a comparatively spacious hut for the kitchen and dining hall. The members conducted an acrimonious correspondence with Dr. Ruppin, demanding that Jewish workers carry out the building, but it did not prove practical. Yemenite Jewish stonemasons, brought from Jerusalem, departed hastily when they learned of the danger of cholera.

When the members of the *kvutza* moved into their permanent buildings, they resolved to call their village Degania, both after *dagan,* Hebrew for the cereals they were growing, and after *degania,* the cornflowers that grew in the area. Shortly afterward, Miriam and Yosef Baratz were married.

Every evening the whole group participated in a general discussion around the rough dining room table, at which the following day's work was allocated. They also discussed the general organization of life in the *kvutza*. No votes were taken in those early days, and they went on talking until consensus was reached. The debates tended to be fierce and long, sometimes lasting until the morning. One discussion that began on Friday afternoon went on for more than twenty-four hours!

As the *kvutza* attracted more members, there were disputes between the original Hadera Commune and the newcomers. The two groups met separately—one in the barn, the other in the vineyard—and at one point the newcomers demanded that control of the communal purse be handed over to them. The account books of the early years indicate that Degania was not a complete commune. The members of the Hadera Commune *did* function collectively. They were treated in the accounts as an individual unit, but the other members were credited for the days they worked and debited for the purchase of food and other items. So for the first decade or so it is true to describe Degania as a community containing a commune rather than a commune as such. It was only in 1923 that individual accounts disappeared from the Degania balance sheet, and the comprehensive communal structure was properly established.

At the same time, the *kvutza* did operate on the basis of common ownership. The young pioneers did not own the animals, tools, or equipment—not even their own clothes. Everything was the property of the *kvutza*. Work clothes were issued on need, and when a member had to travel, he or she would be issued with a set of slightly more respectable garments. A small amount of petty cash was also available for necessary journeys. It was kept in an unlocked box in the dining hall and taken as needed. Often the money was untouched for weeks on end. Members who joined gave all their possessions to the community, and any presents received from outside were also handed in.

The nature of agricultural work necessitated the employment of casual labor in the harvesting season. The "exploitation" of these temporary workers caused some members of the *kvutza* considerable anguish, but in time livestock, fruit trees, and other branches were added, the membership grew, and the *kvutza* was able to organize its labor force without the need of outsiders.

Some of the fiercest arguments concerned the work performed by the two women, Miriam and Sara. Although they saw themselves as revolutionaries, creating a new way of life based on equality, it never occurred to the male members of the *kvutza* that women should change their traditional roles. Miriam had acted as a house mother since the Hadera days. She and Sara were expected to continue cooking, washing, and sewing for the men under intolerable conditions. At first, they did not even have kerosene stoves but cooked over an open fire, suffering from the heat in the summer and soaked by the rain in winter.

The women insisted that the *kvutza* should plant a vegetable garden and buy poultry and cattle, to enable them to take part in the farming alongside the men. When the first two cows were bought, Miriam was away, and she returned to find them being cared for by the men. Furthermore, the men would not let her near the "large and dangerous beasts." Refusing to accept the situation, Miriam went to a nearby Arab village, where the women taught her how to milk cows. One morning she got up before the cow men, and when they arrived she had already done the job. From then on, Miriam worked in the dairy, and subsequently women took all sorts of jobs, even plowing and standing guard.

Despite being in revolt against the orthodox Judaism of their parents, the youngsters were intensely Jewish. Bussel had studied for the rabbinate in Lithuania. He and the others aspired to reform Jewish life rather than abandon it. In the early days, the Sabbath was observed strictly as a day of rest, a custom that continued for many years in all the early *kvutzot* and kibbutzim. They marked Friday night with as fine a meal as they could afford and celebrated it with singing and dancing.

Often the members of the *kvutza* found release from the tensions of the intimate communal life and the unremitting work in song and dance. They brought folk songs and dances from Russia and Eastern Europe and created new Hebrew songs. They would dance the hora in a circle, arms on each other's shoulders, until they dropped.

They looked for meaningful ways to revitalize the Jewish festivals, reviving the agricultural features that had been lost in the Diaspora. In particular, Pessah (Passover) was given a new meaning as the festival of spring and freedom; Shavuot (Weeks), the festival of the first fruits; and Succot (Tabernacles), the harvest festival. They perceived the just society they were creating as a manifestation of the vision of the prophets of ancient Israel, where there would be no rich or poor, no oppressed or oppressors. In the early years a lot of Yiddish was spoken, but they hired Baruch Ben-Yehuda, a special teacher from Jerusalem, to teach Hebrew evening classes. Ben-Yehuda later became headmaster of the Gymnasia Herzliya, the country's leading school.

Although Miriam and Yosef Baratz were married, it was essentially a youth community, without children. Shmuel Dayan proposed that no other marriages take place for five years, to preserve the communal way of life, but he soon broke the rule himself after falling for the beautiful Dvora, a new immigrant from Russia. The *kvutza* was not really ready for the first child, Gideon, born to Miriam Baratz. Suddenly, in a society where all property was held in common, there was a child who belonged to one couple. And what about the obligation of every member to contribute a day's work to the community? Miriam, a strong woman in every sense of the word, continued milking the cows, singing happily as the milk squirted into the pail, with her baby by her side, his face covered with flies.

Yosef Bussel spoke out about the need for partnership in the raising of the children. "There must be no privacy," he said, according to an early protocol of Degania. "All privacy interferes with our communal life. All of us are obligated to participate in the expense of raising the children—not just the parents." Dvora Dayan was the second mother. Her son Moshe would become famous as an army commander and one of the leaders of the State of Israel. She asked the general meeting whether a member of the group should raise the children. Wouldn't it be better to bring in an outsider, who would just look after the children and would not feel obligated to other work? The possibility of firing Ben-Yehuda, the Hebrew teacher, and replacing him with a woman educator, who would also care for the children, was discussed.

Unlike Miriam, Dvora found it hard to continue the communal life after becoming a mother. She acquired a kerosene stove and a few pots, announcing that she would cook at home and that she should not be written down for either work or meals. It was the normally quiet Tanhum Tanpilov who took drastic action. He ascended to the upper story where Dvora and Shmuel lived and threw their stove and pots out of the window. Tanpilov's extreme (and uncharacteristic) action did not, of course, solve the problem, and the discussion continued. In time, special houses were built for the children, where they were cared for by a member of the group, but in Degania (in contrast to other kibbutzim) they always slept in their parents' rooms.

Degania in those years was a magnet for many leading personalities of Palestine's Jewish community. Yosef Trumpeldor, the one-armed Russian war hero who was to die defending a kibbutz in Galilee in 1921, worked there for a time, as did Berl Katznelson, later to become the preeminent ideological leader of the Jewish Labor Movement in Palestine, and Moshe Sharett, who became the first foreign minister of the State of Israel.

One of the most remarkable characters to be associated with Degania was Aharon David Gordon, a frail, middle-aged Russian Jew with a long white beard, a mystic and follower of Tolstoy. He never became a member, not believing in membership of anything, but he had an enormous influence on the young group. Gordon grew up in a Ukrainian forest, where his father worked in the timber trade and where he became aware of a "covenant between man and nature." He came to Palestine with a wife and daughter, but his wife died and he arrived in Degania, where he insisted on doing a full day's work. An intellectual and a writer, Gordon believed fervently that everyone should perform physical labor. He would write by candlelight on an upturned crate for a desk, using a pencil carefully sharpened with his pocket knife, and the following day report for work as usual. He was a pacifist and vegetarian, a lover of children and animals. When a rest period was called in the middle of a day's plowing, he would pick grass for the mules and feed them before taking his break.

A famous story tells of how, before he came to Degania, Gordon was working with a labor gang planting trees on the basis of piecework. As the other workers raced ahead, planting as many trees as they could, they suddenly noticed Gordon far behind. He was concentrating on digging deep and neat holes, planting the trees straight, and lovingly shaping the irrigation concavity around the tree.

He believed in the redeeming force of physical work, particularly work on the soil, and thought that the Jewish revival in Palestine depended on it. He was one of the first Jewish immigrants to become aware of the potential confrontation between Arabs and Jews in Palestine and predicted that the people who most suffered for and worked on the land would inherit it.

"An alienated people with no roots in the soil," he wrote, "deprived of the power of creativity, we must return to the soil, to independence, to nature, to a regenerated life of work." But his influence came more from his personal example, his gentle personality, and his gift for friendship with the young than from his writing. He lived in Degania, on and off, until his death in 1921. One of the kibbutz museums is named after him. It contains his papers and reflects his love of nature and agriculture.

By 1914 Degania had grown to a commune of some forty people. World War I was a particularly tough period for the Jewish community of Palestine. It was a time of economic stagnation and even starvation. The farming villages of the coastal plain, which owed their prosperity to citrus and viticulture exports, collapsed. In 1917, the Turkish army expelled Jews from Tel Aviv and the coastal plain. Thousands of hungry Jews, many of them children, were homeless in Galilee and the Jordan Valley.

Degania, with its mixed farming and successful grain production, survived the war relatively well, but the village was occupied for a time by the Turkish army, with its members forced to live in tents nearby. During this period, two candidates for membership, a man and a woman, committed suicide. The young man left a message saying, "You hope for a better future. I leave you my part in it. You have faith. I have lost mine." Suicides were characteristic of many early communes. Life in the country was hard, and several young pioneers took their own lives. Clearly there were always personal reasons, but something in the physical hardship and the intensity of the communal life seems to have pushed a number of people past their breaking points.

The expulsion of Jews from the coastal plain put enormous pressure on the settlements in Galilee, and Yosef Bussel was among those who worked feverishly to find homes and work for the refugees. In 1919 he was drowned while returning home by boat across the Kinneret, after attending a meeting in Tiberias to set up an orphanage for the homeless children.

In 1919, Degania formally became independent, leasing its land directly from the Jewish National Fund. By then the *kvutza* owned its own equipment, and it had become too large to run itself by consensus. A committee of four was elected to make decisions on a daily basis. Many members saw this as a perversion of the original dream and suggested the *kvutza* should limit itself to ten families. Although this proved impractical, Degania did remain relatively intimate. In 1920, Degania B was formed nearby, and in 1922 the third Degania commune was established. It soon became clear, however, that the land was insufficient for three *kvutzot,* and the third group moved to the Nazareth area, establishing the *kvutza* of Ginegar.

These developments were seen as natural, but there was great bitterness when Shmuel Dayan and several other members of the *kvutza* announced that they were planning to leave Degania and found a *moshav ovdim* (workers' cooperative village). The first *moshav,* a small village with individual households and farms and cooperative marketing, was established in 1914, and at the time many Zionist officials saw it as a more suitable model for settling the land than the *kvutza.* These men thought that the *kvutza* should have the role of initiating settlement but that, once the village was established, the commune should convert to a *moshav* or hand it over to a *moshav* group. In any event, the first *moshav* did not succeed, but after the war Dayan and his comrades sought to revive the idea.

Dayan recalled that Gordon received their decision with great sadness but, in contrast to many of the others at Degania, with love and understanding. He described a luminous evening, sitting by the Kinneret, with the white-bearded elder resting his hand on the shoulder of one of the those leaving and gently inquiring, "What is the reason for leaving the *kvutza?* What hurts you? What has not been improved? How can we improve it? What will happen to the *kvutza* if you, who have given it your youth and strength, abandon it? What will be the social content in your new form of cooperative? How can you be sure it will not degenerate like the other villages?"

In fact, the *moshav* answered a distinct need for farmers who believed in cooperation but rejected the intense communal way of life of the *kvutza.* The first successful *moshav ovdim,* Nahalal, was established by Dayan and his comrades from Degania in 1922, and the kibbutz and *moshav* existed side by side in Palestine thereafter.

After the war, the Zionist venture in general, and Jewish settlement on the land in particular, took giant steps forward as a result of the Balfour Declaration. Proclaimed in 1917, in an attempt to enlist Jewish support for the allied cause, the declaration stated:

> His Majesty's Government view with favor the establishment in Palestine of a National Home for the Jewish people, and will use their best endeavors to facilitate the achievement of this object, it being clearly understood that nothing shall be done which may prejudice the civil and religious rights of the non-Jewish communities in Palestine.

It was the most significant political development in the history of the Zionist movement. Furthermore, it was followed, after the war, by the League of Nations, awarding the mandate for Palestine to Britain. Although the British, once they started ruling Palestine, sought to balance their promise to the Jews with reassurances to the Arabs, Jewish immigration escalated. The Jewish population, which had declined to less than sixty thousand by the end of the war, more than doubled in the next five years. Among those entering the country from Russia, Poland, and other parts of Eastern Europe were thousands of idealistic pioneers, who established new *kvutzot* and also larger communal settlements called *kibbutzim.* Others settled in *moshavim,* like Nahalal, and still more in the towns.

Weakened by the loss of some of its best members to Nahalal, Degania now became a full commune, abolishing individual accounts. It was to be an inspiration in the subsequent development of the communal movement in Palestine, but new ideas were emerging to challenge the "family" model of the first *kvutza.* Proponents of the large kibbutz criticized the *kvutza* as a sterile introverted society. They argued that it must expand to meet the challenges of the Zionist enterprise. Degania stuck to its guns, continuing to believe in the way of the intimate commune, and even those who disagreed looked on the *kvutza* as an example of idealism and practical achievement.

Degania grew and developed, with a wide range of agricultural branches, including orchards, fish farming, and eventually a factory. Unlike some kibbutzim, which took extensive loans for their development, Degania always paid its way. It was lucky in its choice of its factory for diamond-cutting tools, based mainly on exports, but it also preserved a relatively modest way of life.

The first *kvutza* had never seen its primary role as that of defense, but from its earliest days it was an outpost on the border of Jewish settlement. The first member of Degania to be killed, Moshe Barsky, lost his life in a battle with Bedouin raiders in the early years, and in the period leading up to the creation of the State of Israel, the kibbutz movement played a leading role in defending the Jewish community and forming the embryo army of the new nation.

In Israel's 1948 War of Independence, Degania's members were to play a heroic role, stopping the Syrian armored advance with homemade gasoline bombs. The British Mandate ended on May 15, 1948, and the State of Israel was proclaimed the same day. Arab regular armies, advancing on all fronts, invaded the new state. At Degania members dug trenches and prepared to resist the onslaught. The women and children were evacuated, but even the men who remained were virtually untrained, as the more experienced fighters were mobilized on other fronts. The Degania defenders were armed with rifles, Sten guns (locally manufactured submachine guns of very short range), and beer bottles filled with gasoline.

The first attacks by infantry and armored cars were driven off by gunfire, but then eight tanks advanced on the kibbutz. Two kibbutz members threw the gasoline bottles at the advancing tanks from point-blank range, immobilizing one and setting two on fire. The others retreated. One of the destroyed tanks remains in Degania to this day, a memorial to the role of the *kvutza* in the defense of Israel. Today Degania remains a symbol of the idealistic, pioneering past, but like a majority of the country's kibbutzim, the Mother of the *Kvutzot* is in the throes of change.

Yom Kippur, the Day of Atonement, has always been the holiest day in the Jewish calendar. It is a day of fasting, of repentance, of rendering accounts to God. Not widely observed in the early days of the kibbutzim, it has in recent years become customary for many members to fast and abstain from work on that day. One of the ways in which many kibbutzim have sought to infuse contemporary significance into ancient Jewish festivals is to hold a serious discussion about the kibbutz and its problems around the time of Yom Kippur, a sort of accounting of the past year. This has been the custom at Degania for many years.

When he was first elected to the post, the present general manager of Degania spoke about Umm Juni, the earliest days. After two years of managing the *kvutza,* however, he found that he was not in the mood for nostalgia, and he chose a different topic: whither Degania?

"We cannot go on like this," he told the assembled members, declaring that it was absolutely vital to change the way the *kvutza* was organized. "The almost total dependence of the individual on the community cannot continue," he insisted. "We have to transfer responsibility to the individual member."

In the early days, Yosef Bussel wrote in a letter to a friend who had left Degania:

> I am fully aware that people will not revolutionize their behavior in a short while in the *kvutza.* For people to feel and think as they should in a life of complete equality and complete partnership, they have to be born into it, and for that to happen generations will have to pass. Many things that we cannot achieve today will be achieved by comrades who have grown up in the new environment of the *kvutza.*

Today, Bussel's grandson, Chen Vardi, declares forthrightly, "I don't know what my grandfather would say if he were alive today, but I know what I would say to him. 'You were a revolutionary,' I would point out. 'You changed things. Now I want to change them in *my* way.' What was right in Umm Juni in 1910 is not necessarily right in Degania in 1999."

Vardi has the thick curly hair and broad brow of his grandfather, but he has not inherited his "thin stringy build," and, in contrast to the early photos of the founder, his hair is cropped short. No one could possibly suggest that he looks incapable of physical labor, as was said of his illustrious grandfather. He is chunky, broad shouldered, and ruddy faced, a true son of the soil. As chairman of the Committee for Manpower, Consumption, and Services, he is in the forefront of those pushing for changes in the system.

"I can't tell you exactly how we are going to do it," he admits, "but it must include a prize for the hard worker and a fine for the slacker. Public pressure doesn't work any more; we need incentives and penalties."

The contrast with his grandfather's prediction is evident, but not all the members of Degania go along with his ideas. Of course, Vardi does not remember his grandfather, who died in 1919, but Yoya Shapiro, one of the first children to be born in the *kvutza,* remembers her parents, Yosef and Miriam Baratz, very well. In her late seventies, with an outdoor complexion from her thirty years in the vegetable gardens, Yoya looks sturdy and strong. She wears simple clothes, socks and sensible shoes, and no makeup. She continues to work, putting in a five-hour day in the communal clothing store.

"I always knew there would be changes," she says. "I remember arguing with fellow members while we were planting vegetables and warning them that there would have to be changes in our way of life. I realized that we had to worry more about the individual, but I never thought it would come to this."

It is very difficult for her, she confesses. Her parents always said that the *kvutza* was not for everyone, but now she wonders whether it is for anyone at all. The world has changed, and specifically Israeli society has changed, and become more materialistic. Outside influences on Degania have notably increased. Not that the *kvutza* was ever cut off from society, but in the old days the world used to come back to the *kvutza* every Friday, when the members who worked in Tel Aviv came home. Now it comes into the living room every day via the television screen.

Yoya's father believed in equality and simplicity, and he was totally sincere. One member who worked in Tel Aviv used to bring his daughters toys and dresses and take them for days out in the big town, but not Yosef Baratz.

"My father also worked away from Degania," she recalls, "but he never bought anything for his own children. When he bought things, it was for the whole *kvutza*. He once bought sixty blouses for all the women. On another occasion he brought hats for everyone. Once he was given half a dozen radio sets. Do you think that *we* got one? It was distributed according to need and seniority. That was my father."

At the same time she recalls a row with her father over the "privatization" of the clothing budget. Many of the members of the commune objected to the fact that they did not own their clothes, which were distributed from the central clothing store according to need. Every member, man or woman, received one pair of working clothes every week. For the Sabbath, the men got white shirts and clean trousers and the women received dresses, but very often the garments did not fit. Many of the members felt that this was pushing the principle of equality to ridiculous lengths.

Yoya's father was one of those opposing the change, seeing it as an infringement of the principle of "to each according to his needs," and she told him, "You don't really live in Degania; how can you judge the situation? You receive the clothes that you need for your work in town and your journeys abroad. You don't have to put up with the idiocy of the clothing store!"

Her father was dreadfully offended, she remembers, but it was true that he spent a great deal of time away from the *kvutza,* performing various public duties. It was not just that the members often received clothes of the wrong size, she recalls. "We wanted to buy our own clothes—why not?"

On the other hand, she stresses that her father never took advantage of his outside work. He was famous for traveling on buses, always refusing the use of an official car. In Tel Aviv he never stayed at a hotel, preferring to sleep on a camp bed in the offices of the Soldiers' Welfare Association, of which he was the chairman. Once she visited him in the United States and was utterly appalled at the squalor of his hotel in Harlem. He saw nothing wrong with it. He did not want to waste public money on more comfortable accommodation.

Like many Jewish men and women in Palestine, Yoya joined the British army in World War II and was stationed in Cairo. As head of the Soldiers' Welfare Association, her father arrived on a visit to Palestinian troops in Egypt. All her friends were envious, sure that she would be treated to a meal and a room at the famous Shepherd's Hotel. She knew better. Her father did not go anywhere near Shepherd's, preferring to sleep on a couch at the Soldiers' Club.

In contrast to her father, her mother was always in Degania, working in the dairy until she was quite old. Yoya deeply admired both her parents and the other Degania veterans, accepting their values without question.

"They believed in equality, simplicity, and hard work, and so did I," she notes. "I still do." She is emphatic that she was not jealous of the children whose fathers brought them toys or dresses. "It was never important to me," she says simply.

Her first encounter with money was when she served in the British army. Promoted to sergeant, she refused to wear her stripes, which conflicted with her belief in equality, and as a consequence she was underpaid. When the mistake was discovered, she was awarded back pay and became the lending bank for her fellow women soldiers from Palestine.

"I have no idea whether they paid me back or not," she laughs. "I never worried about money. Even today I don't know how much anything costs, and I don't care.

"We now pay for meals in the dining hall," she says with the hint of a sneer, "but I can't be bothered to learn how to use the magnetic card. Somebody writes me down, I guess. I really don't know. I just take what I need. One couple at our table seem to spend all their time discussing the price of everything. It has never interested me."

Her son, Ron, has left the kibbutz. He studied law at a university, and for a time his law practice, in partnership with another member of Degania and members from other kibbutzim, provided a significant source of income for the *kvutza*. "He saw that he was bringing in a lot of money," says Yoya,

> and that some members were not working all that hard. He left. He has rejected our way of life. Not that he is entirely materialistic. He earned much more as an attorney than he does as a magistrate, but his ambition is to be a Supreme Court judge, not a highly paid attorney. At least he lives nearby, and I see my grandchildren, but I still find it very difficult. My father would climb out of his grave if he heard some of the things that Ron says about the kibbutz and the labor movement, but he couldn't have done anything about it, just as I can't. The world has changed; the country has changed. Young people are different today.

Yoya recalls that she never had proper furniture in her room at Degania—just wooden chairs, a kitchen table, and iron beds for her and her husband. When Ron came home from the army, he couldn't understand why their room was so sparsely furnished compared to other rooms. "So we bought a sofa and two armchairs," recalls Yoya with amusement. "We have never changed them. You are sitting in one of the armchairs now."

The Shapiro room remains modestly furnished, with very little in it apart from the sofa, armchairs, and books. It is air-conditioned, they have a television set, and her husband Avraham, a university lecturer and part-time journalist, has a computer for his writing; but otherwise there is no sign of the relative affluence of Degania.

Yoya's eldest brother, Gideon, the first child of Degania, married a South African woman and left the *kvutza*. He has since died. Her younger brother left the *kvutza* for more than twenty years but eventually came back. She has two sisters living in Degania, both of whom strongly opposed the changes that were implemented, and they are horrified by some of the ideas being proposed by some of the youngsters.

"We live here and work here," Yoya says with a big shrug. "Our ideas are no longer popular. What can we do about it? Bang the table? It won't change anything. People arrived in Degania in many different ways, for many different reasons, and they have different attitudes. Speaking for myself, I was born here, and I always accepted our way of life."

Yehezkel (Hezi) Dar arrived in Degania by a very different route from Yoya. He came in 1943 in the midst of World War II as part of a famous group called the "Teheran Children." Some nine hundred orphans from Poland, whose parents had been murdered by the Nazis, arrived in Russia after wandering with thousands of other refugees through the war-torn territory of Eastern Europe. They were sent on to Teheran, where they were cared for by the Jewish Joint Distribution Committee and the Polish Red Cross. From there they traveled by train to Karachi and then in troop ships to Suez, where they boarded a train for Palestine. The Youth Aliya organization, which looked after Jewish refugee children, found homes for them in various children's villages, homes, and kibbutzim. Eighteen of them arrived in Degania.

Most of them left after high school or army service, but Dar and two others remained and eventually became members of the *kvutza*. Dar worked in the banana plantation and other agricultural branches but graduated to youth leadership and teaching. He studied at Degania's expense, and today he is a professor of the sociology of education at Jerusalem's Hebrew University. He has also served as the secretary of the *kvutza* on three separate occasions.

Dar remained because he liked it, he explains, but he also very much believed in the communal way of life. During his first term as secretary of the *kvutza* in the 1960s, he decided to conduct a private research project on the feelings and motivations of the young generation, most of them born in Degania. He was appalled to discover that the reason they remained was because it was a pleasant way of life, or because their parents lived there, or because their friends were there, or simply because it was convenient. Not one of them gave him an ideological reason or even said that they believed in the communal way of life.

A bald, genial man in his late sixties, with a tendency to peer over his reading glasses, Dar divides his time between Degania and the university. His room at the *kvutza* is even more sparsely furnished than that of the Shapiros. His four children have all left, a fact he accepts with amused resignation.

"They are all individualists," he explains. They did not leave so much because of the communal way of life but because Degania is a small village. They wanted to live in a larger and more sophisticated society. "I don't know whether the changes now being discussed would have prevented their leaving. Possibly in one case; possibly not."

Looking back on his experience as *kvutza* secretary, Dar regrets what he calls "my insufficient sensitivity toward the individual's personal needs and feelings." His terms of office were several years apart, and he is aware of the changes in attitude in the different periods. In the earlier period, the individual was expected to suppress his own desires in the interests of the community. He recalls one case in which a veteran member wanted to study. He was prepared to leave Degania and work to support himself until he had raised the money, but his request was refused.

"Appalling," he pronounces it. "Today it would definitely be accepted."

Dar is sanguine about the current changes being discussed in Degania and in the kibbutz movement as a whole. He hopes and believes that Degania, and a majority of Israel's kibbutzim, will remain communities, "where there is more mutual assistance and responsibility for one another than in other communities."

He forecasts that Degania will remain relatively egalitarian: equality will be preserved in basic things such as housing, education, and health care, which will continue to be paid for by the community. He foresees adjustments "at the margins." Food, electricity, vacations, and hobbies are already paid for out of personal budgets, and the list will be extended. Personal budgets will be unequal, but not exaggeratedly so. For instance, if members earn more from work outside, they will be allowed to keep a small percentage of the extra amount. The next stage will be to evaluate the work members do in the kibbutz and extend the same principle to that, but Dar voices a note of skepticism.

"To be frank with you, I don't think it will solve our main problem of motivation," he says. "The ones who will get a bit more money are the holders of the responsible positions, such as the secretary, treasurer, farm manager, factory manager. In my opinion, they accept these tasks because of their personalities and possibly also for the prestige and power they entail. The extra money is not going to make much difference to them. The problem here, and in all kibbutzim, is the weaker members, who don't contribute enough. How do we get *them* to work harder?"

At the same time, Dar asserts that making people pay for their food and electricity has saved money. "People used to feed their dogs and cats on good food from the dining hall," he notes. "Degania has cut its food bill by 25 percent. We have saved thousands of shekels, and the members feel the benefit in their personal budgets." He adds with a smile, "If you ask me, the animals are much healthier!"

Degania has not lowered its standard of living, he observes, but it has saved money by cutting out waste and duplication. There is no economic crisis in the *kvutza,* mainly because the factory, with 80 percent of its produce going for export, was always very profitable. For many years, members of Degania did not inquire how much things cost or how much a branch earned. A successful branch was a happy branch that produced a good crop and whose members worked hard and were contented. Profit or loss? That was the problem of the treasurer. Now the *kvutza* is forced to be more practical.

Chen Vardi, at thirty-nine already eleven years older than his legendary grandfather when he died, is very conscious of his heritage. Legends are powerful in a place like Degania, and he can feel the ghost of Yosef Bussel looking over his shoulder, but he is undeterred.

When he left the army in 1980, he was very enthusiastic about life in the *kvutza.* Many kibbutz children spend years seeing the world, but Vardi only spent a few months abroad and returned to take up his life in Degania. It was only after about five years that he began having doubts. His biggest problem was with what he saw as the mediocrity and dependence of the members, particularly those born and brought up at Degania. He concluded that the kibbutz education created mediocrity. Anyone striving for excellence was derided as a *shvitzer,* a boaster. He thinks that the situation would be worse if it were not for the outside society. The society outside the kibbutz provides a stimulant, he believes.

"There are kibbutzniks who strive for excellence," he concedes, "but that is because of stimulus from outside. If all of Israel were one big kibbutz, the situation would be catastrophic."

The other side of that coin, he maintains, is dependence. As an office holder on various committees, he saw how members came to him for assistance about all sorts of petty matters that they should have handled themselves. He gives an example of how several members decided to wall in their balconies to give themselves extra rooms. This practice was discussed, banned, approved, banned again, and finally approved.

"What has it got to do with the community?" he asks angrily. "It should be left to the individual."

He is sure that the system has built-in deficiencies. According to the principles of the *kvutza,* everyone is equal; everyone is equally entitled to a person's time or attention.

"At Degania you can't say that X is an idiot or that Y is wasting your time," he points out.

> As a result, as the secretary of a committee, you spend 95 percent of your time on 5 percent of the problems. The weaker members of the community are the ones with the problems, and your job is to help them to function better. What happens is that you spend endless time with people who *create* problems, so when someone comes along with a *solution* to a problem, you don't have the time for him. Under the *kvutza* system, if somebody has a new idea, an initiative, a scheme for a new enterprise, a solution to a problem, or a way of doing something better, you never get around to discussing it!

Many kibbutzim have been forced to reexamine their priorities and principles because of their economic situation, points out Vardi. A member was entitled to a certain budget for expenses, a foreign vacation every few years, an extension of his home. Suddenly the kibbutz couldn't afford it. There was a painful confrontation between reality and the norms that were in force for years. Degania has not yet faced this problem. It has been shielded by the success of its factory. It can afford more or less whatever it wants.

Vardi sees a major weakness in the imbalance between contribution and reward. He wants to abolish what he sees as the exaggerated sense of entitlement. Too many members think that they have a right to everything without regard to what it costs, he maintains. There is no awareness that what is bought must be paid for. He wants to foster a sense of responsibility, a feeling of obligation. He hopes to redefine the boundaries so that a member is aware of the limits of the partnership. He cannot justify a system in which somebody who does not work receives exactly the same as somebody who does.

He wants to cut out wastage. Electricity was a case in point. His next target is psychotherapy. Quite a number of *kvutza* residents go for treatment to town. They get the day off, their travel expenses, and Degania foots the (very high) psychologist's bill. "Shouldn't members be expected to pay at least *some* of it out of their personal allowance?" he demands.

A lot of hitherto sacred cows are going to be slaughtered, he says, and so they should be. The system isn't working, and it hasn't been working for years. Did it ever work? He is sure that it did, but times were different, circumstances were different, and demands and expectations were different. It cannot go on as it is today.

"Yosef Bussel built Degania," quipped a cynical veteran. "Now his grandson is taking it apart!"

Vardi does not agree. He maintains that he is fighting to maintain the existence of Degania, which is not as assured as it may seem.

"We cannot return to Umm Juni," he declares,

and of course I am not talking about the conditions. We're not going to go back to living in tents or huts, without electricity or running water. That's obvious. But 80 percent of what they decided at Umm Juni was because of the conditions. If they had not been crazy, they would not have stuck it out.

They had a vision, and they were prepared to sacrifice everything to accomplish that vision. Today we have a different situation. We have a task and a different vision. The task is to ensure that Degania survives. To that end, we have to make it more normal, more in tune with the rest of the world. The proportion of older members is rising all the time. If all the young leave, Degania will become an old-age home. So that is the task: we have to retain the younger members by making Degania more normal.

The vision is to maintain quality values. I am fighting for economic realism; but we should not assess *everything* from an economic point of view. We should be prepared to do certain things even if they do not make sense economically, but if they contribute to our members, to society, to the nation. That is my vision.

Partly because of its relative economic success, Degania, the first kibbutz, has not gone as far with the changes as many others. There is something very enduring about the place. It manifestly possesses a future as well as a past.

The past can be seen in the old basalt courtyard, where weddings and celebrations are still held, and in the museum. Looking at the old sepia-

Figure 1.5.   Degania in the 1990s.

Source: (Yad Tabenkin Archives)

colored photographs with Yoya Shapiro is an exercise in living history. "There is Bussel," she says, pointing to the long-haired youth, posing in a group by the River Jordan. "That one is Tanhum, a good-looking man, he was. There is my father, and that's my mother over here. That is the cowshed, where mother worked. That is the old dining hall."

Less than half a kilometer from the photo museum is the future: Toolgal Degania Ltd., the *kvutza's* state-of-the-art diamond tool factory, which manufactures saws; for marble and granite; dry-cutting laser-welded saws; diamond chain saws; core drills; grinding tools for the optical, ceramics, and glass industries; and diamond wheels for the gem-stone industries. Toolgal employs 130 people, and its sales are about $16 million annually, over 70 percent of it earned from exports.

Although the factory's air-conditioned offices and high-tech work benches are light-years from the hand-dug irrigation channels of the founders, the basic principles by which the members live remain relatively unchanged. Wandering along the paths, under the tall shady trees, and over the manicured lawns, one gets the feeling that the kibbutz is permanent, that apart from a few cosmetic alterations, a few changes of nuance, everything will remain very much the same.

The relaxed, rural calm is deceptive. The sleepy, bucolic village by the River Jordan, where the kibbutz dream was launched nine decades ago, is not what it seems to be. Even here in the Mother of the Kvutzot, the symbol of the Israeli kibbutz movement, the winds of change are blowing. In the subsequent chapters we will see that in other kibbutzim they are blowing harder and that in some they have reached gale force.

2

גבעת ברנר

GIVAT BRENNER
FLAGSHIP IN STORMY SEAS

If Degania is an enlarged family, an idyllic village commune, Givat Brenner is something altogether more ambitious. Almost three times the size of Degania, it is the biggest kibbutz in Israel, or, as its members proudly declare, "the biggest kibbutz in the world!" An entire community enclosed by green lawns, shady trees, and flowering shrubs, it is a miniature cosmos, encompassing agriculture and industry, labor and leisure, tourism and technology. Givat Brenner has four factories, two theaters, a regional high school, library, archive, research center, museum, gymnasium, ball fields, swimming pool, post office, communal dining hall, health center, and an entire complex dedicated to catering to its aged members, including around-the-clock care where necessary.

On the surface it is, like Degania, tranquil and pleasant. The thunder of the jet fighters from the nearby air force base roaring overhead occasionally mars the rural ambiance, but nobody seems to notice the intermediate bursts of noise. The elderly—and there are many of them—swish around on their silent rubber-tired electric carts or sit outside the clinic or the veteran's club, chatting in the sun. Young mothers push strollers. Children play on the lawns or ride their bicycles down the shady paths. Adults, from teenagers to veterans in their midsixties, speed around on motor scooters. Buses and private cars bring adults to lectures and children to concerts. The place is bustling with activity, bursting with life. If ever there was William Morris World, this seems to be it. Under the surface, though, the currents are churning, the foundations are trembling, the building blocks are shifting.

Similar to Degania in many ways, Givat Brenner is nevertheless a different prototype. The period from 1910 to 1928 is a relatively short interlude, but a great deal happened in those eighteen years. With the end of World War I, the Balfour Declaration, and the assumption of the Palestine mandate by Britain, thousands of Jews entered the country, mostly from Eastern Europe. Many of the immigrants were idealistic young pioneers, strongly influenced by the creation of the Soviet Union and by the socialist movements in their countries of origin. This influx, known as the Third *Aliya* (the third wave of immigration), was to have a profound influence on the Jewish community of Palestine and the development of the kibbutz as an institution.

Degania, although today far larger than originally envisioned, retains the atmosphere of an intimate commune, a *kvutza;* Givat Brenner represents the all-embracing *kibbutz.* Although the two terms are used interchangeably, and Degania is almost always described as "the first kibbutz," this was not always the case. Degania was the first permanent communal settlement and remained the concrete proof that a community based on equality and cooperation could work, but other forms of communalism and cooperation were emerging in the wake of the new wave of immigration. Two in particular contributed to the development of the kibbutz idea: Kehillatenu (Our Community) and Gedud Avoda (the Labor Battalion.) The first lasted only a few months, the second a few years; both are a vital part of the kibbutz heritage.

"Our Community" was in fact the title of a collection of personal diaries of a group of youngsters of the Hashomer Hatzair youth movement, who lived for less than a year in a small, isolated settlement called Upper Bittania, situated on a hill above Lake Kinneret. There were several such communes in the early 1920s, but only Bittania published its memoir, thereby becoming a symbol.

Middle-class youngsters from Eastern Europe, fired with the ideals of the youth movement, familiar with the writings of Marx and Freud, Buber and Gordon, genuinely thought that they might be "the first generation to remain eternally young." They labored all day clearing the rocks from their hillside to prepare it for plowing, but their real life was at night, when they conducted their *sicha.* The word literally means "conversation," and some kibbutzim still use the word for their general meetings, but in Upper Bittania, the *sicha* was more of a communal confession. Everything was shared: not just accommodation, food, and clothing but doubts and fears, pain and joy, anger and ecstasy. In the *sicha* nothing was off-limits; there were no secrets, and the members shared their most intimate feelings with the whole group. All members disclosed their thoughts, exposed their anxieties, and laid bare their character. If two members made love, they were expected to share the experience with the entire community.

"Oh, how beautiful it was when we all took part in the discussions," wrote Shulamit, one of the four girls in the twenty-six-member group. "Nights of searching for one another—that is what I call those hallowed nights. During the moments of silence, it seemed to me that from each heart a spark would burst forth, and the sparks would unite in one great flame penetrating the heavens."

And in another passage: "There were other nights: nights of shouting, excitement and wildness. At the center of our camp a fire burns, and under the weight of the hora [circle dance] the earth groans a rhythmic groan, accompanied by wild songs."

David Horowitz, who decades later was to become the first governor of the Bank of Israel, described Upper Bittania as "the solitary monastery of some religious sect or order." Continuing the analogy, he wrote:

> Our ritual was that of public confession, that which often brings to mind the attempts of religious mystics to come to terms with both God and the Devil at the same time. Often it seemed we were a far cry from being a kibbutz of pioneer workers, we were an order of knights of the spirit, suffering not only physical hardships, but mental torture too, eternally searching for something, though with no compass to guide us.
>
> All of us who lived on that peak can never forget the wonderful experience, which is for ever engraved on our hearts. Those were days filled with beauty, the innocence of youth and the magic of friendship, the search for truth and for a new way of life.

This was a far cry from the pragmatic farmers of Degania, but when the youngsters of Bittania came down from the hillside, some of them were to establish Beit Alpha, a successful and prosperous kibbutz, with a population of more than eight hundred at its peak and the prototype for the Kibbutz Artzi federation of communal settlements. Kibbutz Artzi, which was for many years dogmatically Marxist, has always stood on the "left" of the kibbutz movement. Even today, its Marxism long abandoned, it is half a step behind the others in the current drive to modify the socialism of the kibbutz.

Horowitz himself joined the Labor Battalion, a group of workers who hoped to convert the entire Jewish community of Palestine into one vast kibbutz. Starting with a membership of forty, it quickly grew to over five hundred, and some three thousand passed through its ranks. It was named after Joseph Trumpeldor, the one-armed Russian Jewish war hero.

Trumpeldor, one of the few Jews to obtain a commission in the czar's army, was influenced by the ideas of Leo Tolstoy. He brought a group of Russian Jews to Palestine in 1913 and worked at Degania and other places. When World War I broke out, he led a group to Alexandria in Egypt to volunteer for service in the British army. Serving under an Irish officer, Trumpeldor and his fellow soldiers of the Zion Mule Corps distinguished themselves at Gallipoli.

After the war he returned to Russia, where he organized Jewish self-defense groups in the chaos of the revolution and was among the founders of Hehalutz, the Pioneer movement. Groups of Hehalutz started arriving in Palestine, and, in 1919, Trumpeldor returned. He was appalled at the political divisions in the Jewish workers' movement and managed to persuade them to unite and form the Histadrut Labor Federation in 1920.

The same year Trumpeldor rushed to take command of the defense of two communes in northern Galilee. Kfar Giladi and Tel Hai had been caught up in the cross fire between rival Arab forces, which were involved in a postwar border dispute between the British-ruled Palestine and French-controlled Syria. Trumpeldor was killed at Tel Hai and became a legend, celebrated as a figure of Jewish self-defense and labor unity. The colorful Russian officer had long advocated the establishment of a communal labor force, ready to take on any task, "metal that can be molded to whatever is needed." Within a year the Labor Battalion, named after him, had groups of workers all over the country.

Far more ambitious—it could be said more presumptuous—than the members of Degania, its comrades undertook the toughest missions, such as building roads and railways and draining swamps. They lived in tented camps and shared everything on a communal basis, declaring their aim to be no less than "the reconstruction of the country through the creation of a general commune of Jewish workers."

The philosophy of the battalion was different from that of the *kvutza* in that it rejected any sort of selective approach and aspired to be a mass movement. The members of the *kvutza* saw themselves as a pioneering elite and said openly that *kvutza* life was not for everybody. The Labor Battalion embraced everyone.

It was initially conceived as a mobile group, sending units wherever work was available, but early on it was joined by Shlomo Lavi and a group of his followers. Lavi had worked in several communes and had come to the conclusion that the *kvutza* was too small and introverted. He doubted whether it was economically viable and advocated a larger framework, which would engage in industry as well as agriculture. In 1921, he and other members of the battalion founded a permanent settlement at Ein Harod (the Well of Harod) in the Jezreel Valley. Ein Harod, the first kibbutz, or large *kvutza,* extended the principles of the Labor Battalion to a project of permanent land settlement. Whereas Degania had deliberately split up when it reached a certain size, Ein Harod saw itself as a nationwide collective of unlimited size. All the new kibbutzim of the movement considered themselves as part of Ein Harod, or Kibbutz Meuhad (the United Kibbutz).

Kibbutz Meuhad later became one of the three kibbutz federations, consisting of settlements that aimed at continuous expansion. The others were Hever Hakvutzot, comprising Degania and the other small settlements, and Kibbutz Artzi, of the Hashomer Hatzair youth movement, the successors of Our Community.

When Givat Brenner was founded in 1928, it initially regarded itself as a *pluga* (unit) of Ein Harod (and in fact several years would pass before it adopted its present name). The previous year had been a bad one for the Zionist enterprise in Palestine. The flow of pioneering immigrants of the first years after World War I had started to wind down, and in 1927 there were more emigrants than immigrants. There was considerable unemployment and even hunger among the Jewish workers.

A pioneer group from Galicia in Eastern Europe had bought land near Rehovot, south of Tel Aviv, and settled there in Kvutzat Schiller, which later became Kibbutz Gan Shlomo. Groups from Lithuania, Russia, and Ukraine, who had been living and working as day laborers in the villages of Rehovot, Ness Ziona, and Hadera, merged to form the settlement group that would eventually become Givat Brenner. There was no land available from the settlement office, and the members of the new group resolved to purchase fifty acres of land bordering on Schiller. There was also a possibility of an additional 250 acres later on. They had no money—indeed, they were almost starving—and they were opposed by the official settlement authorities, who wanted the fifty acres for private farmers. A famous story is still told about how Avraham Harzfeld, the doyen of Zionist settlement, screamed at two of the group who came to see him: "*Shmendriks* (Good-for-nothings), I'll throw you out of the labor federation, if you settle that land!" Initially, their only support came from Ein Harod, of which they saw themselves as a part, even though it was situated in the Jezreel Plain almost one hundred miles to the northeast.

Two important personalities were among the most prominent members: Russian-born Haim Ben-Asher, who had been sent from Ein Harod as a "veteran" of three years in the country to reinforce the group, and Enzo Sereni, the scion of an ancient Jewish family from Rome. Ben-Asher went for a Saturday hike with some of the members to the thorn-covered hill where they wished to build their new settlement. Looking toward the Mediterranean, some eight miles away, he declared boldly, "We'll develop all the land up to the seashore."

"He certainly knows how to talk and to fantasize," one of his fellow hikers confided to his diary.

Sereni, a married man with two daughters, was a unique figure among the Russian and Eastern European pioneers of that time, most of whom were single. Short, stocky, with horn-rimmed glasses, he had earned a doctorate of philosophy at the University of Rome, with his thesis on the Apocryphal book of Tobit. An intellectual who came to socialism and Zionism through a process of analytical thought, Sereni was a dynamic personality, a doer as well as a thinker. His wife, Ada, a notable beauty, was also from the Rome Jewish community. They joined the Rehovot group after his dream of establishing a Sereni family commune collapsed.

Sereni and Ben-Asher went to see David Ben-Gurion, who would later become the first prime minister of Israel. At that time he was head of the Histadrut Labor Federation. An account of their meeting from the kibbutz archive relates how the two of them got past Ben-Gurion's wife, the formidable Paula, who fought like a lioness to defend her husband's afternoon siesta. Ben-Gurion promised them his full support and told them to go ahead and occupy the fifty-acre site. They had already enlisted the backing of labor leader Berl Katznelson and, as mentioned, were encouraged in their endeavor by Ein Harod.

Locally, though, they were on their own. Moshe Smilansky, a Rehovot citrus grower who had been Sereni's employer, wanted the land. Even their fellow communards of Kvutzat Schiller opposed them, refusing to allow their mule carts, loaded with tents and sections of huts, to pass through their land. Consequently, they were forced to take a roundabout route via a steep-sided *wadi,* but they were undeterred. In the spring of 1928, there were a number of moves toward settlement, with the youngsters erecting tents and setting guards. At the end of March, the Histadrut newspaper *Davar* (edited by Berl Katznelson) reported the establishment of "a new settlement near Rehovot, neighbors of Kvutzat Schiller." However, the official date of the founding of the kibbutz seems to have been June 29, 1928, when some thirty members of the unified group erected a hut for the dining hall and a number of tents for sleeping accommodation.

The settlers felt isolated and vulnerable. They were forced to carry water in cans on donkeys from a pipeline nearly a mile away and had to walk through the sands for more than an hour to their work in Rehovot. Many left during those first hard months to the scorn of their comrades.

"I can excuse doubts and disappointment," Ben-Asher told a general meeting, "but not leaving. One of the deserters has been with us for two years and has shared our dream. Leaving us now is unforgivable." Toward the end of the year one of the founding members, who contracted malaria, was treated abroad, returned to the kibbutz, and died of typhus.

Sereni, who had been given the equivalent of five hundred pounds sterling by his father to celebrate the birth of his second daughter, Hagar (given this "Arab" name to emphasize a desire for Jewish-Arab friendship), handed over the money toward the purchase of the land and the following year, 1929, saw the purchase of all three hundred acres with a thousand-pound loan from Bank Hapoalim (the Workers' Bank) for the down payment, on the assumption that the balance of the money would be raised by Sereni from the Jewish community of Rome. The energetic Italian took on this enormous financial obligation with characteristic panache.

Also in 1929, Givat Brenner was reinforced by a group of immigrants from Germany. The Eastern European founding group found the newcomers difficult to absorb. They felt that the Germans were patronizing them with their Western culture and love of art and music. They thought that the newcomers lacked a Jewish tradition, they criticized their ignorance of Hebrew, and they did not really believe these "intellectuals" capable of hard physical labor. Members of the groups managed to work together but did not mix socially, even sitting separately in the communal dining room.

The cultural difference between the two groups is vividly illustrated by an anecdote that has found its way into several accounts of the earliest years. There was only one public shower, and the rule was that the gender in occupation finished showering, while the opposite sex waited patiently outside. Soon after the arrival of the German group however, a male of the original group was scandalized when, in the middle of taking a shower, he was confronted by a liberated German female, who stripped with a notable lack of self-consciousness. "Naturally I fled!" he told his wife. Several years were to pass before the two communities merged into one.

That year, 1929, also saw the greatest outbreak of Arab violence since the onset of the Zionist enterprise. The rioting started as the result of a dispute concerning Muslim and Jewish holy sites in Jerusalem, but it soon escalated to armed clashes around the country. The religious quarrel was, of course, just the trigger. The underlying reason for the violence was the continued progress of Jewish settlement, the purchase of Arab land leading to the dispossession of Arab farmers, and the emerging national character of the Jewish community in Palestine. The British rulers of Palestine were trying to balance their obligations to both Jews and Arabs, with the result that they annoyed both sides.

The violence spread from Jerusalem to other locations. A total of 133 Jews were killed, mostly in religious centers such as Jerusalem, Hebron, and Safed, and many isolated settlements came under attack. The new kibbutz south of Rehovot was forced to evacuate the site for several days but returned with increased membership. Sixty members left, but seventy-five reoccupied the site the following week with some twenty hunting rifles, which they had now been trained to use. The reinforcements consisted of a group of fifteen recent immigrants from Lithuania.

Their one hut had been burned down, and during the following months all the members had to live in tents. On the other hand, the violence, which came unexpectedly after almost a decade of relative quiet, led to greater employment possibilities for the members of the kibbutz. Rehovot farmers now preferred Jewish workers over Arabs.

By 1930 the membership had grown to 150, and, while retaining its link to Ein Harod, the new settlement cut loose from actual membership of that kibbutz and became an independent unit. The general meeting voted in favor of the name Givat Brenner, Brenner's Hill, after the writer Joseph Haim Brenner, who was killed in earlier Arab riots in Jaffa. The same year a well was dug, a water tank was erected, and the first permanent building was constructed, a two-story house with reinforced walls, built to withstand attacks. Despite this, many of the members would continue to live in the white bell tents for a number of years.

Figure 2.1. Givat Brenner in the 1930s.

Source: (Israel Government Press Office)

Reflecting the growing size of the kibbutz, a council was elected as an intermediate body between the management committee and the *asefa,* the general meeting of all members. In addition, there was a daily news sheet to keep the members up-to-date. Such ideas would have been unthinkable in a kvutza like Degania, where everyone knew everyone else and anything that happened was general knowledge. The news sheet reported discussions and decisions of the management committee and the council—but not of the general meeting, which everyone was expected to attend—gave information about developments, and announced forthcoming events. Even in its early days, Givat Brenner had a rich cultural life, including Hebrew lessons, literary discussions, an advanced poetry group, gymnastics, and a choir.

No less than twenty committees assisted the management committee in organizing the life of the kibbutz, among them committees for housing, manpower, security, culture, sport, education, health, and even a "smoking committee" in charge of the distribution of cigarettes.

Enzo Sereni was ahead of his time in demanding individual autonomy for the members. He rejected the *kvutza* ideal of the commune as a large family, believing that the kibbutz ought to be a "community of individual families." He openly scorned the intimate confessional society disclosed by the diary of Our Community, which he regarded as "suffocating the individual instead of liberating him."

Sereni argued that unless the kibbutz remained an open society, it was liable to petrify, but he also aimed to limit that openness by proposing the admission of new members by secret ballot. He pointed out that the overly frank discussions on candidates up for membership exposed their weaknesses for all to hear and often caused potential members to walk out of the community even before a vote was taken. His proposal was firmly rejected, although secret ballots would eventually be adopted by all kibbutzim. Sereni also failed in his efforts to introduce a system of equal personal allowances, which would give the members the freedom to spend their money as they saw fit. This was rejected on the grounds of being incompatible with the principle of "from each according to his ability, to each according to his needs." Here again the mercurial Italian was proved to be ahead of his time. Today the "privatization" of budgets, more or less along the lines proposed by Sereni, is at the top of the agenda for change in every kibbutz. His wife, Ada, who was in charge of the clothing store in the early years, proposed personal allowances for clothing. This suggestion that members "possess private property" (which would also subsequently be universally adopted) was rejected with horror by the purists. It may be noted that the socialist convictions of the members did not prevent some of them from "removing" garments from the communal clothing store and (as disclosed in a news sheet of the time) even "sewing a patch over another person's number" to conceal the theft.

For the most part, though, Givat Brenner was occupied with its physical survival, and 1931 was remembered as "the year of hunger and idealism." The kibbutz continued to rely on the income it received from members working outside. As work again became more scarce, Sereni discovered that there was a possibility of work at the Dead Sea potash plant, where the unusually high temperatures made conditions extremely difficult. Hitherto only Arabs from Transjordan had been employed in the blistering heat of the carnallite pans. The Histadrut Labor Federation wanted Jews to be part of this industry and appealed to the kibbutzim for volunteers. There was little enthusiasm for the idea at Givat Brenner, but Sereni persuaded the general meeting and personally led a gang of twenty laborers to the site. Their shoes disintegrated, and they developed sores on their feet and legs. Sereni demanded rubber boots for his workers, and they were provided. After that, the pro-

Figure 2.2. Givat Brenner in the 1950s.

Source: (Yad Tabenkin Archives)

ductivity of the Givat Brenner workers increased, eventually surpassing that of the Transjordanians.

Many members continued to work at the tree nursery in Rehovot, but now the kibbutz established its own nursery, along with a vegetable garden, a citrus grove, and cereal crops, and it opened a bakery in what had been the stable. Discussions raged in the group regarding absorption of newcomers. Some argued that new members should be limited according to the accommodation and work available, but the pro-expansion party, which sought to maximize absorption of newcomers, regardless of "practical" considerations, repeatedly won the argument. When the Nazis came to power in Germany in 1933, Givat Brenner took in its share of the newcomers who fled from that country, increasing the number of its members to 280, and two years later membership was approaching 400.

Like all the other kibbutzim, Givat Brenner was faced with the question of how to educate its children. The reaction to the arrival of the first children of the first *kvutza,* Degania, has already been chronicled. It is clear that, from the earliest stages, the second generation must be a prime concern of every communal society. The members of Degania were the first to face the question of what to do with their children, and they made arrangements for raising them together in a social peer group. From the earliest age, the infants were supposed to learn to live in a community, to make allowances, to tolerate their fellows, to work together, to cooperate. The Society of Children illustrated the principle articulated by Joseph Bussel that the community as a whole should be responsible for raising the children.

One of the communes defended by Trumpeldor, Kfar Giladi, was forced to evacuate its site for a prolonged period, during which its members lived in the village of Rosh Pina, a few miles to the south. The shortage of accommodation necessitated the placing of all the children in a single room at night, apart from their parents. This improvisation subsequently became the general pattern. In all the communal settlements (with the notable exception of Degania) the children slept in special children's houses, away from their parents. It meant that they could have decent accommodation, while their parents were still forced to live in tents. As time went on, it became a doctrine, an article of faith, that to create a genuine Society of Children, the children should live with their own peer group, even at night.

Givat Brenner, as part of the Kibbutz Meuhad, followed the way of Ein Harod, which evolved the idea of the school as an integral part of each kibbutz. From an early age, the children were expected to help clean and tidy their own quarters, and older children worked for several hours each day in the various farming branches. Kibbutz teachers and educators were also influenced by the ideas of progressive educators in Europe and the United States, in particular by John Dewey. At a general meeting in 1935, Givat Brenner voted to establish its own school, and it was opened the following year.

By then Givat Brenner possessed, in addition to the branches already mentioned, a vineyard, fruit trees, poultry, and a dairy herd. Striking out in new directions, the members also established a carpentry shop, a foundry, and a workers' canteen in Rehovot. The rapid expansion and the inclusion of industrial and service branches had been the policy of Kibbutz Meuhad from its earliest days, but it had been implemented only to a limited extent. In this, as in much else, Givat Brenner was a pioneer.

Typical of the new thinking was the construction in 1934 of a convalescent home. It was the brainchild of Jessie Sampter, an American writer who joined the kibbutz with her adopted daughter after the 1929 Arab riots. A lady of means, she sold the house that she had built in Rehovot and gave the proceeds to Givat Brenner for the construction of "a rest home for workers." Sampter, who published several books of poetry and prose in English, had immigrated to Palestine in 1919. A passionate idealist—she was a pacifist and vegetarian, as well as a Zionist and socialist—she persuaded the kibbutz to make the rest home a vegetarian institution.

When she died in 1938, the rest home was named "Beit Yesha" (Jessie House) in her memory. Although many years later the management altered its vegetarian character after potential customers started canceling bookings unless they received meat meals, Jessie House continued to function into the 1980s. Today its rooms are rented to non-member residents of Givat Brenner.

Sampter wrote extensively about kibbutz life. In this letter to her sister, she explains the egalitarian system of the kibbutz and conveys something of the atmosphere of Givat Brenner in the 1930s:

> Everyone works here. One could not live here and not work, it would be a spiritual impossibility. All work is done without remuneration. All pay goes to the common fund. Life here is very free and there is a great deal of personal consideration. Each is treated according to his needs. The ideal which guides us is, as far as possible, to give to each according to his needs and get from each whatever he can give. As you say, it does not always work out so well. Still I would call this experiment a great success, not in relation to the ideal, but in comparison with other societies.

Another passage illustrates the continuous drive to absorb more members: "We are terribly short of buildings, and dreadfully overcrowded, but we want to take in as many as possible, particularly German youth."

This rapid growth had a negative side, however. Housing was inadequate, forcing new members to live in packing crates and tents. The public shower was too small, there were insufficient toilets, garbage was often dumped in the open. These deplorable standards resulted in an outbreak of typhus. A delegation from the Histadrut health department, which came to inspect the kibbutz, pronounced it "unfit for the absorption of refugee youth from Germany."

In addition, spurred on by the enthusiasm of Sereni, among others, Givat Brenner spent more money than it had. A Kibbutz Meuhad committee criticized the kibbutz for its high rate of investment, in light of its uncertain economic future. Here again Givat Brenner (and Enzo Sereni) were pioneers ahead of their time but in this case in a partly negative sense.

The 1930s saw large-scale Jewish immigration to Palestine, at first as a result of the Polish economic crisis, and then because of the accession to power of Adolf Hitler in Germany. The British continued to juggle their obligations to the Zionist enterprise and to the Arab community of Palestine to the dissatisfaction of both. As the Jewish community grew, the resistance of the Palestinian Arabs escalated, until, in 1936, an

Arab general strike escalated into a full-scale Arab Revolt, which lasted until the outbreak of World War II in 1939.

The first Jewish communes in Palestine, even before Degania, were of Hashomer, the Jewish self-defense organization, and the *kvutzot* had undertaken their own defense from the outset. Many of the members of the Labor Battalion and of Ein Harod were former Hashomer guards, and the Hagana defense force was established in 1920 by the labor movement. In the subsequent years, the communal settlements, often surrounded by Arab villages, had continued to engage in their own defense. Despite this, the Arab Revolt took the kibbutzim by surprise, and it was only in 1936 that they seriously began to develop a defense strategy. Even the *kvutzot*, which were still influenced by the pacifist ideas of Gordon, came to the conclusion that "the rifle is as essential as our working tools—perhaps more so."

Many kibbutz members joined the "Field Squads," based in the kibbutzim, which were demobilized at the end of the Arab Revolt, only to be resuscitated in 1941 as the Palmah, the mobile strike force of the Hagana. During the Arab Revolt, the British authorities set up units of the government-financed "Jewish Settlement Police," the recruits of which were in most cases also members of the Hagana. As the war with Germany approached, there were disputes in the kibbutzim, as in the population at large, as to whether the members should mobilize to defend their own settlements as members of the Hagana or the Palmah or volunteer for the British army. The leadership of Kibbutz Meuhad opposed joining the British forces, and at Givat Brenner the general meeting voted to expel any member who joined up without the consent of the kibbutz.

At the same time, the presence of a considerable British army, stationed in the Middle East, facilitated an enlargement of Givat Brenner's industrial infrastructure. A plant that the kibbutz had set up for pickling surplus cucumbers was expanded into Rimon, a full-scale, mechanized canning factory, manufacturing juice, canned fruit, and preserves from a whole range of fruit and vegetables, mainly for the British army. Rimon was to be a vital source of income for the kibbutz for many years.

With the outbreak of World War II, many members of Givat Brenner defied the vote of the general meeting and volunteered to serve in the British army, leaving the kibbutz short of manpower. The kibbutz was forced to take in hired workers, in particular for its factories. Enzo Sereni, who over the years had served as a Zionist emissary in Germany and the United States, was stationed in Iraq, where he organized

Figure 2.3.   A funeral at Givat Brenner in 1967.

Source: (Yad Tabenkin Archives)

attempts to bring Jews to Palestine. In the final stages of the war, he parachuted into Italy in an attempt to rescue Italian Jews. He was captured and sent to the Dachau concentration camp, where he died.

To commemorate its most illustrious member and his tragically heroic death, Givat Brenner converted the first permanent building, which had been constructed after the Arab riots of 1929, into Beit Sereni (Sereni House). It included a library, a children's library, reading rooms, a lecture hall, and an auditorium. Subsequently, a memorial room was added with a record of every member of Givat Brenner who has died.

After the war, the British were faced with an increasingly explosive situation in Palestine. The Jews, who had lost six million of their people in the Nazi Holocaust, were desperate to bring in the survivors; the Arabs were demanding self-determination and a ban on Jewish immigration. Britain, which had tried to maintain a balanced policy over the years but had in fact fluctuated between support for one or the other side, now came down on the side of the Arabs.

Some elements in the Palestinian Jewish community started taking direct action against British targets as well as Arabs. Strong differences evolved among the Jews, with some backing actions such as blowing up the King David Hotel in Jerusalem, where the British administration was centered, and others favoring a more moderate policy. The British, naturally enough, saw such actions as terrorism, and their hostility toward the Jews increased. Attempts to bring in Jews from Europe and stockpiling arms were seen as subversive activities.

Givat Brenner's members were active in attempts to smuggle Jewish refugees into Palestine against the wishes of the British authorities, and, like other kibbutzim, it served as an unofficial base of the Hagana and the Palmah. The kibbutz was searched by British troops, who discovered the secret arms cache and severely beat a number of members as well as damaging property. Subsequently, they deported fifty members of Givat Brenner to Cyprus.

Kibbutz members played a prominent part in Israel's War of Independence, which broke out when the British left in 1948. The brunt of the fighting against the invading Arab armies and local militias was born by the Hagana and the Palmah. Altogether, forty-four members of Givat Brenner lost their lives in Israel's wars.

After the war, the kibbutz acquired land that had been abandoned by Palestinian Arabs who fled or were expelled during the conflict. Givat Brenner continued to grow and expand. The Rimon preserves factory prospered, and a plant for the manufacture of irrigation equipment was established. Immigrants from more than twenty different nations joined in the years after the war.

The kibbutz enjoyed a rich cultural life. It had members who were writers, poets, artists, and musicians. There was a drama circle, an orchestra, a choir, a chamber group, and performances by the kibbutz children, including a Mozart opera. The kibbutz youngsters excelled in sports, including soccer, swimming, athletics, and gymnastics. The kibbutz basketball team was in the national league. Givat Brenner had a membership of over nine hundred and a population including children, parents, and other residents of some fifteen hundred.

And then, in 1951, in what should have been its finest hour, the kibbutz movement—and with it Givat Brenner—split apart over a question that was entirely theoretical. When it declared its statehood in 1948, Israel won the support of both the United States and the Soviet Union. It therefore adopted a policy of neutrality between East and West. As the cold war intensified, however, David Ben-Gurion, Israel's first prime minister, felt that the nation's survival necessitated a pro-Western stance. He was supported by the members of Hever Hakvutzot, the association of small communes. The avowedly Marxist Kibbutz Artzi dissented from this policy, and some members even declared support for the Soviet Union in the event of an East-West conflict breaking out. Kibbutz Meuhad was split, with a majority opposing Ben-Gurion. Although there are a number of pro-Soviet declarations on record, the kibbutz members who were involved in the split at the time insist the cold war was a side issue and that the pro-Soviet statements were made by a minority of extremists. They maintain that the argument was over Marxist socialism and the right to support the Communist Manifesto.

Although it did affect the education in the kibbutz schools and youth movements, Marxism had absolutely no relevance to the way the kibbutzim conducted their daily lives. Nevertheless, it generated the fiercest quarrel in the movement since the establishment of Degania. In kibbutzim all over Israel, members who had overcome so many difficulties to forge strong successful communities argued to the point of physical violence. Communities were torn asunder; families were split down the middle; communal dining halls had roped off areas to divide Mapam members from supporters of Mapai. Several individual kibbutzim divided their assets and split amoeba-like in two; most went one way or another, with the minority leaving for a kibbutz of their ideological persuasion.

Givat Brenner managed to avoid the excesses of other kibbutzim. There were no violent arguments or physical confrontations, although some families were split. Yaacov Viterbo, an Italian who came to the kibbutz after World War II, recalls that the general meetings continued and that there was no separation in the communal dining hall. There were meetings of the left-wing group, which was in the majority, and the minority that supported Mapai. The result was that Givat Brenner remained in Kibbutz Meuhad, but 120 members, many of them founders of the kibbutz, left to form Kibbutz Netzer Sereni nearby. Those leaving included Germans, Lithuanians, and most of the Italians (though not Viterbo himself). In naming their new kibbutz after Enzo, they were clearly stating that he would have been with them; anyone familiar with the character of the brilliant Italian can only wonder whether he might have prevented the split in Givat Brenner, if only he had survived the war.

The split in the kibbutz movement was only one of the factors leading to its diminished importance. The socialist pioneering endeavor, which had played a leading part in the establishment, defense, and survival of the State of Israel, became increasingly marginalized in the course of the next years. Givat Brenner continued to prosper, but it was only marginally involved in absorbing the new wave of immigrants that swept in from the Muslim countries of the Middle East. Although the new influx doubled Israel's population, less than 4 percent of the new-comers found their homes in the kibbutzim.

Veteran Haim Zeligman, who arrived in Palestine from Germany and joined Givat Brenner eight years after its founding, expresses regret:

> We did not play our part in absorbing the oriental immigration. I blame the East Europeans. We *Yekkes* (German Jews) have a more positive approach to the Middle Eastern Jews. Of course, we were still reeling from the Holocaust, and it was also the time of the big split, and that sapped our energy and reduced our ability to achieve things. When I look back on the split in the kibbutz, I just don't know how we let it happen. We lost 120 of our best members. How did we do it?

Viterbo regards such talk as being wise after the event:

> Although I was a relative newcomer and didn't fully understand all the issues, I did not think the argument was absurd. It was the atmosphere of the times. The dispute was not about money or material things; it was about ideology. I admired both groups, and I still do. I am glad that we avoided the extremes of other kibbutzim, and several families have retained friendly relations with members of Netzer Sereni.

The failure to absorb significant numbers of Middle Eastern immigrants meant that the kibbutzim stopped growing, and their relative strength in the population as a whole declined. The reservoir of pioneering youth from Poland and other parts of Eastern Europe had been wiped out by the Nazis. The local youth movements provided some reinforcements to the kibbutzim, and their groups, along with natural increase, prevented an actual decline in the kibbutz population.

It was in the 1950s and 1960s that the *moshav* cooperative village came into its own. The new immigrants from the Middle Eastern countries found the looser cooperative form of the *moshav* far more to their liking than the tight communal structure of the kibbutz. Hundreds of new *moshavim* were established, the cities expanded, and some twenty new towns, called "development towns," were built in all parts of Israel.

The newcomers, in both the *moshavim* and the towns, needed work, the kibbutzim needed workers, and the government expected the kibbutzim to do their national duty. In the kibbutz movement, a new debate raged over the question of hired labor. As other kibbutzim followed the path of Givat Brenner in setting up industries, the need for labor became ever more urgent, and as the immigrants poured into the new state, unemployment became an increasingly vital problem.

A large majority of the kibbutzim jettisoned their socialist principles in favor of doing their national duty, particularly because in so doing they were bettering their own economic situation. The employment of large numbers of outside workers, however, was a serious intrusion from the world outside. The kibbutzim had never seen themselves (as communes in the United States and elsewhere did) as dropouts from mainstream society. Rather, they aspired to lead society and serve as examples or blueprints. However, with the introduction of hired workers, the kibbutz had manifestly become a capitalist exploiter. Although lip service was still paid to the original idea of a workers' commune, the reality was somewhat different.

As if the kibbutzim did not have enough problems in the 1950s, with the political split, the failure to play a major part in absorbing the mass immigration, and the matter of hired workers, another crisis arrived in the form of German reparations. The Israeli government negotiated an arrangement with West Germany, whereby that nation extended large credits to Israel as a gesture of recognition of the dreadful sufferings of the Jewish people caused by the Nazis. At the same time, refugees and survivors were personally compensated for their property, businesses, and loss of education.

Givat Brenner, with its large number of German Jews, was a major recipient. There had always been marginal inequality in the kibbutz. At a general meeting in the 1930s, objections were raised against a member who was lucky enough to be related to a dentist and went to him for treatment. "We do not have to have equality in toothache!" Enzo Sereni had declared on that occasion, but another objection concerned a visit abroad of a member to visit his parents at their expense. "Is this not a gross infringement of the principle of equality?" asked a member in the daily news sheet.

Possibly it was, but in the 1930s these were marginal matters. Now in the 1950s larger sums of money were involved. Naturally some recipients of German reparations left the kibbutz. In some kibbutzim members were allowed to keep at least a proportion of the money for what was after all very personal loss or suffering. Generally such money was spent on a piece of equipment, such as a record player, or a one-time trip abroad. At Givat Brenner, most of the money was given to the kibbutz, which used it for the building of public facilities, including a swimming pool, a larger dining hall, and an auditorium.

"Thank God it was the *Yekkes* (German Jews) who received the money," said a kibbutz-born member. "They played by the rules."

Veteran Haim Zeligman, himself a recipient, acknowledges that the money helped build much of Givat Brenner, adding that in general German reparations built up the whole State of Israel, but he sees it as the beginning of the end of kibbutz values. "Suddenly we became rich, we in the kibbutzim and everyone else. The collective ethos declined, and all of us became much more materialistic and individualistic. The money that came in from Germany had an enormous influence on everything."

Despite all the problems faced by the kibbutz movement in general, and Givat Brenner in particular, the kibbutz celebrated its twenty-fifth anniversary in 1953, with a grandiose display that illustrated the economic power, the social vitality, and the cultural richness of the community. It presented a spectacular production of *My Glorious Brothers,* the dramatization of a novel by American author Howard Fast about the 166 B.C.E. Jewish revolt against the Greek Empire.

The story of this presentation is recounted by Shula Keshet, a kibbutz member, in the journal *Kibbutz Trends.* The production was staged, regardless of expense. An ancient village (real houses—not a stage set) was built on one of the surrounding hills, and trees were specially planted, creating a natural site for the performance. The "stage" was thirty yards across and fifty deep. The whole community was drafted, with more than three thousand workdays invested in the building, acting, and producing. An announcement in the kibbutz journal said, "Everyone asked by the committee to participate must accept immediately, without resisting." Shulamit Bat-Dori, the producer-director, would use only kibbutz members as actors, even refusing to employ a professional when her lead actor was mobilized for military service. She had been a pupil of Max Reinhart and Ervin Piscator in Germany in the 1930s, when they were experimenting with new forms of theater, producing "happenings" in the streets. She saw the production as a way of commemorating Israel's recent War of Independence by drawing a parallel with the ancient struggle.

In Keshet's view, Bat-Dori was also concerned with reinforcing both the image and the self-image of the kibbutz following the split and the other problems of the early 1950s. People came from all over the country by bus and truck, and the performances were seen by an estimated forty thousand people. Keshet believes Bat-Dori's "manipulation" was only temporarily successful, masking the real issues facing the kibbutz and producing an illusion of kibbutz solidarity. Be that as it may, it was an awesome display of the social and economic power that the kibbutz still possessed at that time.

It is also an example of how the kibbutzim endeavored over the years to re-create the past in a way that made it meaningful in the present. The efforts of the early pioneers to find modern ways of observing the Sabbath and marking the Jewish festivals have been mentioned in the account of Degania. These attempts increased in scope with the growth of the kibbutz movement, particularly with the growing population of children, and they continue until today. Givat Brenner is one of the kibbutzim that has invested energy and resources in reviving Jewish life as a secular culture and making it relevant to the modern era.

The Sabbath, traditionally a day of rest for Jews, often had to be a special workday in the kibbutz, but efforts were made to generate a festive atmosphere, with white cloths spread on the tables, all the members eating together at the same time on Friday night, and blessings over wine and bread. Pessah (Passover) has been re-created as a festival of spring and freedom, with the traditional Haggada, the text that relates the Exodus from Egypt, updated and infused with modern significance. Sometimes the modern Haggada includes humorous passages about the kibbutz members; often the kibbutz choir sings and the folk dance group performs. The ancient custom of the Omer, the offering of new barley brought to the Temple in Jerusalem on the second day of Pessah, has been revived with the creation of a local ceremony with song and dance. Shavuot (Weeks) and Succot (Tabernacles) have been re-created as festivals of the first fruits and the harvest, respectively, particularly significant in a farming community. Observed for centuries in the synagogue, these festivals have been brought back to the fields and orchards of the kibbutzim as joyous modern celebrations with specially written songs and children performing folk dances.

It is at celebrations such as these that the whole kibbutz comes together to create an atmosphere of warmth, friendship, social solidarity, and achievement that gives the members a feeling of elation, a belief that they are rebuilding an ancient identity and creating something enduring, rooted in the soil of their ancient homeland. The renewal of the Jewish festivals by the kibbutzim has revitalized their significance in schools, kindergartens, and private homes throughout Israel.

More prosaically, the 1960s saw the "privatization" of the communal clothing store, with members of Givat Brenner at last owning their own clothes. They also got their own radio sets. In the 1950s, the kibbutz had three radio rooms where members would gather if they wanted to hear the news or listen to a concert. Then members started keeping radio sets that they were given, and in due course the kibbutz bought radios for all the members. In the early days—and even, as we have seen, up to the period of German reparations in the 1950s—members gave anything they received from outside to the kibbutz. But as consumer goods became more plentiful, kibbutz practice became less puritanical. Members started off by keeping radio sets; they continued by keeping televisions, stereo sets, and other items of furniture. This was the case in Givat Brenner and most other kibbutzim, but as long as the kibbutz could afford to "level up" by purchasing items for those members who did not have them, the situation remained under control.

It was not long, however, before members started retaining gifts of money that they received as wedding presents. No formal decision was reached, but the concept of "equality as far as the kibbutz fence" became generally accepted. This meant that the kibbutz did not permit blatant inequality in the kibbutz, such as the purchase of a private automobile, but nobody asked any questions about what happened outside. Some members even inherited apartments without informing the kibbutz treasurer. This situation that prevailed in most kibbutzim probably paved the way for the concept of differential allowances that emerged some two decades later.

Meanwhile, Givat Brenner continued to be a relatively prosperous community. In the 1970s, it was one of the first kibbutzim to have the children sleep in their parents' homes instead of the children's houses, and it began to encourage its youngsters to go in for higher education, even financing their university studies. The kibbutz also developed an impressive infrastructure for caring for its increasing community of veterans. Over two hundred of the fifteen hundred residents were by now of retirement age, and life was good for them. A small hospital offered around-the-clock care for a dozen incapacitated old people.

The fittest veterans continued working at their jobs in farming, the garage, or the metal workshop, often with reduced hours. For those who found their previous work onerous, the Ben-Gali workshop was established, offering part-time employment to those still able to do some work. They could work at their own pace for as long as they liked at wood weaving, bookbinding, raffia work, and other crafts. The plant did not make a profit, but it covered itself. Those who were still capable of managing on their own remained in their individual homes, but where possible they were moved to accommodation nearer the dining hall and cultural center, and they were given assistance in cleaning and maintenance. Those who could no longer get to the communal dining hall had their food brought home. Many of the elderly were able to get about in special battery-powered electric carts. A well-appointed, fully staffed retirement home was established for those who needed continuous care.

Tova Gavrielli, herself a veteran, was sent by the kibbutz to study gerontology in Germany. When I interviewed her for a newspaper article fifteen years ago, she was adamant that her studies did not make her an "expert" in what was good for old people. She aimed, as far as possible, to let the old decide for themselves. "If you make all the decisions for an old person, you finish him off!" she declared. She established Ben-Gali in 1965. "The great thing about the kibbutz is that it is a working society, and people can exercise their right to work to the end of their lives." As an older person herself, she knew that the veterans slept less. "I didn't ask questions," she explains. "I simply made it possible for the Ben-Gali employees to come to work at four in the morning."

Her friend Shulamit Lachish felt that the kibbutz was ideal for old people. "They have friendship, care, security, the possibility of some work, suitable accommodation in beautiful surroundings, and, above all, the presence of children, grandchildren, and great-grandchildren. Even if they do not have their own, they have the pleasure of living in a multi-generation community." In this, as in so much else, Givat Brenner was the trailblazer for the kibbutz movement. Many kibbutzim learned how to care for their old folk from the Givat Brenner example.

"The kibbutz is perfect for old people," remarked a member cynically during this period. "It's also great for children. In between it is awful!"

The reality at Givat Brenner and other kibbutzim seemed to justify the remark. In the mid-1980s, increasing numbers of kibbutz children were leaving on reaching adulthood. The second generation of those born on the kibbutz had, for the most part, continued the path of their parents, but the third and fourth generations were far less inclined to remain, particularly as living standards rose and travel became cheaper. Large numbers of kibbutz youth started to travel abroad after their army service; many of them did not return. If they did return to Israel, they often did not come back to the kibbutz.

As mentioned in the introduction, the big economic crunch for most kibbutzim came in 1985. Many kibbutzim, which had borrowed money rashly, were left with unpayable debts. After negotiations, which lasted several years, the government, the kibbutzim, and the banks worked out the so-called Kibbutz Arrangement, an economic recovery plan for the kibbutzim involving a debt write-off and reschedule. We will take a closer look at the 1985 crisis and its solution in a later chapter, but here it must be pointed out that Givat Brenner, mainly because of the success of its Rimon juice and preserves factory with its annual income of $30 million, was performing relatively well at the time. Consequently, it was not involved in the Kibbutz Arrangement. When Rimon went bankrupt in 1995, it was too late for Givat Brenner to benefit from the Kibbutz Arrangement. The company was eventually sold, and the kibbutz was left with the debts. According to Yosef Rietti, who has served as the kibbutz controller since the early 1980s, the collapse was the result of a combination of bad luck, bad judgment, and the kibbutz system of guaranteeing its enterprises. Unlike a private business, a kibbutz guarantees the loans it takes with its other assets. As a consequence, when Rimon went bankrupt, Givat Brenner was left with debts it cannot repay from its current income.

"Rimon was becoming out-of-date," explains Rietti. "We needed to renew the machinery, and we didn't have the money. We had to look for new ideas, and whatever we tried didn't work."

Unlike some other kibbutzim, Givat Brenner did not try to solve its financial problems by borrowing money from questionable sources, says the controller, but its financial probity did not pay off. Wrong decisions were made, he concedes. For example, the irrigation equipment factory continued to manufacture aluminum equipment, instead of going over to plastic. Nearby Kibbutz Naan converted to plastic, and its factory turns a substantial profit to this day.

At the same time, Rietti believes that a fundamental social malaise had developed at Givat Brenner. The real blow was psychological. Despite their decline in prestige, the kibbutzim have, until recently, been an economic success story. Whatever might be said about them, the kibbutz system worked. Now, after the debt crisis, this impression is no longer clear. Rietti is convinced that social problems lead to economic crises and not vice versa. The kibbutzim with strong communities are the ones that have remained economically successful. Their members also work harder.

"In Hatzerim and Maagan Michael [two economically successful kibbutzim, which we will be visiting in due course], they work harder than we do," Rietti maintains. "Their members are not afraid to work shifts in their factories. If the community is healthy, the members are loyal; the children remain; everyone makes an effort and works hard."

The successful kibbutzim invest in their factories, introduce mechanization and automation, make the work more interesting, and generate money for investment, creating a multiplier effect. In Givat Brenner, on the other hand, there was a vicious circle. The community lost its self-confidence and started to bring in outsiders to manage the factories. As a consequence, many of the kibbutz office holders and managers felt that they had failed and sought work outside Givat Brenner. They had to be replaced by outsiders. Rietti maintains that several outside managers employed by the kibbutz were overpaid and, furthermore, only served for limited periods.

"They departed with nice wads of money, leaving us in the lurch," he charges. He is convinced that Givat Brenner must seek its salvation from within and regain its belief that it can run its own affairs.

The collapse of Rimon, and its subsequent sale, has left the kibbutz in a bad way. The total income of the other factories is around $10 million annually, one-third of what Rimon used to earn. Consequently, this large community, with an extremely high proportion of elderly people, is now facing financial ruin. Today, under duress and with a sense of crisis, it has embarked on a path of reform and restructuring. It is against this background that the current situation must be seen.

One of the first casualties of the reorganization of the economic branches has been Ben-Gali, the marvelous workshop for veteran members. Formerly structured to give the elderly members satisfying work, without too much regard for profits, Ben-Gali has now become a profitable enterprise, earning some $300,000 annually. In itself this success is a good thing, but it has been at the cost of its service to the elderly of Givat Brenner. Today only two veterans still work there. The remainder have to be satisfied with occupational therapy and similar activities. At the other end of the age range, kibbutz children are continuing to leave in increasing numbers. Givat Brenner's membership has declined from a peak of over 900 to 750. The proportion of elderly has increased, and there is a genuine fear about the future of the kibbutz.

Although Givat Brenner as a whole, with its many buildings and well-kept gardens, still gives an impression of prosperity, the kibbutz offices are a bit dilapidated. The furniture is old and shabby, the floor tiles are chipped and worn, and the walls are in need of a lick of paint.

Avner Zacks, the secretary of Givat Brenner, is in his fifties. A lean, worried-looking man, in traditional blue cotton working shirt and jeans, he asks if he can smoke and puffs away nervously. Thoughtful, unpretentious, laceratingly honest, he lays out the facts without hesitation.

"We have a business manager who is not a member of the kibbutz," he remarks.

> And that tells you a lot. I don't like to shout it out loud, but there is a negative selection process at work here. We have lost some of the best and brightest of our young adults. Two-thirds of our members are over fifty years old, more than a third have passed pension age [sixty-five]. We do not have enough members in the twenty-five to forty age group, and, frankly, those who have stayed are not the best. I don't want to run them down. Most of them are decent hard-working people, but too many of our kibbutz-born members with ambition and initiative have left. We *needed* an outside manager.

Avner admits that the kibbutz members simply did not know how to manage their affairs and didn't really want to know. They were not up-to-date, did not change the managers of the factories and farming branches when they needed changing, and have become increasingly incapable of coping with the realities of modern life. He took on the job of kibbutz secretary just over a year ago and quickly obtained approval from the general meeting for an "emergency regime," which enables him to bypass the plethora of committees, which, while guaranteeing democracy and public control, have tended to petrify kibbutz life and prevent change. He accepted the job because the changes that had been approved by the general meeting and the council were not being implemented, and he thought he could do better.

"I came in with high hopes but have lowered my expectations," Avner confesses. "You have to go easy. I am seeking the widest possible consensus. I have come to the conclusion that you can't carry out too many sudden drastic changes. We could destroy our society completely."

Rimon provided more than half of the income of the kibbutz. Today there remain a furniture factory and store, an aluminum workshop that subcontracts for exports, a small plant for computer programming, a dressmaker, Ben-Gali crafts, an amusement park for children, a tree nursery, a sod farm, a dairy, a poultry branch, and an orchard. There is an industrial photographer and a kibbutz team making videos. In addition to all this, the kibbutz rents out its facilities, including apartments, theaters, and land. Some 120 members work at outside jobs, paying their salaries to the kibbutz.

Although Avner does not think that the branch managers have yet been granted sufficient autonomy, Givat Brenner has started to put the factories and farming branches on a businesslike basis. The service branches, though, are still too labor-intensive, and the kibbutz as a whole is still far from efficient.

In an effort to mobilize the necessary capital for their reorganization and economic recovery plan, the members of Givat Brenner have voted to build a new neighborhood. This will double the population of the kibbutz, but the new neighbors will not be kibbutz members, which means that they will not be partners in the kibbutz enterprises. The houses will be put on the market for anyone to buy. In fact, not quite anyone: there will be a selection committee to screen prospective purchasers.

This is going to create a new situation, because the new residents *will* be partners in the village. Clearly, they will have to participate in elections for the local council and will have a say in the way the joint settlement is run. What it actually means, explains Avner, is that Givat Brenner will no longer be a kibbutz but rather a settlement that *includes* a kibbutz. One of the benefits is that it will increase the proportion of residents in the missing twenty-five to forty age group. "We assume they will want to purchase services from the kibbutz," says Avner. "We have a good school and good kindergartens and day care facilities. That will be one of the attractions that the new neighborhood has to offer."

Will the two communities remain separate over the years, or will the barriers come down? It is too early to know the answer, thinks Avner. He believes that several of the features of communal life will be maintained within the kibbutz but concedes that those members "guarding the kibbutz ramparts" consist of a small minority in the Givat Brenner of today. He thinks the new neighborhood will strengthen the kibbutz socially, but the main motivation is economic. Avner is confident that if the project is carried out efficiently, Givat Brenner can solve its economic problems.

"I know people don't *feel* well off," concludes Avner, "but, even today, when you add up the apartments, gardens, dining hall, theaters, library, swimming pool, gymnasium, ball fields, education, health services, care for the aged, and general environment, we still have a pretty high standard of living. It takes a lot of money to maintain it, I can tell you that."

Perhaps the first thing to note about Dov Sherman, the outsider who is paid to be the general business manager of Givat Brenner, is that he is extraordinarily busy. You have to get up early to see him, as the phrase goes—in our case, seven o'clock in the morning. Sherman is not a member of the kibbutz management committee, and his office is situated a hundred yards away from the kibbutz office, as if to demonstrate the separation, to emphasize that he is a paid official, not the head of the kibbutz. He is a lanky, genial man, with a pale, long-nosed face, black mustache, and black shock of hair. He dresses like a kibbutznik, in jeans and leather jacket. He speaks like a kibbutznik, in abrupt, explosive bursts. His plain-talking direct style and body language are also those of a kibbutznik, possibly because he was a kibbutz member for most of his adult life.

Sherman was a member of Neve Ur, a kibbutz in the Jordan Valley, where he was elected to manage the factory, making auto parts for export to the German motor industry. In 1993, the kibbutz decided to raise money for its factory on the Tel Aviv Stock Exchange, and the plant became a modern capitalist business. The kibbutz retained ownership of 75 percent, but it did not interfere in running the concern. An outside board of directors was appointed, but the chairman and general manager were kibbutz members.

The difference, explains Sherman, was that before the change he, as manager, had reported to the kibbutz general meeting, where most of the members had no idea what he was talking about. After the change, he was accountable to a professional board, the members of which understood and scrutinized everything. He had to produce quarterly reports, three-month work plans, proper budgets, and cost and control reports. The board members—businessmen, accountants, engineers—did their homework, read the minutes of previous meetings, examined the balance sheets, and asked awkward but relevant questions.

"We were producing for the German auto market," recalls Sherman. "The competition was murderous. They argued over the price of every item. We had to maintain first-class quality control, and we had to get it right the first time."

Sherman's wife had long wanted to leave Neve Ur for personal reasons, but he resisted the idea of a move, until it dawned on him that in managing the factory he had become alienated from the kibbutz. Although the factory was now run on entirely modern lines, the other kibbutz branches were still organized in the same old way.

"When I came to think about it," recalls Sherman. "I realized that I did not merely reject the kibbutz way of running things. I thought it ridiculous. It is simply irrelevant to the modern world."

Despite this, when he was offered the position of outside general manager at Givat Brenner, Sherman was overawed. Givat Brenner, he explains, was the "Flagship of the Kibbutz Movement." It was the biggest kibbutz, the first with industry, the first with a convalescent home, and a pioneer in many fields. Although he knew that it had economic problems, he still expected to be impressed. What he found when he began the job stunned him.

Rimon had already been sold, so Sherman decided to examine the other industries, starting with the furniture factory and store. He found sixty-year-old machines, operated by sixty-year-old workers, and a balance sheet that showed it was operating at a loss. There was no plan to turn things around and no money for investment, anyway. He proceeded to the irrigation equipment factory, where he found operators walking around in slippers, some machines idle, no work discipline, no safety regulations, no plan of action. In desperation, he went to the "modern" business of Givat Brenner: the computer processing office. There was no computer program for the plant itself. It was still operating on the obsolete DOS system. A gentle inquiry about Windows produced blank stares. He tried agriculture. The tree nursery had a board of directors, with an outside chairman, but it was separate from the sod farm. There were two general managers with an unclear demarcation of authority. There was a marketing framework, but only for the sod farm. There was no research and development, no planning, no minutes of meetings, no meetings.

"I thought they were pulling my leg," Sherman exclaims. "I simply did not believe what I was seeing!"

Sherman compares the managers of the industrial and agricultural branches at Givat Brenner to marathon runners with their hands tied and weights on their legs. They do not have the freedom to make decisions, to set budgets, or to operate at all. If a manager wants to produce a marketing strategy, he will be told by the kibbutz treasurer that there is no money. Formally, the kibbutz has voted to separate the business from the community, but this has not actually been implemented. Everything is mixed up in everything else, and every kibbutz member is a boss who can do as he likes. Whether the kibbutz invests in new machinery for a factory may be unconnected with the factory's needs and very much connected with the fact that Givat Brenner needs the money to pay its medical bills.

Together with an external chairman, who had been appointed by the kibbutz, Sherman set to work to change the way things were organized.

One of the problems has been that some of the members feel that by appointing him they have done their bit. "Now I am supposed to solve all the problems," he says. "That is what I am being paid for, but, without the full participation of the members of Givat Brenner, I can't achieve anything."

He concedes that he has been given full authority and is empowered to negotiate with anyone he chooses. For example, he is negotiating a partnership for the furniture factory. He is confident that the factory's board will support him, but a veto at the kibbutz general meeting is always possible. The meeting can decide that it does not want a partner or even that it does not matter whether the factory makes a profit.

The construction of the new neighborhood will provide the financial means for economic recovery, believes Sherman, but he warns that Givat Brenner is approaching its moment of truth. Although the decision to build has been taken, the general meeting could decide against it when the time comes for signing the contract. Nobody knows how a kibbutz general meeting reaches decisions. From his own experience of kibbutz life, Sherman knows that the considerations are not only professional ones, and all sorts of extraneous and personal factors can influence a decision. That is why the business must be separated from the community.

He is confident that Givat Brenner can be turned around, that the members can be persuaded to change their methods of operating. He is trying to ensure that branch managers have both authority and accountability. He is running a weekly management workshop for members in the thirty to fifty age group, including many of the current office holders, and feels he is getting somewhere. If a new generation of managers can be trained, there is hope. If they see a future, members of that age group will remain at Givat Brenner.

A great deal depends on psychology. The other day a young member told him, "You are the only person around here with a smile on his face. You believe we do have a future. That is why I am with you."

David Zacks, the brother of the secretary, works outside the kibbutz. Formerly headmaster of the regional school, he is now the director of an external study course established in Israel by Britain's University of Derby. Gray haired, with a lively intelligence and a dry humor, he works in an office at the Efal Kibbutz Center, where the university has its Israeli campus. The office is modern, with wall-to-wall carpeting, neon lighting, and computers.

In the past he has played a prominent role in the kibbutz, but he is not overly enthusiastic about the way things are going today. He is worried by the reliance on the outside manager and chairman.

"We have lost the confidence that we can do it better—or even as well," Zacks laments. "We can't make our own decisions anymore."

He tells of a recent proposal to permit outside employees, such as himself, to benefit from the fact that they earn larger-than-average wages. A special kibbutz committee, in consultation with the outside manager and chairman, proposed to allow them an extra 10 percent of their earnings as an increment on their kibbutz allowance. To the chagrin of the committee, the outside employees rejected the offer.

"You can't buy me for 2,400 shekels [$600] a year," Zacks told them.

In general, he is worried about the proposed changes. There were always minor inequities at Givat Brenner, he concedes. People always had small sums of private money, from wedding presents and other gifts, and some had more than others. The equality was not in the personal allowances but in the fact that the kibbutz provided housing, food, education, health, culture, vacations, and hobbies for the members, and it was responsible for finding everyone work.

Zacks acknowledges that socialism often meant waste, and in fact Givat Brenner was one of the first kibbutzim to "privatize" electricity consumption, making all members pay for what they used. He agrees that it is sensible to make the members pay for their food and other things, but he is worried at the long-term effects of abandoning the basic principle of equality.

"Givat Brenner is not Degania," he declares. "It is a large kibbutz, and not homogeneous. We have all types—at least one alcoholic and a number of social cases. I am afraid that, if the collective relinquishes all responsibility for the individual members, we could have homeless people at Givat Brenner."

He would like to preserve at least some kibbutz principles. Housing, education, and health should remain the responsibility of the community. At the same time, he admits that his main concern is for the survival of Givat Brenner as a *place,* even if the kibbutz structure is eventually abandoned. For this reason, he supports the building of the new neighborhood, albeit with some reluctance.

Near the entrance to Givat Brenner is the kibbutz museum. Originally prepared as a one-time exhibit to celebrate the seventieth anniversary of the kibbutz, it was so successful that it has been decided to make it permanent. The main organizer was Moshe Eisen, a gray-bearded, ginger-haired, barrel-chested man of fifty-two; the member who collected most of the exhibits is fifty-four year-old Shlomo Wittenberg, a giant of a man who served for most of his life in the Border Police. In their shorts, sandals, and working shirts, the two of them could easily pose for pictures of "typical kibbutzniks."

"See that cooking pot?" asks Eisen, pointing to a huge cauldron.

We made jelly for the British army in that. We were the first to have an industry. That and those barrels for pickled cucumbers were the start of Rimon. The kids pinched the barrel hoops for rolling. Later, we used sealed empty tin cans for teaching the children to swim. Look at those water sprinklers. We were the first with irrigation equipment. All the others copied us. That insecticide spray for the orchard dates to 1930.

No, that isn't an original tent. None of them survived. I had it made up; it is just like the ones they lived in. That oven was in use until 1982. Until then, we baked our own bread. See those radios? They were in the radio rooms. All the old tractors, plows, and tools will be outside in the yard. We had to put them away for the winter.

Those are all books written by members of the kibbutz. Sereni, of course, and you have met Haim Seligman, another of our authors. There are also lots of artists. And you see that board game. It was invented by one of our teachers. I myself am a sculptor. I have had several personal exhibitions outside the kibbutz.

To be frank with you, we haven't managed to convey the cultural richness of Givat Brenner. You see those photos of the choir, the orchestra, the basketball team, but we don't do it justice. Givat Brenner was a cultural leader in the kibbutz movement.

Eisen is determined to run the museum as a paying concern. He is publicizing it in the media and sending circulars to schools. Like everything else, it has to be marketed. Eisen criticizes the implementation of the current changes in Givat Brenner.

They are doing things the wrong way 'round. They shouldn't be talking about assessing the value of the members' work and awarding differential allowances for effort. First, let's make things more efficient. Let's put everything possible on a profitable basis, as I am doing with the museum, and *then* get onto paying wages or letting members keep some of their earnings.

Only a quarter of our members earn money. We can increase this to 40 percent. I'll give you an example: we have a first-rate modern laundry. Why don't we take in laundry from outside? We could easily turn that into a profitable branch.

Eisen notes that Givat Brenner accepted members over the years without asking them to pay in their money or even to buy a share in the kibbutz, but he doesn't worry about inequality. He thinks that the kibbutz should not deal with the haves, only with the have-nots. The community should concentrate on leveling up and forget about leveling down.

He regards change as inevitable, given the current social climate in the country as a whole. In the 1970s, he recalls, when the Jordan Valley was being shelled daily from across the border, he volunteered to live at a kibbutz in the area.

"Today, I would expect money for doing something like that," he points out. "The era of volunteering is over. Things have changed and we have to change with them."

Eisen could not have established the museum if Shlomo Wittenberg had not obsessively collected items used in the daily life of the kibbutz for decades. He started with tractors from the 1930s and 1940s and then went on to radio sets and other things.

"Everything works," he says proudly. "All the tractors and all the radios. They are all in perfect condition."

Wittenberg was born on the kibbutz but spent most of his working life in the military, starting in the army and later enlisting in the Border Police, where he was wounded and still has some disability. He always felt the obligation to volunteer, he says, to make a contribution. He has retired from the service, but he is still the coordinator of regional security. The collecting and restoration work were a hobby, carried out in his spare time. He points out that his parents received large sums of money from Germany and gave it all to the kibbutz. But times have changed, and today everybody is out for themselves. There used to be at least a semblance of equality, he maintains, but in recent years this has broken down, and inequality has become blatant.

I've given hours to this museum, and my children wonder why I can't help them economically. We thought that the way of life we had at the kibbutz was beautiful, but things have changed. I love Givat Brenner. It is my home, but there is less of a feeling of pride. One of my classmates, who married someone from outside the kibbutz, has invested 80,000 shekels [$20,000] in his room. What about my parents' reparation money that is still paid into the kibbutz?

If I want to buy something, I have to beg from the kibbutz treasurer, and he tells me there is no money. So the people who took advantage are fixed up, but many of us are screwed, because things have changed.

Am I a parasite? I always worked. I never went abroad, but you can't sit around crying. Let people keep their wages. The kibbutz system worked once, but it doesn't work anymore. When did it stop working? Fifteen years ago, twenty, maybe. I don't want to say that I've been swindled, but sometimes I feel like shit!

If Givat Brenner has a future, it is surely with the thirty- and forty-year-olds, many of whom are the current office holders in the kibbutz. They are the ones responsible for pushing through the changes, for running the business and the community for the next few years, for finding the way to keep the next generation at Givat Brenner. It is a heavy responsibility.

Noam and Tali Shamir live with their school-age children in a two-story maisonette in the center of the kibbutz. The furniture is modest, and an attractive spiral staircase winds up to the children's bedroom on the second floor. Noam, relaxed and soft-spoken, has just been elected community secretary, dealing with members' personal problems; Tali, his wife, born at Givat Brenner, is winding up a four-year stint in charge of the youngsters who complete their army service and are entitled to a university education at the expense of the kibbutz.

Tali says that she has remained at Givat Brenner because she likes kibbutz life. She is unenthusiastic about the proposed changes but does not feel able to take a stand against them, particularly after one of the most talented couples of her generation left because things were not changing quickly enough for them.

"You know, a few years ago we had four kindergartens here, and we were about to open a fifth," she remarks. "Today we can hardly fill one kindergarten with our own children. We take in kids from outside the kibbutz. That is fine. I have no quarrel with that. I'm sorry about the lack of Givat Brenner children, though."

She sees her most important task as fostering conditions that will encourage the young generation to remain. The principle of equality has to be moderated to enable members to keep a proportion of their salaries, even though it means some will have more than others. She would like health and education to remain the responsibility of the kibbutz, although some health care and certain special classes are already paid for out of personal allowances. There are about two hundred army or postarmy children of Givat Brenner who have not yet decided about their future. Some of them are still traveling the world; many of them are studying. The kibbutz undertook to give every kibbutz child education to undergraduate level and to pay them an allowance while they studied. Recently the financial situation forced members to retrench. Tuition fees are still paid, but the students have to work to support themselves.

"About 3 percent of the Israeli population live on kibbutzim," notes Tali, "but I don't think the way of life is suitable for even as much as 3 percent. It was founded by people who believed in the ideal, but the next generation were born into it or joined it by marriage. Those people just don't believe in the kibbutz way."

Growing up in the Society of Children was a marvelous experience, she remembers. When the kibbutz decided to bring the children to sleep at home, she was sorry for them. She thought they were missing out on a lot of fun, but she is pleased her own children live at home.

"I still think that the kibbutz is the best society in the world for raising children," she says, "but we have to acknowledge that the individual family has become much more important than the group."

Noam, who comes from another kibbutz, remembers being frightened when he slept in the children's house away from his parents. He used to wake up and wait anxiously for the birds to start singing so he knew it was morning, but the fear passed, and he remembers his childhood positively for the most part.

Despite the move to make members more self-reliant and less dependent on the community, Noam does not feel his job as community secretary will become obsolete. He agrees that, as secretary, he should cut down his involvement in the details of members' lives, but the community has to help the members, particularly the youngsters.

"After the army and some travel, lots of them want to come back here to take advantage of our financing their studies," he notes. "Even though they now have to work to support themselves, it is still a pretty good deal. Nevertheless, they don't want to become members right away with the responsibility that it entails. What should I do? Should I frighten them off by insisting that they join? It won't work today. We have to be flexible."

One couple is hesitating about joining, explains Noam. They want to be residents and keep their wages. He is trying to persuade them to become members and take part in the process of changing the kibbutz in the direction that will satisfy them, but he is not going to be dogmatic. He wants to work something out with the couple, some sort of compromise.

Tomorrow he has a meeting with the landscape gardening team. A few empty houses can be rented out and bring valuable income to the kibbutz, but the gardens around them are neglected. For some reason, the landscape team refuses to clean up the area. Noam plans to meet with them, find out the reasons for their obstinacy, and persuade them to do the job.

Another important task as community secretary is arranging funerals. Accidents, divorces, and family breakups are also in his province. Sometimes the problem for him to resolve is trivial—even farcical—such as when a member's dog bites another member.

Noam studied administration at the kibbutz movement's Ruppin College; Tali studied food technology at the Hebrew University. She has an outside job in a soft drink factory. Most of the kibbutz children in their age group studied. Many of them also traveled extensively in Asia or South America after the army. They regard the age group a few years older than themselves them as problematic. If changes are made in the kibbutz structure and the higher earners keep a proportion of their salaries, many of that generation—those in their fifties and sixties—will find themselves with less money than their fellows.

"They didn't study and didn't travel," says Tali. "They feel they missed out. Unlike us, they are not qualified, so they feel trapped. They pass on their disillusionment to their children, who are now completing school or serving in the army, encouraging them to leave."

This theme is taken up energetically by Neri Lahad. Also in her thirties, Neri is married to a nonmember resident of Givat Brenner. Her husband worked most of his life in the security services and "never got around" to joining the kibbutz.

"The over-fifties are frightened, and with good reason," she states emphatically. "They are not equipped for the new-style kibbutz. The kibbutz made a dreadful mistake with that generation. They grew up in a bubble and had no contact with the life outside." Neri concedes that they served in the army but maintains that they were insulated there also.

They did not travel abroad and see the world. They never tried living outside the kibbutz, never had to pay rent, go to the bank, or do any of the everyday things that a citizen in a modern state does automatically.

She calls it the "*metapelet* complex." The *metapelet* (the child care worker) lays out the clothes for the kibbutz children, decides what they wear, and tells them what to eat and how to behave. Some adult members, thinks Neri, continue to regard the kibbutz secretary and other office holders in the same way as they used to regard their child care worker. They are dependent. They are incapable of making their own decisions. They wait to be told what to do.

The members of her generation are different, she maintains. They lived outside the kibbutz, competed in the labor market, traveled the world, studied, and gained qualifications. Today's young generation are more career oriented, she says. They tend to study first and only then travel, but the essential thing is that, like her generation, they gain outside experience. She is worried about the future and also mentions the talented couple of their generation who left Givat Brenner. This departure was clearly traumatic for her and Tali's age group.

Neri is a strong proponent of "lowering the kibbutz wall" and affording more contact between Givat Brenner and the world outside. She thinks it is a good thing that there are children from fifteen other settlements in the Givat Brenner Regional School; likewise, she is enthusiastic about the proposed new neighborhood. She thinks it will strengthen Givat Brenner as a settlement and be good for the school and other activities. She is not worried about the existence of two separate communities and expresses confidence that the relationship can be worked out without too much difficulty. With regard to the future, she predicts that Givat Brenner will be different from the traditional kibbutz, but not the same as an ordinary village. The future population will have to decide what they want, just like anywhere else in the world.

If Noam, Tali, and Neri and their generation hold the present of Givat Brenner in their hands, the future depends on the current batch of postarmy children in their twenties, and right now it does not look too bright. Netta and Rotem live in kibbutz rooms behind the museum. Articulate and intelligent, they express considerable affection toward their kibbutz, but both of them are pretty clear that they see their future outside Givat Brenner.

Netta is studying infant education at the Kibbutz College in Tel Aviv. She works in the kibbutz furniture factory and at the veteran's club, for which she is paid a salary by the kibbutz. Rotem, a student of political science at Tel Aviv University, prefers to work outside the kibbutz, cleaning apartments, which she says is very well paying.

Netta explains that if children of the kibbutz work for a year after their army service, they receive university tuition fees at the undergraduate level and a kibbutz room at a subsidized rent; those who don't work the year pay full rent. Rotem is pleased with the current system, which affords her a feeling of independence.

"The difference between Rotem and me is that I am the youngest child in my family, whereas she is the oldest," explains Netta. "I know what my brothers got from the kibbutz and what I am missing. My eldest brother studied at Ben-Gurion University in Beersheba. He got an apartment there, a room in the kibbutz, full tuition fees, a living allowance—he didn't even have to work on his vacations!"

Rotem says forthrightly that the members of Givat Brenner lived above their means. They had a very high standard of living but used to finish their day's work at two o'clock and go to sleep. She is very much in favor of the proposed changes. The old kibbutz was a beautiful idea, but it has had its day. It worked in the early years because all the members were struggling to survive.

"It can't continue," she says. "You can't force people to be equal if they don't want to be equal!"

Netta thinks that the kibbutz works well in extreme situations: when there is no money or when there is lots of money. It also shows its good points in abnormal situations. Death, divorce, one-parent families—in those situations the kibbutz system is great. The community helps. Unlike Rotem, she thinks that Givat Brenner is going about the changes in the wrong way. The kibbutz always invested too much. Her mother came from another kibbutz, where at the time of her leaving they had one tractor. She arrived in Givat Brenner to find that they already had a dozen.

"We have to do everything on a large scale," she protests. "It drives me crazy. Why can't we tackle the small problems and advance one step at a time? Why do we have to have this neighborhood? The building contractor will make all the money, and we'll be left with a whole gang of people we don't know."

"No, there will be an absorption committee," Rotem contradicts her. "I'm in favor. The new residents will pay taxes, buy services, enlarge the school and kindergartens. It will bring in money."

They both enjoyed growing up in the Children's Society and regret its absence today. Rotem thinks it is a good thing that the balance has moved in the direction of the family and away from the group, but they both feel it has gone too far. The young children today do not experience the group solidarity that they had.

"We were together all the time," points out Netta. "We were a real group."

At the same time, Rotem feels that in a way it did encourage mediocrity. When anyone had outstanding talent, he or she tended to be "squashed" by the others. She agrees that the kibbutz system produced outstanding people but says they did not remain in the kibbutz. She herself does not want to stay. She wants to live where she can be more independent. Netta also does not see her future in the kibbutz.

"It's really sad," she says. "We were brought up here and received everything; now we want to leave."

"It's natural," counters Rotem. "Children always leave home, and Givat Brenner is our home."

Netta looks back to the celebrations of the seventieth anniversary last year and the feeling she had of the tremendous strength of Givat Brenner, and Rotem agrees that enormous latent forces still exist in the kibbutz.

"The kibbutz was a beautiful experiment," declares Rotem. "It was worth doing, but now we have to find a new way. From each according to his ability to each according to his needs may have worked once, but it against human nature. If they thought they could change it through education, they were dead wrong."

Rotem and Netta have the impression that most of their age group will leave. The children of Givat Brenner do not have good contacts with the older generation, they say. They do not speak at the general meeting; they don't participate in the life of the kibbutz. Both of them compare the kibbutz to the nation as a whole.

"It used to be more innocent," suggests Netta. "People used to worry about the community as a whole. Now they think about themselves first."

Ronen and Maor are still at school. Maor, who wears an eyebrow ring, has no doubts about his future. His parents are divorced. His mother lives at Givat Brenner, but his father lives in Los Angeles, and he plans to join him there. He has visited him several times and sees a better future there. He thinks there is too much gossip in the kibbutz. When he shaved his head, no one said anything to him personally, but they all made remarks to his mother.

"I was insulted that they talked to my mother behind my back," he says. "A few of us have motorbikes, and we ride them in the fields. There is gossip about that also."

Despite that, he loves the kibbutz, and he will remain in touch. He will definitely come for visits.

Ronen has no plans beyond his army service, which is due shortly. He may study, may live in the kibbutz, may live elsewhere. His parents are among those in favor of the changes. He thinks that eventually the kibbutz will be like any other village. He is a little jealous of Maor having a father in America but not at all sure that he wants to live abroad.

The views of the schoolchildren are probably not significant. Like youth anywhere, they are not really thinking about the future, but the student generation must be a serious cause of concern at Givat Brenner. If too many of them leave, the future is uncertain.

Kibbutz Naan is a neighbor of Givat Brenner, founded only two years later, on which fortune has smiled. Well organized and prosperous, it is facing the future with a certain amount of confidence, partly because it is economically viable, partly as the result of a basic process of change that a special committee has been implementing over the past four years. This is not to say, however, that Naan is free of problems.

Yair Shavit, an impressive man, with an incisive, forceful style of speech, studied management at Ruppin College. His specialty is the process of administrative change. He has been working as a management consultant, mostly outside the kibbutz, for twenty-five years. Three and a half years ago, the kibbutz general meeting gave him and four colleagues the authority to introduce their program of change. They have another six months.

Their basic plan was to separate the business side of Naan from the community, so that the kibbutz lives off the wages of its members. They also aimed to improve management procedures, to establish a proper control mechanism, to make each family responsible for itself, and to establish a connection between members' jobs and their income. Most of the plan has been implemented, but the general meeting balked at one of the key proposals. The job of every kibbutz member has been valued by an outside expert, but allowances are still distributed in the classic kibbutz way, according to family size, seniority, and special needs. The general meeting refused to approve differential allowances partly based on "salary."

(N.B.: It is not unusual for a kibbutz community, after it has implemented many changes, to balk at the legitimization of inequality, which seems to them the final abandonment of their lifelong values. At Naan, the general meeting voted against. At Beit Hashita in the Jezreel Plain, the general meeting approved "linking effort and reward." But a relatively large—and vocal—minority kicked up such a fuss that the general meeting reversed itself and voted to "reconsider" the matter.)

Not that Shavit and his colleagues planned to abandon the kibbutz system entirely. The kibbutz remains responsible for accommodation, health, education, culture, and care for the elderly and the disabled.

"We still want a kibbutz," explains Shavit, "but a kibbutz where members take on more personal responsibility, where there is less dependence on committees and office holders, where families are more independent. We undertook to set off down a clearly defined road, but we emphasized that we do not know what the final version will be."

They took on two outside advisers to assist them but implemented the program by themselves. Many of the items formerly supplied by the kibbutz have been "privatized," including food, energy, vacations, and recreation. There is much more flexibility with regard to how the members spend their money. Enormous sums have been invested in a pension plan so that every member, including those too old to join national or private pension schemes, will have a pension. Naan has been lucky in that its irrigation equipment factory, which earns 80 percent of its income, has remained profitable, but Shavit is not complacent.

"We are lucky that we are implementing our changes without the pressure that they have at Givat Brenner," he says, "but it wouldn't take very much to put us in a similar position to them. We need some $700,000 a month to keep Naan going at its present level. If something went wrong, we could get into debt very quickly indeed."

Some five hundred of Naan's members go to work every day of whom, only three hundred actually earn money. The others work in services that save money. The factory employees 150 kibbutz members (and the same number of outsiders), 100 members work at outside jobs, some 200 are in services, and only about 20 are employed in the various farming branches.

Today the children born in kibbutzim only become members after their army service, which in effect usually means after extensive travel and study. Naan is the only kibbutz in Israel that still admits its children to membership immediately after they finish high school and before they go in the army. Consequently, it has three hundred members between the age of nineteen and twenty-seven, which is the hope of the future but also a huge financial burden. The students get their tuition fees and a living allowance throughout their studies, sometimes to postgraduate level.

They can work on the kibbutz or outside, as they wish, and they receive half of their living expenses.

Some say that the comparatively large number of young members at Naan is an optical illusion, that it is just a question of labels. At Givat Brenner, for example, there are some two hundred soldiers, students, and others living outside the kibbutz or traveling, but they are not *called* members until they make a formal application to join and are accepted by a vote of the general meeting. Naan stands by its system, which it sees as the guarantee of its future.

Looking ahead, Shavit sees a kibbutz with a looser framework but still a kibbutz. He points out that in much of the Western world, there is a search for greater cooperation and social responsibility. The paradox of the Israeli kibbutz movement, he says, is that it has to dismantle the old form of cooperation to build new forms. Despite the fact that, with the changes, the members of Naan are better off financially and now only work a five-day week instead of the former six days, they are not happy about it, concedes Shavit.

"It is a painful process," he asserts. "There is a feeling of loss, of uncertainty. Nobody knows where it will end."

Eventually, he believes, the general meeting will approve at least a partial link between wages and income. After all, he stresses, there has always been a measure of inequality within the equality.

> My father had a Jeep for his work, and that was in the 1950s. My wife is a consultant, and she has a private car at her disposal. When I leave my job here and return to outside consulting, I'll also have a car. You can't call that equality. I think Utopia is a nice idea, but it is unattainable. If you want a "title" for the kibbutz of the future, I would take that of a recent videocassette put out by the United Kibbutz Movement. It's called *Modest Dreams.*

To return to Givat Brenner, a reading of the latest kibbutz news sheet gives some idea of what is happening today at the kibbutz. A poem by one of Israel's leading poets is quoted on the cover:

> Something is fleeing,
> Or already is not what it was,
> And it will not return, like the seasons,
> The heat, the cold, the ice, and the laughter.

Inside, an editorial laments the fact that the kibbutz is so introverted: "We are enclosed in our own conch shell, uninterested in what is going on outside our fence. It is strange: outsiders anxiously ask us what is going on inside the kibbutz, and we, who were once so involved in the nation as a whole, are busy worrying about our own problems."

A report of the field crops branch relates that it is growing cauliflower, which is a more reliable crop than tomatoes and cucumbers, and has just started growing chicory, of which there are high hopes. In what seems like a flashback to former times, the branch manager thanks "those experienced members who participated in special voluntary work-days to harvest the cotton crop."

A report of a recent general meeting records a discussion regarding the location of the new neighborhood and quotes a member who called the construction project "the most cynical of all cynical decisions, but absolutely correct, as there is no alternative."

At another general meeting it was resolved that "the member of Givat Brenner is responsible for finding profitable work commensurate with his talents, which will contribute to Givat Brenner. On the other hand the Human Resources Committee is *obligated* to assist the member in the process of looking for work."

An announcement proclaims that the kibbutz has saved six thousand shekels (about $1,500) in electricity consumption, noting that the money will be passed on to the members. Members are urged that further cutting down on electricity, as well as water, food, travel, cigarettes, and "bad atmosphere" (!), is possible and desirable.

Finally, the kibbutz commemorates one of its veteran members, Yael Lanir, who died at the end of the year, lauding her contribution over the years as a nurse. Yael was born in Holland and rescued by a brave Dutch family, who hid her in their attic. After the war, she came to Israel. She is praised for her work as a nurse, notably with new immigrants in nearby Rishon Lezion. Her family also thanks those members who looked after her in her final years in the Givat Brenner old age facility.

Let us conclude this chapter with observations from four Givat Brenner veterans. Haim Zeligman, a pioneer and farmer turned teacher and researcher, points out that the kibbutz has always been a society that changed and developed but concedes that in recent years there have been much more dynamic and basic changes. He attributes this to changes in the nation and the world at large. In the 1980s, the idealistic collective ethos collapsed, he says, and Israel as a whole became more egotistical and individualistic.

Yosef Rietti confesses to a feeling of bitter disappointment. He does not believe that anything of the kibbutz, with the total interdependence of its members on each other, will be preserved.

"It is irreversible," he says. "I believed in the kibbutz way of life, but I cannot say I believe today. I'm afraid that all the examples of socialism have failed. Where did it succeed?"

"I just don't want to know about the current changes," says kibbutz archivist Yaacov Viterbo gently but firmly. "I am already past the biblical three score years and ten. Every day is a present. Why should I make my last years bitter? I can't change anything, so why get involved?"

"I pray that the kibbutz will not lose its special character," says Shulamit Lachish. "I have lost a husband and a daughter-in-law during the last decade, and the kibbutz gave me strength and support. I felt the most wonderful community solidarity. Maybe the youngsters who grew up here take it for granted, but it is beautiful. For my age group the kibbutz is marvelous."

Each kibbutz has its own story, its own members, its own problems, and its own solutions. Even in the past, with all the similarities, each kibbutz was unique. Today, as pointed out in the introduction, kibbutzim are becoming increasingly different from each other. Having made that point, let us suggest that Givat Brenner does have something to tell us about the kibbutz movement as a whole. Something about the place makes it illustrative of the kibbutz as an institution. In the tradition of its illustrious founder, Enzo Sereni, Givat Brenner has always operated on a grand scale. Its achievements are enormous, and its failures are on the same scale. It has been ambitious, presumptuous, and possibly arrogant; today it is facing mind-boggling problems.

Many of its sons and daughters have deserted what they see as a "sinking ship." The remaining "crew members" have taken a "pilot" on board to help them navigate. They deserve credit for struggling to keep afloat. The responsibility is great, the challenge daunting, yet Givat Brenner seems determined to forge ahead, even though a clear course has yet to be set. Bearing in mind the sentiments of its younger members, it seems unlikely that the collective way of life will survive for long, but some sort of settlement will continue to exist.

In the next chapter, we will turn to a much smaller kibbutz but one that has set a definite course, with crucial help from an outside "pilot." Its former secretary, who helped chart the route, compares it not to a ship but to an airliner, the crew of which conducted repairs in midflight. It has undeniably undergone a transformation, a change so radical that many question whether it should still be called a kibbutz.

3

הסוללים

HASOLELIM
REPAIRS IN MIDFLIGHT

Was Hasolelim more of a kibbutz when each member thought that he was doing all the work and the other members were living on his back? I ask myself: Was it more of a kibbutz when we were forced to stop calling volunteer work days because no one turned up? Was it a kibbutz when we couldn't persuade members to help prepare for the celebration of a festival, and, if we did get a celebration organized, nobody cleaned up afterward? Is a kibbutz simply a joint bank account, or is it rather a good quality of life and a cooperative partnership?

Rita Aurbach, a vital, energetic, auburn-haired woman in her forties, speaks with some heat. She was a believer in the old-fashioned kibbutz and admits that, had she known where Hasolelim was going, she might have chosen another settlement, but now that its members have implemented the big change, she is heartily fed up with being told by secretaries of other kibbutzim that Hasolelim is "no longer a kibbutz."

The Argentina-born Rita is secretary of Hasolelim, except that nowadays she is called the "community manager." She only joined the fifty-year-old kibbutz a dozen years ago, after living with her husband at another kibbutz and later in the development town of Upper Nazareth.

"I came here to live in a kibbutz," she explains, "but I don't think we had a real partnership here, just a joint bank account. For years we took everything for granted. We had to sit back and take stock of our values and our way of life."

Despite Rita's manifest sincerity, an objective observer must indeed wonder whether Hasolelim is a kibbutz today. It is certainly not a kibbutz in the hitherto accepted sense of the word, where the community owns the property and means of production; where the kibbutz is responsible for providing work, housing, food, education, health care, and cultural activities; and where the available resources are distributed according to the needs of the members, as determined by the general meeting and the various committees answerable to it.

Today the members of Hasolelim receive wages, according to their earning ability, and they pay for most of the services provided by the kibbutz. They are responsible for finding their own work, whether on the kibbutz or outside. They manage their own budgets, make their own decisions, and are on the way to owning their own homes. They pay for food, electricity, transportation, medicines, and a large part of their children's education. All that remains of the original kibbutz is the common ownership of the various agricultural and industrial enterprises, a mutual assistance fund to help those members in need, and (for the time being) collective payment of income tax.

Hasolelim was established in Lower Galilee in June 1949, when the State of Israel was just over one year old, by a joint group of Israelis and American immigrants on land that until Israel's 1948 War of Independence belonged to the Arab village of Tzippori. The land was divided up between the kibbutz and Moshav Tzippori. Although their pioneering era was shorter than that of Degania or Givat Brenner, the founders of Hasolelim also started out by living in tents and prefabricated huts.

Hasolelim (rough translation: The Trailblazers) started with a membership of 70 and never exceeded 120. Today it has 116 members. It did not remain small, as Degania did in its early years, for ideological reasons. Although the members wanted their kibbutz to expand, it just never happened. Many of the original group left over the years, and many other groups joined the kibbutz, both from Israel and abroad, but the membership always remained at around the hundred mark.

Hasolelim started out with the conventional mixed farming, including poultry, dairy, field crops, and orchards. In the early years, both male and female members earned money for the collective by working on afforestation projects for the Jewish National Fund. There is no special climatic or topographical advantage in Lower Galilee, explains a veteran member. Hasolelim is not blessed with the cool climate of Upper

Galilee, with its bumper crop of apples, plums, and cherries, or with the heat of the Jordan Valley and the southern desert, where bananas, dates, and winter vegetables flourish. At the same time, the kibbutz enjoys a reasonable rainfall, making the area green and fertile.

Hasolelim developed its poultry branch into a sophisticated breeding concern and acquired Linero, a factory for producing drawing equipment and light-display cabinets. Along with its field crops, those are its two main branches. The kibbutz children attend a regional kibbutz school nearby, but an educational enrichment center for children with learning problems, established by the kibbutz five years ago, has proved a profitable branch and attracts children from outside.

Although Hasolelim made no drastic mistakes, it was never economically successful, and in the crisis of 1985 it was on the list of nineteen worst-off kibbutzim, regarded by the United Kibbutz Movement leaders as being "without hope." Morale was low, some members left, and the survival of the kibbutz was far from assured. Nevertheless, it still took another decade before the members embarked on the radical, comprehensive, far-reaching reform program that has brought Hasolelim to its current situation.

Starting the process in 1995, the members spent the whole of 1996 in intensive discussions, during which each paragraph of the plan was debated, amended, and voted on by the general meeting of the kibbutz. In November the new structure was approved at the ballot box by a vote of ninety-eight to fifteen, with one abstention and two members away at the time. On January 1, 1997, the new system was put into practice. Of course, not all the decisions could be implemented on the spot, but the big changeover occurred on that date. Last year six kibbutz-born children, encouraged by the new developments, returned and became members of Hasolelim.

In the words of Michael Mensky, who served as kibbutz secretary and main facilitator throughout the process, "Our Boeing 747 was transformed into a Boeing 767 in midflight. We couldn't bring it down into the hangar for repairs!"

Mensky, a slim, youthful South African, joined Hasolelim in 1988. Within three years, he was pitched into the "privatization" of the communal dining hall. He was not involved in the actual decision, but he was picked to implement it. He brought in a private contractor to cook the meals and arranged for members to buy their food by means of magnetic cards. Previously, members had taken to eating their evening meals at home, but there was no proper arrangement for that, and it cost them money. There was a feeling that people wanted more control over their personal expenditure, explains Mensky.

The contractor eventually left them because Hasolelim was too small a community to make a profit, and the idea of attracting outsiders to eat there proved impractical. The transfer of food to individual budgets, however, saved the kibbutz money, and the members were satisfied. It prompted them to extend the system to electricity.

"The introduction of individual electricity meters cut consumption by almost a third, even though members were not at first asked to pay for their electricity," recalls Mensky.

During the following three years, Mensky worked outside the kibbutz as a community worker at a trailer park for new immigrants, most of them from Ethiopia. It was his first real experience of Israel outside the kibbutz, and it gave him an insight into how local government works. After three years with the Ethiopian newcomers, one of the veterans of Hasolelim suggested that he stand for election as kibbutz secretary.

"I ran on a program for change," he recounts with a smile. "Until then the accepted style of becoming secretary, as in most kibbutzim, was that a member was drafted, showed reluctance, and finally 'bowed to the will of the community.' I was the first person to compete against another member with a program. That in itself was a revolution."

During his few years at the kibbutz, Mensky had been struck by the ambivalence of the members toward their way of life. He saw that there was a strong feeling that the system was not working. Although it had benefited from the rescue program agreed by the government, the banks, and the kibbutz movements for the write-off and rescheduling of its debts, Hasolelim was still heavily in debt. There was a sense that something new was needed.

Mensky was elected secretary in 1995, and he discovered that a group of members had already arranged to meet with Yigal Orbach, the managing director of Tmurot, a Tel Aviv–based consulting firm specializing in the process of change. Hasolelim had already availed itself of the services of Tmurot in reorganizing Linero. Tmurot had done a good job with the factory, so the members returned to that company to consult with its advisers about the larger picture.

Mensky and a dozen other members participated in an all-day discussion, during which every aspect of the situation in Hasolelim was discussed. Orbach, a social psychologist, says it was a particularly fascinating process because the members started out by disagreeing but came to perceive during the course of the day that they basically wanted the same things.

"Once that became clear," he says, not without satisfaction, "it was certain that Hasolelim was setting out on the path of change."

Yigal Orbach founded Tmurot thirteen years ago. Today it is situated in an almost aggressively high-tech building—all green glass and smooth elevators—in Petah-Tikva, near Tel Aviv. The hallway is floored in blond wood (unusual in Israel), and miniskirted secretaries offer coffee, fruit, and pastries to the visitors. The offices are modern and gleaming, and the well-appointed conference room has a giant computer screen to display organizational charts and other management techniques.

Orbach is an energetic man: dynamic, fluent, and cogent. Tmurot works in the public domain, with businesses and municipalities. The kibbutz, "a whole world in itself, with municipal authority, community, business, education, and welfare all in one package," is a particularly interesting field to work in. Orbach was born and raised at Regba, a *moshav shitufi* that is a sort of *moshav*-kibbutz hybrid, and admits to an underlying sympathy for the kibbutz. He thinks that if it can manage to give the individual more independence and autonomy, the kibbutz can be very competitive compared to other ways of life, taking advantage of the partnership to provide a feeling of community and togetherness.

"The kibbutz is green, pleasant, and safe; it is what everyone wants, basically," he says. "At the same time, the process of change there is unbelievably complex. In a business you have to convince one manager and maybe six board members. In a kibbutz you have to convince 75 percent of the members of the community."

Recalling that first day with the members of Hasolelim, Orbach says that the initial differences among them were a result of the fact that they argued about solutions rather than aspirations.

"One member said he wanted differential wages; another was opposed. I asked the first member why he wanted the differential. He replied that he wanted there to be a fairer relationship between effort and reward. I turned to the second man and asked him what he thought about that, and he replied that he 'could live with it.' I then wrote it down."

Two other members wanted to "privatize" all the branches, an idea that other members rejected. Orbach demanded to know their reasons. One "privatizer" said it was to afford more independence in purchasing goods and services; the other said he thought it was the only way to ensure that all the branches would be run efficiently. Orbach wrote down "More independence and better administration." Everyone agreed.

"I remember we were in our previous offices in Tel Aviv," recounts Orbach. "We were cramped in our small conference room, and it was very hot. I had to go to a funeral at three o'clock that afternoon. There was a lot of pressure, but they discovered that they could agree on a list of desired results. I pointed out that there were many different ways of achieving those results, and the process was launched."

The meeting gave Mensky, the newly elected secretary of Hasolelim, an overwhelming feeling that it was time to take action. He perceived his election as a mandate for change. To explain the process, he again resorts to the aircraft metaphor: "Yigal Orbach was in the control tower; I was the pilot. If we got it wrong, I would die in the crash. He would remain unhurt, so his stake wasn't the same as mine. Nevertheless, his role was invaluable."

Mensky decided to bypass the kibbutz secretariat, leaving it to get on with the day-to-day running of the settlement. He divided the entire community into six discussion groups of twenty-five members each for one-time discussions lasting from four to five hours. More than 100 of the 116 members participated in the discussions, with Mensky and Orbach attending every meeting. They did not start off talking about change; initially, the members were invited to state what they did and did not like about the kibbutz. Orbach chaired the sessions; Mensky maintained a low profile, mainly listening. After airing their likes and dislikes, the members were asked to envisage the future model of Hasolelim.

Based on the discussions, Mensky and Orbach came up with a number of general objectives. The kibbutz office holders and heads of branches were invited to a two-day discussion, which was also open to any member who wished to attend. Some thirty members were present for most of the deliberations, which resulted in the appointment of five teams to work out the details of what should be done. Teams were created for economics, organizational structure, property, social security, and community services.

The teams worked for nine months before coming up with their suggestions. Following that, Mensky and Orbach sat down for a further three months to write a comprehensive report. This report was brought to a series of more than thirty general meetings of the kibbutz, where it was thrashed out paragraph by paragraph. Attendance at the meetings, which were held twice a week, was good, and many valuable suggestions were made, amending the various clauses.

Another step was to determine salaries, based on their market value. Orbach, who carried out the initial survey, stresses that it is vital to value the *job* and not the *person,* because one of the most traumatic parts of the process of change is when the members start thinking that they are "worth" a certain wage. In some kibbutzim, he has found instances in which members changed their jobs after being assessed, calculating (quite rightly) that they were capable of earning more.

With an estimate of salaries, every family's economic situation was determined *in advance of the vote.* Orbach was uneasy about this. He thought it would lead to further delays and felt that the series of general meetings had already gone on too long. Summoned back to the discussions, which had been proceeding without him, he urged the members to move to a decision.

On November 20, 1996, the twenty-three-page "Plan for the Development of Kibbutz Hasolelim" was brought for final approval to a vote of the entire kibbutz, resulting in its overwhelming approval. Someone suggested breaking out the champagne. Mensky, mindful of the fact that many of the members, particularly the veterans, had cast their positive votes with heavy hearts, managed to veto that proposal.

The plan starts off by noting that it is the culmination of two years of discussions, which considered the needs and wishes of the members, and that more than a quarter of the membership participated in the five working teams. The different committees made sure that the plan was economically feasible, that the various elements were properly coordinated, and that as far as possible no member would be damaged by the proposals.

The next sections deal with practical details of implementation, including reorganization of the kibbutz and its various enterprises under the new system, training of the various office holders, and discussions with all members individually to ensure that they would be able to cope with the new situation. The seven general principles of the new regime were spelled out:

1. All members will be responsible for their place of work and their livelihood.
2. The amount of money received by all members will be directly related to their earnings.
3. The members will have the maximum independence in living their own lives, and the community will interfere as little as possible in the lives of the members.
4. The members will have a minimal guarantee of their livelihood as members of the kibbutz.

5. The rights of the veteran members will be guaranteed in preference to all other expenses, including personal allowances of members. Ditto with regard to invalid or disabled members.
6. Certain services will continue to be supplied by the community, such as education, health, and local services such as landscape gardening.
7. The new system will lead to greater efficiency and economic expansion, which will increase the income of the kibbutz.

The members wanted cooperation and mutual assistance to continue, notes the report, as well as a guaranteed livelihood for all, but in a different way than in the past. The individual should be less dependent on the various committees, with more personal responsibility and freedom at the expense of absolute equality (which in any case many members claim no longer exists).

The basis of the new system was in the separation of the community from its productive branches and the running of these for profit as efficiently as possible. Although cooperation will be maintained, including subsidies at an agreed level, allowances will be "privatized," to ensure that all members have the freedom to spend their money as they wish. The allowances paid to the individual member will be based on his or her earnings.

Mensky recalls that he was at first alarmed at the extreme line taken by the majority. In other kibbutzim that are going through the process of change, the personal allowances—hitherto based on estimated needs—are now based on a combination of needs, seniority, and earnings. Hasolelim, while maintaining some of the general services, decided to base allowances *solely* on earnings. Rita Aurbach, the current community manager, says the decision was correct.

"In kibbutzim where they have complex combinations, there is unanimity," she remarks with a hint of sarcasm. "*Everyone* is unhappy with the results!"

It should not be thought, however, that the members of Hasolelim rejected their basic commitment to fairness. The rights of the founding generation are clearly and unambiguously recognized. The obligation to the veteran members of the community is emphasized again and again in the plan. Any income accruing from the combined property is first and foremost to be used to pay pensions.

There follows a section dealing with the new structure, with emphasis on maintaining proper control, bringing in outside professionals, and making maximum use of the talents and abilities of the members through the establishment of a Unit for Human Resources. Although members will be earning unequal salaries (called in the terminology of the change process "differential salaries"), these will be progressively taxed to provide funds for assistance for exceptional health expenses, care for the aged, education (including nonconventional studies), laundry for serving soldiers, pensions, and extra payments to low earners, the disabled, and those unable to work at all.

With the aid of charts, the new structure of the kibbutz is laid out. Under the new system, the members must pay directly for the dining hall, laundry, clothing store, domestic electricity consumption, village store, and use of automobiles (to be subsidized for a limited period).

"Municipal" services, such as street lighting, landscape gardening, maintenance of paths, mail, culture, sport, and burials, remain the responsibility of the community, which will also subsidize kindergartens, some health services, and home maintenance for the elderly. Biannual reports will be issued to the community, and members who fail to pay the agreed taxes can have services withdrawn.

The productive branches of the kibbutz will be administered by a general manager, supervised by a board of directors, two of whom will be members directly elected by the general meeting. The manager and the board will be responsible to the general meeting and will run the enterprise as a normal business. There will also be a coordinating committee to act as a bridge between the business and the community.

The document then goes into detail about the subsidized services, emphasizing the aspect of personal responsibility for paying for the services (based on a principle that could be described as "no free lunches"). Although the members have health insurance as members of the Kupat Holim health fund, they will now be expected to pay for such items as eyeglasses, medicines, and psychological counseling. At the same time, the mutual assistance fund will be available to help those who need it.

The kibbutz will go on paying for the joint bar mitzvah celebrations of the kibbutz children reaching the age of thirteen, but family parties will be paid for by the families themselves. Weddings and circumcision parties will continue to be the responsibility of the community as a whole.

The plan includes details of the taxes and levies, which the members are called on to pay, with a notable reduction for pensioners. The next sections deal in detail with the pensions, noting that most of the twenty members of pension age do not have pension schemes. These members will receive full pensions from the kibbutz.

Figure 3.1.   Children playing at Hasolelim in 1999.

Source: (Daniel Gavron)

The rights of disabled and others unable to work follow, together with an itemized list of the rights of the kibbutz-born children. The kibbutz sees an obligation to absorb its children into the community. Until the end of their military service, the children are the responsibility of their parents but receive accommodation at the kibbutz. In addition to this, the children are entitled to live rent-free at the kibbutz for five years after their military service, although they will have to pay municipal taxes and service fees. Furthermore, if they do not live at the kibbutz, they are entitled to the income accruing from renting their rooms. The kibbutz children can also apply to the fund for mutual assistance for payment of their university tuition fees. Those who leave are also entitled to three years of tuition fees. The children must settle their status by the end of the five-year period following their army service.

In the event of any profits being available for distribution to the members, this dispersal will be carried out on the basis of seniority, on the grounds that the veterans have contributed more years of effort to the kibbutz. Members will receive payments for extra work days owed to them from the previous system over a ten-year period, but older members will be able to cash in their rights more quickly.

The preceding account is an abbreviated digest of the "Plan for the Development of Kibbutz Hasolelim," conveying an idea of what the kibbutz members decided, without going into too much technical detail. Though somewhat repetitive, the original document is a sincere and serious effort to reform the way of life of the community, while preserving many of its former values.

As in many kibbutzim, the financial underpinning of the plan will come from developing a new neighborhood, on lines similar to that proposed at Givat Brenner. In this, too, Hasolelim is further along the road than the larger kibbutz, with purchasers already signing up and building plans well advanced.

Yigal Orbach of Tmurot is proud of his project with the members of Hasolelim. In a follow-up questionnaire, he found general satisfaction with the changes, although some members expressed annoyance that he had not been more involved with each stage of the discussions. Interestingly, he has started working with Degania, but in that case he is working with the Team for Change, which then works on its own with the kibbutz membership. Thus, he is less involved there than he was with Hasolelim.

Many people have observed that Hasolelim was able to carry out the changes because of its small size and relative homogeneity, but Orbach believes that even large kibbutzim such as Givat Brenner can do it because basically everyone wants the same things. He is convinced that changes such as occurred at Hasolelim return the kibbutz to what it was supposed to be. He believes that the kibbutzim can keep their values by changing the system and also that the members will accept the resulting inequalities, provided there is equality of opportunity.

Clearly, Michael Mensky, the member most responsible for the changes, is pleased, although he concedes it went further than he had originally wanted. He is now working outside the kibbutz, advising other kibbutzim that are embarking on a process of change. Rita Aurbach, the community manager, is convinced that the changes were inevitable. During the first year, she says, there was a period when members were traumatized. Communal activities, which had declined during the difficult years, became even less common, as people remained at home, worrying about their own lives. Once they saw that they were all managing economically, however, they came out of their shells and started organizing community celebrations, hikes, and festivals, as they did in the past. So-called kibbutz values were often simply habits that became rationalized, she thinks. Optimistic about the future, she thinks that the new neighborhood will be good for Hasolelim socially as well as financially.

Sixty-six-year-old Yumbo Tzaller is the veteran most identified with the changes at Hasolelim. Relaxing in an elegant black and green tracksuit in his room, the crew-cut, bespectacled Tzaller explains that he initiated the process but quickly adopted a low profile in the face of the younger more energetic members who forced the process through.

"I have had no training whatever," he proclaims with a smile, "whereas they all have at least two degrees, and some have doctorates."

The Hungarian-born Tzaller and his mother were saved from the Nazis by the legendary Swedish diplomat Raoul Wallenberg. He joined the Noar Hatzioni youth movement in Hungary after the war, arriving in Israel in 1950. After becoming a member of Hasolelim, he went straight into the army. After his army service, he returned to the kibbutz to work in the fields. He was a truck driver for eleven years and kibbutz treasurer for separate periods of seven and eight years. His second term of office saw the economic crisis of the mid-1980s, following which he did a course in human resources at the Kibbutz Movement's Ruppin College.

"I didn't learn a damn thing," he maintains. "I'm lousy at human relations. I was the one who set up the meeting with Tmurot, but afterward I played a very minor role in the process of change."

Tzaller makes no bones about the current status of Hasolelim. "It's not a kibbutz," he states baldly. He believes that all the kibbutzim should go through the same process and thinks it a shame that Hasolelim didn't do it twenty years earlier. He is quite sure the old kibbutz system is against human nature.

"The system only works when you are in a state of extreme poverty," he opines. "I was against it ever since the 1960s. The idea that every member could take on any job—it drove me crazy!"

Two of his children are living in Tel Aviv and the third in the United States. He looks back without regret but admits that he would not have opted for life on a kibbutz "if I had known what I now know."

His fellow veteran, American-born Dina Brock, came to Hasolelim in the earliest days. Her husband, born in Germany but brought up in Palestine, died four years ago. A comfortable gray-haired grandmother, she describes herself as "a conformist."

"I accepted everything they handed out," she confesses. "Whatever was voted on, I went along with it." She regrets that she did not stand up more for her rights. She wanted to study nursing and later to become an English teacher, but she always accepted the kibbutz demand that she work as a *metapelet* (a child care worker). She was not enthusiastic about the children sleeping away from home but accepted it as she accepted everything else.

Her husband established the poultry-breeding enterprise that is one of the three pillars of the kibbutz today. She is convinced that he would have been bitterly opposed to the changes, and she herself thinks the old system was better, but she voted in favor of the plan because her own children wanted it. Not that she is totally opposed—she concedes that the new system has improved some things at Hasolelim.

"There were parasites among our members," she admits. "Some members took too much food from the communal dining hall, others exploited the laundry. One couple, who worked reduced hours, refused to apply for national insurance benefits. Two years ago, when they saw their paychecks under the new system, you should have seen them running to the National Insurance Institute!"

Dina feels economically secure: her pension and other payments are more than adequate, and she supplements her income by working in the clothing store. Two of her children live at the kibbutz, and the third is only ten minutes away by car. Basically, she is content but maintains Hasolelim went too far too fast.

"People often come here from other kibbutzim to ask our advice," she notes. "I always tell them: do it, but go more slowly than we did; do one thing at a time."

Heading the opposition to the new regime is veteran Hiki Caspi, who is waging an almost lone campaign against the implementation of the decisions that started being carried out in January 1997. He was not the only member voting against the plan, but he is the only one actively opposing it.

"They have stolen the kibbutz from me," he declares. "I came here to live a certain way of life, and it has been turned on its head. If the others want a nonkibbutz, so be it, but at least they should give me—and anyone else who wants it—the option of living in the old way."

Caspi's demand for a two-track system is based on a belief that, if there is a group in each kibbutz—even a small group—living in the classical kibbutz manner, it will maintain an option for a revival of socialist values when the cycle comes around again, which he is confident will happen. He intends to take Hasolelim to court in support of his demand.

"I won't be any better off economically," he concedes. "It is simply a question of principle. The original agreement of all the members was to live according to the principle of 'from each according to his ability to each according to his needs.' I think the courts should back me up on that principle."

Hiki Caspi is a gnarled old pioneer, with a white goatee beard and mustache. Had Leon Trotsky survived into old age, he might have looked very much like Caspi. His wife died of cancer five years ago, and most of his activities these days are connected with support groups for the relatives of the terminally ill.

One of the founders of Hasolelim, he has been secretary, farm manager, work organizer, head of field crops, and factory manager. He is still a fervent believer in the classical kibbutz. He accepted changes such as the children sleeping at home, payment for meals and electricity, and the general privatization of budgets. For him the "red line" was differential wages. In his view, that is what has destroyed the kibbutz.

"I still don't see why a manager should get more than a worker," he insists. "I don't accept that *anyone* should get more than anyone else, except where the need is greater. Where will it end? You may start with a wage differentials of three to one, but you'll quickly get to twenty to one."

Weren't there always inequalities—private money, presents from relatives, and so on? Caspi is indignant. Of course, there was inequality, he admits. People are human beings, not angels. Anyone who thought that the kibbutz would create a new human being was deluded. He never thought that, but to take minor distortions as proof that equality cannot exist is nonsense. The kibbutz was still far more equal than the surrounding society. The trouble is that some people tried to make an ideology based on the fact that kibbutz society was imperfect.

"The point is that it was better than other systems," he insists.

Hiki has no quarrel with the actual process of change. He agrees that the discussions were thorough and systematic, but he is skeptical about the success of the new system. He maintains that the promised financial reports have not been issued, and "nobody really knows whether it is working or not." He expects the whole system to collapse economically sometime soon, but that is not the basis of his complaint.

"I accept the right of the others to alter the way they live," he sums up. "All I'm asking for is the right to live in the way I want to live."

Things are not static in today's world, he maintains. The kibbutzim are rejecting cooperation just as the Western world is searching for new communal forms. In another twenty years, everything will turn around again. Caspi concedes that the kibbutzim made many mistakes in the past. There was too little consideration of the individual, he admits, and the group was elevated to an exaggerated degree. Now it has gone too far in the other direction. Ways must be sought to give individuals a chance to express their creativity and initiative, while still maintaining the community.

Mira Carmon is the village nurse. A compact, self-assured figure in her white coat, she grew up on the kibbutz and has every intention of remaining there.

"I don't say that everything is perfect," she says, "but, really, we did it very well. Of course, the fact that we are relatively small made it much easier."

"Why did you never expand?"

"We did!" Bright smile. "We expanded from 100 to 116. No, really, I don't know the reason. People came; people left. Hasolelim was a bit of a 'railway station.' We were amateurs regarding administration and money matters."

"What was it like growing up in such a small community?"

There were positive and negative aspects. She, personally, was traumatized by the communal sleeping system. She was sick as a small child and missed her mother. She remembers lying awake at night, terrified. Her sister used to run home to the parental room, but she was too scared to do the same. Although things improved, as she grew older, she vowed she would not inflict the system on her own children. In her view, at the age of sixteen children benefit from living together, although she thinks even then it is vital to have good teachers and counselors. She still looks on her peer group as brothers and sisters; her real siblings are not as close.

Mira spent eighteen months outside the kibbutz after her military service, working in Haifa, the port city some twenty miles to the west of Hasolelim, before traveling in South America with her boyfriend. They came back and married, and she enrolled as a student nurse at the nearby Afula Hospital. Her husband came to the kibbutz with his youth movement group and remained. Both of them have pursued academic studies with some avidity. Mira followed her nursing course with an undergraduate degree in life sciences at the Open University and is now studying for a second degree in public health administration, offered externally in Israel by Clark University, Boston. Her husband studied farm management and economics at Ruppin College, following up with an M.B.A. at the Hebrew University of Jerusalem. Today he works in the poultry-breeding plant, which has expanded considerably under his leadership, making contacts with Cyprus, Jordan, and the Palestinian Authority.

While generally positive about the changes at Hasolelim, Mira does on occasion contradict her own thesis. She was always annoyed by the fact that everyone received the same, no matter how hard they worked.

"Why should someone who just puts in his eight hours get the same as a member who works all hours of the day and night?" she demands.

She wanted to decide what to do with her own money. She resented a situation whereby the kibbutz decided to buy everyone toaster ovens. Maybe she preferred a computer. She was horrified by the dependence of everybody on committees. If she wanted to buy a dishwasher, she saw no need to justify her decision before a committee. Questions such as "Did you get me my medicine?" or "Did you order me a car?" disgusted her. She is certain people prefer to do things for themselves. Of course, she concedes, people who need help should get it. The mutual assistance fund takes care of that.

On the other hand, she has written an essay for her public health degree on the differences in motivation at Hasolelim before and after the changes. She discovered that a member who was lazy before is still lazy. She also found that money is not such an important motivation for working hard. She now thinks that interest and pleasure in the work are more vital components.

She has herself been affected: there used to be two full-time nurses at Hasolelim. First they reduced the second nurse, an outside employee, to half-time. Now they have cut her out altogether, except for special duty. Naturally Mira now has to work harder and has made herself more efficient. She concedes that in the old days she and her colleague would sometimes gossip, but they would also discuss genuine problems and reach solutions to them. Furthermore, she now devotes less time to her patients. She cannot make lengthy home visits as she used to and is not sure that this is a good thing.

"Is Hasolelim still a kibbutz?"

"Yes," she is emphatic. "It is a *different* kibbutz. Equality is bullshit. I am not the same as you, and you are not the same as him. There is no point in buying computers for everybody. Maybe some people don't want them."

Hasolelim is an example of a kibbutz that has transformed itself radically, but also smoothly and efficiently. An examination of its present situation must lead to the conclusion that it is very different from the classical kibbutz, even though it still retains many of its elements. This is not to deliver a value judgement. The kibbutz is a democratic society; the overwhelming majority of the members approved the changes and are still in favor of them, but if Hasolelim still calls itself a kibbutz, it must be admitted that the meaning of the word has been changed. Only the future will show how much is preserved of the original way of life, but with all one's admiration for the decisiveness and sensitivity of Michael Mensky, Rita Aurbach, and their colleagues, the verdict must be that Hasolelim is a new category of settlement. Maybe it is the first *kibbutz kehillati* (community kibbutz).

In the next chapter we will examine a kibbutz that failed to read the danger signs and, as a result, is no longer a self-governing community.

4

נוה ים

NEVE YAM
SURVIVING COLLAPSE

In 1994 Neve Yam faced bankruptcy and collapse. It was forced to agree to the appointment of a special committee, including two members from outside the kibbutz, to run is affairs. The field crops and the fish farming, the poultry branch and the dining hall are rented out to private contractors. The elected committees that normally regulate the life of every kibbutz member no longer exist at Neve Yam. There is no general economic committee, housing committee, or education committee, nor are there committees for health, security, absorption of newcomers, personal problems, culture, or sport. The kibbutz general meeting is still sovereign; it will eventually approve decisions about the future of the community. It does not meet weekly, however, as in the past, or even monthly. It will be called into session only when the time arrives for major decisions.

The members still live according to the hallowed principle of "from each according to his ability, to each according to his needs," which is more than can be said of many kibbutzim today, including the one described in the previous chapter. The wages earned by those members who still work are paid into a communal purse, and allowances are distributed to all, including retired veterans, on the basis of equality, with a 10 percent increment allotted to the wage earners. But this situation is temporary. Neve Yam is planning to turn itself into a noncooperative village.

Neve Yam (Dwelling by the Sea) was established as a Fisherman's Commune in 1939 on one of the prettiest stretches of the Mediterranean

Figure 4.1.   Vessels of Neve Yam in Nahariya 1938.

Source: (Yad Tabenkin Archives)

coast by a group of immigrants from the Gordonia youth movement. They had undergone training in the Polish port city of Gedinya, with a German fishing instructor, Captain Gustav Peach. Peach, a gentile and a fervent socialist, accompanied the group of Jewish pioneers to Palestine and remained with them for some years.

The group called themselves "Gordonia-*Ma'apilim*" (the Gordonia Blockade Runners), because by then the British mandate authorities, under pressure of the Arab Revolt, were limiting the number of immigration certificates to Palestine. In 1938, the group settled temporarily in Nahariya, some fifty miles north of today's Neve Yam. There they built three fishing boats under Peach's instructions from wood imported from Poland. The following year they settled at their present site. Initially they were granted a strip of sandy shoreline. They did not mind the fact that they had no land suitable for farming, as they aspired to make their living from fishing.

"We were incredibly naive and totally inexperienced," says Benzion Kagan, a veteran in his eighties who left some years ago and today lives in the city of Haifa. "We did not realize that we could not establish a village based only on fishing, and we did not realize that we needed land."

The fishing boats were unsuitable for the Mediterranean. Moreover, the fishing nets and other equipment brought in by the German fisherman were useless in the local conditions. "It was not that Peach was impractical," recalls Kagan with a smile. "He was practical—but for the Baltic, not the Mediterranean!"

The young pioneers acquired a new instructor, Abu-Shafik, a local Arab fisherman. With his help they bought light boats and locally made nets and began to fish for sardines. The old-timers remember the early days as very tough. Although the Mediterranean is a relatively calm sea, it has its storms, and the see breezes often blew down the tents of the new settlement. The veterans also recall nights when they spent hour after hour on their fragile vessels, unable to land until the waves calmed down. Some of the members worked in the salt factory in nearby Atlit. Both the fishing and the work in the salt pans caused swift deterioration of their working clothes. The women in charge of the clothing store patched the clothes with remains of other clothes and even made garments out of tent canvas.

Their troubles were only just beginning. The strip of shore that they occupied belonged to PICA, the pre-Zionist Jewish Colonization Association, of the Barons Hirsh and Rothschild. It transpired that the Zionist Settlement Office only made a temporary agreement with PICA for the settlement of the Gordonia group. Within two years, PICA decided not to renew the lease and tried to expel them.

Kagan describes the subsequent period of litigation as terribly disillusioning—even traumatic—and says the members took a long time to recover from it. In the end, they were allowed to stay, but it was a long time before there was a clear-cut decision, and meanwhile their sense of security had been seriously undermined. A further blow was the failure of sixty more members of their pioneer group from Gedinya to arrive in Palestine. These young men and women, trapped in Poland by the outbreak of Word War II, eventually perished in the Nazi death camps.

Members of Gordonia, named after and influenced by Aharon David Gordon of Degania fame, the Neve Yam settlers initially espoused the intimate *kvutza* as their model. Ultimately, though, Neve Yam's failure to grow was, like that of Hasolelim, the result of chance and circumstance rather than ideology. Kagan also cites the loss of the sixty left behind in Europe and the experience of almost being turned off their land as possible reasons for their failure to attract and absorb more members. For most of its existence Neve Yam had a membership of around eighty, and today it has only sixty, one-third of them pensioners.

A visitor to Neve Yam can immediately perceive that it is different. It looks like a kibbutz on the back burner: not abandoned, but by the standards one has come to expect from kibbutzim, a little forlorn. The lawns have not run wild, but they are not tended the way kibbutz lawns usually are. The flower beds, though not neglected, are far from luxuriant. The trees and shrubs are roughly trimmed. The plaster on some of the houses is peeling, and the paths are somewhat overgrown. There are dilapidated corners, with rusting machinery and broken furniture scattered around. On the other hand, the garbage is regularly collected.

The area of the Marine Recreation Center looks rather better. Although empty in the off-season, it is neat and tidy. The grass is noticeably greener than in other parts of the village, the buildings fresher and better maintained. The bay is beautiful, with white sands and a black stone breakwater jutting into the royal blue sea. The vacation houses and water park appear in excellent condition.

Nurit Bruner, a small, neat, energetic woman in her fifties, was born at Neve Yam to parents from the original founding group. She grew up in the kibbutz and went to school there and then to high school at the youth village of Kfar Galim in Haifa. After military service, she married a member of a nearby kibbutz, and the couple elected to live at Neve Yam. They have three children—two at home, one at her husband's kibbutz—and two grandchildren.

"We were always a very small kibbutz, and we never had much money," she remarks with a sad smile. "I don't know whether we were just naive or what, but we were content. Growing up here, we felt that we had everything we needed."

Despite its small size, Neve Yam enjoyed a rich cultural life, Nurit notes, and was famous for its choir. When Kibbutz Meuhad split in 1951, Yehuda Sharett, the celebrated kibbutz conductor who led choirs in many kibbutzim (including Givat Brenner), left his kibbutz, Yagur, and came to live in Neve Yam. Although the kibbutz acquired several families from Yagur, most of them eventually left.

Despite its beautiful location, bad luck seems to have plagued Neve Yam almost from the outset. Early on the kibbutz attempted to enhance its fishing branch by establishing a factory for processing and canning sardines, but during the land dispute with PICA, work was stopped by a court order. The members managed to acquire some land from the

Figure 4.2.   Neve Yam in the 1960s.

Source: (Yad Tabenkin Archives)

nearby village of Atlit and made a new start, building. They subsequently extended their operations to other products, canning citrus, corn, and other fruit and vegetables. Neve Yam's "Noon" became a large factory, with more than six hundred employees at its peak, and in time it became the largest manufacturer in the world of the Jewish delicacy gefilte fish, made from the produce of carp ponds, which were established at the kibbutz.

Benzion Kagan, who founded Noon and ran it until he left Neve Yam in 1961, disputes the statement that Neve Yam "never had money." He maintains that the factory guaranteed the survival of the kibbutz, with exports worth millions of dollars. Other veterans say that it was always struggling to pay back loans. It is not impossible that both versions are true: that Neve Yam did earn large sums of money with its factory but also had large expenditures and never managed to balance its books.

Regarding Noon's sale at the beginning of the 1980s, there is general agreement that it was mishandled. The man in charge of the factory after Kagan, an extremely capable member called David Levy, was killed in a road accident, and no suitable successor was found. It is stated, with the wisdom of hindsight, that Neve Yam should have sold only part of Noon and remained a partner in the factory. Instead, the kibbutz insisted on selling out entirely, which was a mistake. Even today, with the Noon factory relocated away from Neve Yam, its former premises earn money. The factory buildings are rented out to several workshops and small factories, but the kibbutz doesn't benefit from the rent.

From its early years, Neve Yam took advantage of its location, renting out holiday homes. The vacation enterprise earned good money, as long as the investment was minimal. In the summer, the vacationers would eat in the communal dining hall, while the kibbutz members ate outside in a large thatched hut. However, when the kibbutz invested in a convalescent home, with high-quality buildings and a restaurant, the kibbutz found it difficult to repay the investment. One of the veterans maintains that the season was too short, but the Israeli summer extends from May to October, with plenty of good weather in November and December, so that excuse is unconvincing. No more persuasive is the contention of another veteran that Neve Yam suffered from being too near to Haifa. The proximity of a large town should have been an advantage rather than a liability. The fish ponds, where carp are still raised, and the field crops were more successful, but they did not suffice to keep Neve Yam solvent in the face of its other problems.

Figure 4.3.   The Neve Yam management committee in 1975.

Source: (Yad Tabenkin Archives)

"We had good people here," maintains Nurit, "but somehow we never took off economically."

Bad luck may have been the lot of the kibbutz in the past, but today, despite its debts, which amount to millions of dollars, Neve Yam is in the fortunate category of a "real estate kibbutz." It will relinquish part of its prime land to the government to pay off its debt and build a new neighborhood on what remains. As of November 1999, the government has frozen the situation with regard to all kibbutzim planning to build neighborhoods. Hopefully, the necessary authorizations will be granted. In relinquishing land Neve Yam is taking action similar to that of Givat Brenner and Hasolelim, but there are two major differences: first, Neve Yam, with its idyllic location on the seashore, will definitely attract purchasers; second, there will not be two separate communities. Nurit is certain that Neve Yam's period as a kibbutz is over, and the entire village, including the new neighborhood, will become a *yishuv kehillati,* or "community settlement."

This is a category that has become popular in Israel during the past two decades, particularly in Galilee, when young people from the towns are unwilling to join kibbutzim or *moshavim* but keen to live in small communities in the countryside. The community settlement has more collective responsibility than the ordinary village, but there is no aspiration to equality, and its communalism is minimal, leaving the residents very much the masters of their own fates. They are members of an association, which admits new residents, licenses local stores, approves development plans (together with the relevant national and regional planning committees), arranges education for the children, encourages and supports business enterprises, organizes cultural events, and, in many cases, exercises a certain supervision over the style of the houses. However, in contrast to a traditional kibbutz, the residents are almost completely independent.

Many kibbutzim may eventually end up as community settlements, although most of them will probably retain some form of joint ownership of their farming branches and factories. Neve Yam has already given up on its assets and is on the way to being a community settlement. The members are waiting for Kibbutz Arrangement Authority to grant the requisite permission, following the completion of agreements with the government and the banks.

Once dissolving the partnership becomes a practical proposition, Neve Yam's general meeting will have to give its assent, and Nurit is confident that it will go through. She has no regrets. The kibbutz was a nice idea, she says, but it did not manage to guarantee the members a living. The new framework will enable people to own their homes, earn their living, and grow old with self-respect. She does not believe that the Neve Yam community settlement will retain any traces of the old kibbutz system.

"Once people were prepared to pay the price to live communally," she says simply. "Today they are not. It no longer works."

For the time being, as mentioned, Neve Yam is run on kibbutz principles. The committee administering the settlement was appointed by the Registrar of Cooperative Societies, following the intervention of Bank Hapoalim (Neve Yam's bank) and the Auditing Division of the Cooperative Organizations Association. They came to the conclusion that the kibbutz was no longer managing its affairs competently. There were reports of malpractice in kibbutz terms: members who worked at outside jobs were said to be withholding part of their income from the public purse; kibbutz money was allegedly used for private purposes; some of the bookkeeping was misleading. Although it is difficult to check the details of these allegations today, there is no doubt that the mutual trust among members that is an essential feature of kibbutz life collapsed.

The committee that runs Neve Yam today consists of an outside chairman, a resident of a nearby town; Nurit Broner, who serves as the secretary; and two other members: one from Neve Yam, one from a neighboring kibbutz. There is also a village administrator, who collects the income from the rented enterprises and attends to the everyday problems of the community. The administrator works with the committee, but he is not formally a member.

The Marine Recreation Center, with its vacation houses, restaurant, and water park, is still half the property of Neve Yam. Long before the appointment of the present committee, the kibbutz went into partnership with a private company on a fifty-fifty basis. The chairman is from the outside company; half the board are members of Neve Yam.

As noted, the other branches of the kibbutz have been rented out to private companies, and all income is distributed according to kibbutz principles. The veterans, who receive their allowances in lieu of pensions, also receive full health care, free electricity, laundry, and transportation. They have their homes cleaned every week and are provided with any other services they need. Beit Oren is less than ten miles away, and the lesson of that kibbutz, where the veteran founders were abandoned, seems to have been learned.

"Although most of the veterans no longer have children at Neve Yam, their needs are given priority," points out Nurit, "I think we can be proud of that."

Her claim is backed up by Abrasha Kahal, a founder of Neve Yam and today a widower in his eighties. Abrasha, a bald man with wings of gray hair and large horn-rimmed glasses, underwent open-heart surgery in 1991. A former treasurer of the kibbutz, he still puts in a day's work in the accounting office.

"There is a nice young lady who comes every week to clean and tidy my room," he notes. "I have my allowance and health insurance, and everything I need." Unlike many of the veterans, Abrasha has two sons at Neve Yam. He is content with his life and philosophical about the collapse of the kibbutz idea. He is clearly saddened but does not seem to regard it as a tragedy.

"Things have changed," he says. "That is a fact of life: the youngsters don't want a collective life. They don't want the responsibility. The age of ideals is over. We have to face the fact that many of our children did not come back to Neve Yam after their army service."

Rachel Rawner is the archivist and librarian of Neve Yam. A well-preserved woman in her midseventies, she arrived at Neve Yam in 1943 as part of a group of Austrian immigrants that trained at Kvutzat Schiller (neighbors of Givat Brenner). Her husband Dan, who died three years ago, arrived in Palestine in 1940 as an "illegal" immigrant. He was one of those transferred by British soldiers to the *Patria,* which was scheduled to deport them to the Indian Ocean island of Mauritius. In an operation that is still the subject of controversy, the Hagana defense force detonated explosives in an attempt to disable the vessel, but the charge was so powerful that the *Patria* sank, and 250 of the immigrants were drowned. Dan, a graduate of Gordonia, was one of those who managed to swim ashore. He was imprisoned for almost a year at Atlit (less than a mile from Neve Yam) before joining Rachel's group at Kvutzat Schiller and then coming with her to Neve Yam.

The couple had three sons, one of whom was killed in the 1973 Yom Kippur War. The other two live at Neve Yam. Rachel still works in the library but admits that she has neglected the archives.

"It was so hot this summer," she explains, "I just couldn't find the energy. I'll get back to it, though."

She says flatly that Neve Yam is no longer a kibbutz, but it doesn't seem to trouble her. She is content with her children and grandchildren. Every Friday night she makes a meal for the whole family.

Ayal Rawner, Rachel's son, runs the field crops branch, as he did in the past, when Neve Yam was a normal kibbutz, but today he is an employee of SDS Production & Marketing Ltd., which rents the fields from Neve Yam. As in the case of the other wage earners, his salary is paid in to the kibbutz and he receives his allowance, plus 10 percent.

Ayal is manifestly a farm worker, although he laughingly insists that he is a "manager, not a laborer." He has strong callused hands, and his clothes are work stained. Only the fashionably modern sunglasses perched on his iron-gray crew cut are at odds with the image.

"I always wanted to live here," he declares with an impish grin. "A house by the sea—surely it is everyone's dream."

After his military service, Ayal studied practical engineering at the Ruppin College and later took a short course in financial administration. He married a volunteer from England and served as farm manager. He now runs the fields of irrigated crops, as a paid manager, with the help of four agricultural workers from Thailand. They have 250 acres of cotton, with the remaining 125 devoted to corn and chickpeas. There is a certain amount of crop rotation, which he plans together with the company. It is no longer Neve Yam's business, provided the kibbutz receives the rent. Ayal regards the kibbutz ideal as "a nice idea that was never really tried." He maintains there was never any real equality, at least not at Neve Yam: some people studied and others didn't; some traveled; some had perks; some were "more equal than others."

"It's all bullshit," he states. "You don't need the complicated kibbutz structure for people to cooperate. A home, a reasonable living, honorable old age, friendship—what more do you need?"

Ayal concedes that Neve Yam's Noon factory was probably incompetently managed and failed to keep up with the times, but he points out that many factories have collapsed for these reasons, not only kibbutz enterprises. He is hopeful about the future, believing that Neve Yam will be able build its new neighborhood and pay off its debts.

"It's worth hanging on," he says. "I've been through the difficult times. I have been working for twenty years and still haven't really established my home. Hopefully it will all work out. We have a beautiful location here. I think it will be popular."

Despite everything, Neve Yam is somehow not depressing. Although it has broken down as a kibbutz, those members who still live there have not abdicated. They are planning their future, which will be different from their past, and, most important, they are fulfilling their obligations to the founding generation.

There is no doubt that several kibbutzim, with similar insoluble economic problems, will take the same path as Neve Yam. Many others, while managing to avoid economic collapse, will nevertheless gradually dismantle their cooperative structures. At the same time there are still kibbutzim that continue to function as they did in the past. In the next chapter, we will visit a kibbutz that has retained all the principles and most of the features of a classical kibbutz, proving that given competent management, hard work, a strong community, and a measure of luck, the kibbutz system can work even today.

5

חצרים

HATZERIM
PROVING IT CAN WORK

It owns a factory and twenty-two subsidiaries all over the world, with annual earnings of a quarter of a billion dollars. Its members have spacious modern homes, computers, cellular phones, credit cards, and the use of private cars. They can travel abroad every year. Their children are entitled to free education up to the undergraduate level, no matter where they live. Conversely, the members own nothing; earn the same whether they are executives, engineers or garbage collectors; and all of them—whatever their profession or position—are obligated to put in a weekly shift on the factory production line.

Welcome to Hatzerim in the Negev Desert, a wealthy kibbutz with a flourishing advanced economy. It is entrepreneurial, profitable, competitive, efficient, and adapted to the modern era. It is also a traditional kibbutz, which practices the principle (pronounced obsolete by an increasing number of members of other kibbutzim) "from each according to his ability, to each according to his needs."

In its outward appearance, Hatzerim is not very different from Degania or Givat Brenner: the same well-tended gardens, the same shady paths, the same trees and shrubs, gymnasium, swimming pool, and ball fields. Yet the success of this kibbutz is almost tangible, from the moment you walk through the tinted-glass electronic doors into the inviting communal dining hall, with its spotless marble floor, tasteful furnishings, and simple but superb food. Its factory, with its vast manufacturing space, its humming computerized machines, its research lab-

Figure 5.1. Hatzerim in the early days.

Source: (Yad Tabenkin Archives)

oratories, and its gleaming modern offices would not disgrace a high-tech plant anywhere in the world.

Hatzerim is as modern as Microsoft and as old-fashioned as Umm Juni: a remarkable illustration of the fact that the classical kibbutz format can work, even at the start of the twenty-first century.

Why? Why has Hatzerim succeeded, whereas so many of Israel's kibbutzim have failed? Possibly its success cannot be adequately explained, but an examination of its history and present situation does provide a number of clues. Despite what has been described in the previous chapters, Hatzerim, and other kibbutzim like it, could yet justify adapting Mark Twain's adage to describe the reports of the death of the kibbutz as "premature."

Hatzerim (Walled Villages in biblical Hebrew) was established in the fall of 1946, on the night after Yom Kippur, the Day of Atonement, as part of a Zionist operation for the simultaneous placing of eleven new kibbutzim at strategic locations in the western Negev Desert. Carried out in the dying days of the British mandate for Palestine, it was a determined coup, which helped claim the area for the State of Israel.

Twenty-five young men and five young women from the Israeli Scout Movement tramped through the desert, avoiding Beersheba, which at that time was an Arab town, to pitch their tents on an arid desert hilltop. On the following afternoon, after an eighteen-hour day, as they were struggling to haul a water tank onto the top of an improvised wooden tower, a party of Zionist officials arrived, led by the redoubtable Avraham Harzfeld, the same man who had told the pioneers of Givat Brenner that he would throw them out of the labor federation because they were acting alone instead of fitting in with his overall settlement plan.

Although Harzfeld was eighteen years older and the settlers of Hatzerim were (unlike the Givat Brenner pioneers, who took a private initiative) acting under orders, he was no less emotional. He stood on a packing case to address the young settlers, but he did not make a speech. Instead he sang:

> This is our fate,
> Thus we are commanded,
> This is the road,
> This our aim,
> We have not labored in vain.

As the diminutive Zionist leader repeated the popular song, one or two began to join in, until, by the third repetition, all the young pioneers and their guests were singing with fervor and hope. It was, said one of the founders of Hatzerim, more effective than any speech could have been. They felt that they were making history.

Although the youngsters were infected with an enormous sense of achievement, their euphoria was short-lived. The United Nations voted to partition Palestine between Jews and Arabs in November 1947. Seven months later the British rulers left, and the State of Israel was declared in borders that included Hatzerim. The Arabs of Palestine did not accept the UN decision, though, and the new kibbutz soon found itself with its water cut off, under siege from hostile forces. One of the early settlers recalls that she was not able to leave Hatzerim all that year; in the burning heat of the Negev Desert the water was measured out in cups.

This phase was only temporary: following the 1948 War of Independence, Hatzerim found itself with a lot more land. Moreover, the land was good for farming. The problem was that it was more than twenty miles to the north. The location meant that the rainfall there was

Figure 5.2.   Hatzerim in 1956.

Source: (Yad Tabenkin Archives)

measurably higher, but the members had to sleep in a hut near the fields all week, only returning to their kibbutz at weekends.

In due course, water was piped to Hatzerim and other Negev settlements. Fields were sown and orchards planted, but in every diligently claimed plot of green there appeared large patches of brown. Hatzerim's land was too saline for farming.

"Even in those days we had a strong sense of fiscal responsibility," recalls a veteran. "We resolved that we would not stay there unless we could make a living."

The head of the Jewish Agency's settlement department, Levi Eshkol, told the young settlers that it would be cheaper to put them up at the new luxurious Dan Hotel in Tel Aviv than to maintain them in Hatzerim. Eshkol, who would later be Israel's finance minister and prime minister, suggested that cotton might be grown despite the saline conditions. Prime Minister Ben-Gurion, a strong believer in settling the desert, told them, "Leave Hatzerim by all means, but go further south!"

The arguments raged back and forth. In a fateful general meeting of the kibbutz on February 7, 1959, the members who wanted to remain argued that they already felt emotional ties to the place; that, with patience, success could be achieved; that they could establish a dairy and a chicken house. Their opponents said that it was a hopeless struggle, that they should join forces with another kibbutz, that the money and effort could be better invested elsewhere. Out of the sixty-four members, twenty-nine voted to remain, seventeen wanted to leave, fourteen abstained, and four did not vote. They resolved to give it another three years. In any event, the members of Hatzerim discovered that they could farm successfully, provided they carried out the very laborious process of washing the salt from the soil. They realized, however, that they would never survive on agriculture alone, and they began the search for an industry.

Water engineer Simha Blas, a former managing director of Israel's Mekkorot Water Company, had conceived a revolutionary new method of irrigation and was trying to hawk it around the Negev kibbutzim, where water shortages were endemic. The story that has been told repeatedly is that Blas saw an enormous palm tree growing by a leaking faucet, which planted the idea in his mind. Although the story is probably apocryphal, the concept of drip irrigation has revolutionized agriculture in Israel and all over the world.

The principle is straightforward: instead of spraying water from sprinklers, in an approximate imitation of rain, the water is fed directly to the plant's roots by means of a gradual drip. The basic simplicity of the concept turned out to be somewhat deceptive. The technical problems were formidable, but the potential was enormous. Apart from saving water, improving efficiency, and increasing productivity, the drip system would in time enable farmers to fertilize their crops directly through the water pipes. Subsequently, Hatzerim teamed up with another inventor, Rafi Mehudar, who was responsible for the refinement and development of the system, which has kept it one step ahead of its competitors. Another important factor in the success of the enterprise was the concept.

"We didn't sell a system," explains one of the members. "We sold a service. We were farmers who understood our customers. We came with the product, set it up, made sure it worked, and continued to maintain it over the years."

Today Hatzerim still has a profitable dairy, a poultry branch, and field crops, including jojoba, from which it manufactures oil for the cosmetics industry. It also has a legal office, headed by a member who is an attorney, which makes good money for the kibbutz, but the major part of its income comes from its irrigation enterprise.

According to Yigal Stav, the current chief executive officer of Netafim Irrigation Equipment and Drip Systems, the kibbutz initially made every possible business mistake. It was not only the pipes that leaked; the technology "leaked" to rivals all over Israel and the world. Hatzerim made coproduction arrangements with two other kibbutzim "based on a handshake," without written contracts.

Stav was completing his second degree in physics and working as an assistant lecturer at Ben-Gurion University when he was called back to Netafim after a management crisis in the early 1980s. Burly, gray haired, decisive, with a relaxed, assured manner, he presides confidently over an international concern, with factories in three kibbutzim in Israel, manufacturing centers in Australia and the United States, and twenty-two wholly owned subsidiaries in countries as varied as China, Mexico, Poland, Zimbabwe, and Thailand. Netafim's annual income is a quarter of a billion dollars, some two-thirds of which is earned by Hatzerim.

"In the final analysis, our ideology protected our economic interests," notes another veteran. "We insisted that our industry would be connected with farming, because of our belief in the Jewish people's return to the soil; we rejected anything that would necessitate outside hired workers, because we refused to exploit the labor of others."

Today Hatzerim does employ some twenty outsiders in various capacities, but—unlike many kibbutzim—it never agreed to take on significant numbers of hired workers. Even in the 1950s, when Prime Minister Ben-Gurion was insisting that the kibbutzim give employment to the new immigrants who had flooded into the country, Hatzerim held firm to its socialist principles. When it needed more manufacturing capacity, it farmed out its production to two other kibbutzim, Magal and Yiftah.

Possibly what most characterized the kibbutz was its fiscal caution. The initial investment in Netafim was minimal. It started with six workers and one machine, and the concern never borrowed money it could not repay. Netafim has always worked with its own capital. The kibbutz did not even take on mortgages: the houses at Hatzerim were built with profits from the factory.

Netafim is a high-tech, state-of-the-art concern, constantly expanding and diversifying. Its marketing is dynamic, its quality control is superb, and its follow-up and support services are efficient and comprehensive. More than 5 percent of Netafim's annual turnover is invested in research and development, which has served to keep the company competitive. Its local agents and representatives maintain continuous

Figure 5.3. Hatzerim's Netafim factory in 1986.

Source: (Yad Tabenkin Archives)

contact with customers, and they are backed up by an international team of agronomists, geologists, soil experts, and water engineers.

In a move toward increased diversification, the kibbutz has set up a new company, Waternet, focusing on gardening. A key product is the Plantsitter, a computerized system for watering houseplants, which can also be operated while the homeowner is on vacation. Waternet also manufactures special nozzles, power sprays, nontwist hoses, connectors, and irrigation computers. These products also come with a comprehensive customer follow-up service.

In 1999, conditions in the world market prompted Hatzerim to combine with Magal and Yiftah, the other two kibbutzim with Netafim plants, to form a unified company. To an extent, this move will involve a division between the company and the community, as the Netafim board will now be answerable to all three kibbutzim. However, the system at Hatzerim is diametrically opposed to the idea of the New Kibbutz, which advocates separation of the business from the community.

"We have been concerned to create an *identity* between the factory and the kibbutz," stresses Netafim CEO Yigal Stav.

Figure 5.4.   Hatzerim in 1994.

Source: (Yad Tabenkin Archives)

We insist that every member of Hatzerim, whether his regular work is
in Netafim or not, puts in a weekly shift on the factory production line.
I do so myself. It sometimes causes problems, but, even from a purely
business point of view, it pays off. Our members feel a sense of ownership and involvement. In some kibbutzim, they organize special visits to the factory; but our members know what's going on at Netafim,
and that is a major motivation for working hard.

In the communal dining hall, all the kibbutz members were voting
for Hatzerim's representatives on the board of the new company, and
Stav insists this is entirely consistent with efficiency. The members do
not have the expertise of a professional board of management, he concedes, but the candidates have been preselected by a special panel, and
the voting process adds to the sense of involvement with the factory.

There are "parasites" at Hatzerim, as there are on every kibbutz.
Everybody agrees on that. There are also quite a few who simply do their
jobs, without any special effort, but a remarkably high proportion of the
kibbutz members are prepared to give their all. Everyone puts in his

weekly shift in the factory, and, when the demand is especially large, members willingly work on the Sabbath to fill the orders. The work ethic is unusually strong at Hatzerim; the manifest success of the kibbutz and its factory has tended to attract talented people.

The downside is that, despite its prosperity, Hatzerim, like most kibbutzim, finds it difficult to retain its young generation. Only some 40 percent of the kibbutz children choose to remain. At the same time, the waiting list of outsiders wanting to join is long, and the age range is evenly distributed.

For the members, most of whom do work very hard, life is extremely comfortable. The dining hall has already been mentioned. The individual homes have recently been expanded to more than eight hundred square feet of living space, with extra rooms for larger families. Recently, every member who wanted one received a computer. Prior to that, all members were issued cell phones, apart from their ordinary telephones. Every member is entitled to six days abroad per year, which is accumulative, and, in addition, members who have families living abroad are entitled to visit them at the kibbutz's expense. All members have an allowance of some $5,000 per year, which they can spend with their own credit cards. Cars are freely available at a subsidized rate. The members do not have to pay separately for health care, education, furniture, food, local phone calls, electricity, or water, and, of course, they have free use of the swimming pool, gymnasium, ball field, and other facilities. All children born at Hatzerim are entitled to fifteen years of education (even if they leave the kibbutz), which give them an undergraduate degree or its equivalent. Every member has a pension and can bequeath descendants $100,000. Although children who leave the kibbutz receive a financial grant in addition to funds for their education, a proportion of the $100,000 bequest can be taken out early and used to assist children living outside Hatzerim.

At the same time, members do not own their homes, nor do they have shares in the kibbutz enterprises, all of which are the property of the commune. They are not allowed to have private bank accounts or to receive gifts of money or even airline tickets. Many of the members travel abroad on Netafim business, but there is a rigid separation between business trips and vacations.

Hatzerim is the classical commune brought up-to-date. Stav concedes that there is a certain contradiction between the traditional kibbutz values and modern business practices, but he maintains that they are not irreconcilable. In his view, it all boils down to what the members want.

In many kibbutzim, the members resent having to live and work together. In Hatzerim the members still want a partnership. He has no doubt that hierarchy and comradeship can go hand in hand. Members can tell other members what to do by virtue of their position or expertise. There is no reason that a community based on cooperation and equality cannot also be an organism that shows initiative and adapts to change. In some ways it is more difficult for a communal group to map out strategy and set targets, but in other ways it is easier.

"It did happen in the past that somebody continued in a job because of reasons that were not strictly business," Stav admits. "We left the member in place because, if he was kicked out, he wouldn't have anywhere to go. That sort of humane approach will be more difficult now that we have to answer to a board representing three kibbutzim. But we never exaggerated; we always managed to behave with a measure of flexibility and wisdom."

One problem might be that, unlike Hatzerim, Magal and Yiftah have both made serious changes. The Magal plant of Netafim has five grades of salary. Hatzerim will now have to grade its own workers for the accounts of the joint company, but the "wages" will be averaged out and distributed on the basis of equality.

Stav believes that the experience of Hatzerim proves that a kibbutz can run a profitable modern business, but he stops short of saying that it is a model that others should follow. He points out that it is often difficult to find the necessary talents in a small community of fewer than four hundred members and notes that Hatzerim had a very strong leadership group from the outset. Furthermore, possibly because of this feature, the kibbutz managed to attract and absorb other talented members over the years.

"I cannot predict the future," Stav admits. "We are not an isolated island, and I don't know how long we can hold out with different values from the surrounding environment, whether in the kibbutz movement or the nation as a whole, but I still believe we can carry on living together and achieving great things, without giving up our values and our way of life."

A Team for Change was created at Hatzerim and held a few meetings in 1998, but very few members turned up, and it was wound up after less than a year. "Apparently the time was not yet ripe," concedes Rafi Zimmerman, who initiated and chaired the committee, "although compared to what is happening elsewhere, my proposals were a joke. I have to be honest: at Hatzerim we buy equality with money. That's not cynicism; it's a fact."

Zimmerman was not proposing separation of business and community, or home ownership, or making the member responsible for earning his own living. He was certainly not suggesting payment for overtime or the legitimization of any sort of inequality. He simply wanted to introduce a general allowance. In other words, instead of separate allowances for foreign travel, visits to families abroad, furniture, vacations, and such items, everything should all be lumped together in a general allowance that members could spend any way they wished. The allowance would continue to be allocated on the basis of strict equality of needs, according to seniority, family size, and special requirements. Even that idea was too radical for today's Hatzerim, although Zimmerman is sure it will eventually come.

"You can't run a community of almost one thousand people the same way you ran one of two hundred," he maintains. "And anyway, many people know how to use the present system to gain extra from it, which is also a sort of inequality."

Zimmerman does not have time to brood on the failure of his Team for Change. He is busy setting up a new kibbutz company, Hatzerim International Trade (HIT), which will deal in trading of agriculture-related products. The project is in its early days, and he will not go into detail beyond saying that he will use the contacts of his years in Netafim, but he will not compete with the company in any way.

Zimmerman is a wiry, youthful-looking man of fifty-eight, with a sandy gray mustache and a wry, humorous manner. He arrived at the kibbutz in 1964 as part of an army settlement group, sponsored by the scout movement. After working in the fields for a number of years, he was sent to study farm management at Ruppin College and started working in Netafim in 1969.

With interruptions for university studies, he worked in marketing in Israel and abroad. He spent two years in Costa Rica, trying to develop a market there, but the big breakthrough came in 1981 with the establishment of Nefatim's first foreign subsidiary in the United States. By 1990, he was in charge of exports, but in 1998 he found himself differing with his colleagues over future development and stepped down. He spent the subsequent five months "washing dishes in the communal dining hall and thinking." During that time, he also chaired the short-lived Team for Change. In 1999 he began setting up his new company. He had to secure the agreement of the Kibbutz Economic Committee, but once he convinced them that he had no intention of competing with Netafim, they agreed.

Whatever his differences with the current management of Netafim, Zimmerman is convinced there is no better company around. Like Stav, he sees no reason that a kibbutz structure should not be compatible with business efficiency. At the same time, he also points out that the founding group of Hatzerim was an exceptional group. In particular, he cites Abie Ron, a member who died in 1998 and who he thinks was largely responsible for the ideological purity and fiscal responsibility that has characterized Hatzerim. He describes himself as "one of the pragmatists" of the kibbutz, rather than an idealist, but maintains that the secret of Hatzerim's success has been its ability to combine realism with ideology.

At thirty-two, Arnon Columbus is one of the kibbutz-born children who decided to remain. He is also one of the youngsters who failed to turn up to discussions of the Team for Change. Indeed, he expressed himself as opposed to a general allowance: "You won't be able to control what people have in their rooms, and that could be a mistake." At the same time he allows there can be some measure of rationalizing the allowance to include more items.

As head of Netafim's warehouse, he handles thirty people (all but one of them members of Hatzerim) responsible for receiving and dispatching raw materials and manufactured goods. Another team of fifteen people is responsible for assembling and packaging. Arnon, a university-trained production engineer, admits he has ambivalent feelings about the kibbutz principle that makes every member work a shift per week on the Netafim production line.

"It is not always efficient," he says, adding with a smile that he sometimes advises some of his key employees not to show up for their turn if it interferes too much with the warehouse administration. He also admits that he has enlarged his teams to compensate for the weekly absences. In his view, the various production tasks take between two and eight months to learn, which means that "you can't simply put a person into any job."

In his view, some more serious thinking about the system is required, and possibly the weekly stint should be reduced to half a shift, in at least some cases. At the same time, Arnon admits that the arrangement works and improves motivation by giving the members a sense of identification with the factory.

"The fact is that everyone in Hatzerim has a sense of ownership," he says, "and that is what creates our unusually high work ethic."

Arnon does not deny that he and his girlfriend (today his wife) thought long and hard before deciding to make their life in the kibbutz. After leaving school, he spent a year of "national service" working in the scout movement before joining the army. He regards that year as very important, as it gave him a view of an Israel he had not known at the kibbutz, even at the regional school, which was not exclusively for kibbutz children.

Subsequently, like many kibbutz-born children, Arnon served as an officer in an elite combat unit. His girlfriend was from another kibbutz, but it was to Hazterim that the two came for a trial year after their army service and subsequent travel in North and South America. Although Arnon considered an interesting job in the regular army and signed up for a smart new neighborhood in the center of the country, he and his wife eventually opted for Hatzerim.

"I am still not certain I made the right decision," he confesses,

> but I think I did. Most of my friends outside the kibbutz are working like mad to get the things I already have. I work hard in the warehouse, but even if I'm here until midnight—and that does happen quite often—I am close to home and can nip off to see my wife and children. I really value kibbutz life and specifically love Hatzerim. Any small community contains pettiness and nit-picking, but here it is at a minimum.

When Arnon was fifteen, the kibbutz decided that the children should sleep at home rather than in the children's house. He and his classmates organized a protest demonstration outside the general meeting that was debating the decision.

"We demanded that the members should not make a decision which would deprive the children of the best experience of kibbutz life," he recalls with a smile. "I thought our parents were crazy to abolish the communal sleeping for their children. Now that I am a parent myself, I can't understand how they ever permitted it."

Arnon is actively involved in a program to bring back children born on Hatzerim who have left. He is in touch with some thirty kibbutz-born singles and couples in Israel and abroad. He feels that many who left may want to come back, but they have to be convinced that they are welcome.

Many kibbutz children who serve as officers in the army are frustrated when they return to the kibbutz by the dependence on a plethora of committees. In the army they were able to make decisions, they say; on the kibbutz they find that they need the authorization of some committee "every time they want to sneeze." Arnon rejects this complaint. On the contrary, he notes, apart from himself, three other recently appointed Netafim branch managers were relatively senior officers in the army.

"Officers appreciate the value of systems, or frameworks, for getting things done," he suggests. "I think the kibbutz children who leave are the ones who hate being part of a system, who want to be completely individualistic."

Chen has just joined the army, and he hasn't the faintest idea whether he will live in Hatzerim. He is serving in military intelligence, which he enjoys. He belongs to a later generation of kibbutz children, who slept at home with their parents. He feels that because of this, he has a greater intimacy with his parents, brother, and sister. He points out that, even under the new system, the children receive their own rooms away from the parental home at the age of sixteen.

"I think the Children's Society is important," Chen says, "but I think you can achieve it by other methods than sleeping away from home." He thinks that the kibbutz is a marvelous place in which to grow up but also concedes that "there is some truth in" the contention that the kibbutz education creates mediocrity.

"You won't hear a kibbutz kid saying he wants to be the best or to earn the most," he notes. "Is that a bad thing? I don't know."

He and his girlfriend do not spend much time thinking about whether they want to live in a kibbutz. Nor is the future a topic of conversation among his classmates and other friends. The decision is a long way off, and there is simply no point worrying about it now, although he has decided that he will remain in Israel.

"Of course, I want to travel," he says, "but I have no doubt that this is the country where I want to live."

The positive environment for raising children could be a critical factor in favor of an eventual decision to return to Hatzerim, Chen says, but he thinks his choice of career, which he is not yet prepared to make, will determine his final decision. He is not particularly enthused by the idea of living at Hatzerim and working outside, although he agrees that lifestyle is possible. He feels that anyone who decides to live in a kibbutz should be totally involved. If he opts for a career outside the kibbutz, he probably will not remain.

Gideon Elad is involved in something called the Project for Social Involvement, an offshoot of an earlier project for plowing back some of Hatzerim's profits into Israeli society. In the 1980s, Hatzerim was the initiator and founder of Kedma, a youth village for children with special needs, established on the site of an abandoned kibbutz. For several years the kibbutz provided some of the funds and many of the instructors. As the project became established, however, it received funding from the appropriate government agencies, and Hatzerim gradually reduced its involvement.

In its latest reincarnation, the Project for Social Involvement aims at linking up with the year of national service performed by most of the kibbutz children before they go in the army. Elad wants the project to work like a charitable foundation, with the kibbutz children identifying and assessing worthwhile projects. They will be expected to find the project, write a report, and follow up with their own involvement. In 1998 Hatzerim handed out some $20,000 and over $30,000 in 1999.

Elad has lived at Hatzerim since 1951, and he has always been involved in activities outside the kibbutz as well as within it. He has worked abroad as a youth leader for several periods of two to three years and is responsible for much of the contact between the kibbutz and Zionist youth movements in South America, Europe, and the United States. One of the reasons for the success of Hatzerim, he believes, is the excellent mix of Israelis and immigrants from abroad, notably from South American countries.

Elad spends three days a week working for the CRB Foundation, which awards grants to Israeli educational projects. It is not connected to Hatzerim, and he works there as an outside employee. It was his experience working in the foundation that encouraged him to create something similar for his kibbutz, albeit on a smaller scale. He is also active at the kibbutz in a number of fields. One current project is a weekly Bible discussion group, which has recently worked its way through the Book of Genesis.

He is also trying, with some technical assistance, to enhance voting procedures in the community. Worried by the low attendance at the kibbutz general meetings, which take place every two weeks, some of the members looked into the idea of an elected council to replace or supplement the general meeting. The experience of other kibbutzim that had introduced councils was not reassuring. It was found that the same numbers—and the same people—turned up whether the meeting was termed a "kibbutz council" or a "general meeting." Furthermore, only a small minority turned up in each case. In Hatzerim, only about 40 members of 370 turn up for an average general meeting, but very often as many as 300 watch it over the internal video system. Elad is pressing for the introduction of two measures aimed at improving the situation: a special committee that will provide written background information to all members on every matter that is discussed, and electronic voting, which will enable members to vote from their homes. He also wants to introduce a system allowing members to ask any kibbutz office holder anything they wish to know about his or her job and be guaranteed a proper answer.

"Even in Hatzerim, where motivation is relatively high and members identify strongly with the kibbutz, there is a sense of 'them' and 'us,' " Elad notes. "We have to improve our participatory democracy."

Hatzerim has two secretaries, both in their forties: Dalit Afik and Avi Schweitzer. Dalit, a psychologist, was born on the kibbutz; Avi came in 1972 as part of a group of the scout movement. He is only part-time secretary, working the rest of the time as a production engineer in the factory. He is a fervent exponent of the principle of giving a shift a week on the production line.

"I would recommend it to any factory, not just a kibbutz enterprise," Avi says. "It gives everyone a far better understanding of the plant and how it works. In my opinion, it is worthwhile even from a strictly economic point of view. It gives the work organizer a headache, but that doesn't matter."

"I am afraid that Hatzerim is a very sexist society for all our ideals," says Dalit with an embarrassed laugh, disclosing that she has never worked on the Netafim production line. "It is the *male* members who put in a weekly production shift. There are about five girls working in the factory who have volunteered to give shifts, and they do so. The rest of us volunteer in the children's house, the clothing store, or the kitchen."

Amazingly, it is the first mention of this significant fact, yet consistent with Hatzerim's classical kibbutz character. From the time of Miriam Baratz and her struggle to work in the Degania cow shed, kibbutz egalitarianism has tended only to pay lip service to sexual equality.

In the early days of most kibbutzim, women members worked alongside their male fellows in the fields, but the period of liberation was always relatively short.

Although all the members insist that there *are* problems at Hatzerim, they rarely voice specific complaints. Pressed to come up with a criticism, Avi will say that he feels the kibbutz is too preoccupied with its own problems. He would like to see more outreach. What about the Project for Social Involvement? Yes, he concedes, that is a good idea, but it has only been revived recently after several years of inaction.

Apart from her criticism of the "sexism" of Hatzerim, Dalit notes that the discussions of the Team for Change did not only deal with the rationalization of members' allowances. There was also a proposal to discuss limiting future membership.

"It was not said out loud," she says, "but there was a definite implication that some members felt we should not share our wealth with newcomers. I am strongly against that sort of elitist approach. I still believe in the traditional kibbutz ideal that we should continuously expand, encouraging anyone who shares our beliefs to join."

Both secretaries are concerned at the low turnout for general meetings, and Dalit admits that she was a defaulter herself before becoming secretary. They are not sure how to deal with the problem. Voting from home is an idea, but then members who have not participated in discussions and who consequently do not know the issues may participate in key decisions.

Veteran Ruth Keren, the kibbutz archivist and one of the founders, hotly disputes the suggestion that Hatzerim is sexist. "Absolutely wrong," she insists. "I remember women secretaries and treasurers, women running the poultry branch, the orchards, the dairy. The women have always played their part in Hatzerim."

Today in her seventies, Ruth confesses to being a "defense counsel" for the kibbutz but also concedes that there have been failures. During the period of the mass immigration from the Middle Eastern countries in the 1950s, many groups came to Hatzerim, but few remained. The kibbutz did not succeed in absorbing them. On the other hand, many South American immigrants became members of Hatzerim and remain to this day. She is sorry that more of the kibbutz children did not remain and deeply regrets that farming and a link to the soil is not more a part of kibbutz life. She is not consoled by the fact that the Netafim factory is connected to agriculture. That is not the same.

A teacher at the kibbutz school—and its director for fifteen years—
Ruth is not sure how much kibbutz education has succeeded.

"We definitely did do well with the work ethic," she suggests. "Our
kids are good workers wherever they end up."

Today she would like to see more activities specifically for the older
members. Although some thirty residents are over the age of sixty-five,
and maybe as many as sixty are over fifty-five, no special activities are
organized for them. As a widow, Ruth feels the loneliness, despite living in such an intimate community. Her real disappointment, however,
is that the kibbutz has not managed to abolish hatred and jealousy.

"We wanted to create something better," she says. "I am still upset
when I hear that one member has not been on speaking terms with
another for ten years. That shouldn't happen on a kibbutz."

Among the Argentinian immigrants successfully absorbed into
Hatzerim is fifty-four-year-old Julio Kneidel, who arrived in 1967 as
part of a group of eighty members of the Habonim Youth Movement.
Most of them came between 1964 and 1967, and about sixty remained.
It is an unusually high proportion, but Julio emphasizes that their
absorption was not easy.

"I often tell the veterans, 'We remained in spite of you!' " he says.
"They wanted us very much in theory; but in practice they didn't make
enough allowances for the cultural differences." One is inevitably
reminded of the problems between the Eastern Europeans and the Germans at Givat Brenner. Julio notes that his group was infused with a very
strong socialist-Zionist ideology; but the reality of the small, poor, isolated kibbutz in the desert was traumatic. None of the children of the first
Argentinean immigrants speak Spanish, he notes, because they were
given the feeling they had to speak Hebrew to become real Israelis. The
children of the members who arrived later, though, including some
Brazilians, did speak Spanish and Portuguese to their children. By the
1970s, Hatzerim was a much more open and pluralistic society, he says,
partly because of the influence of his group.

At the same time, Julio holds the veterans in high regard. While his
own group gave valuable reinforcement to the kibbutz, it was the
founders who set the tone. Despite the social and cultural problems, both
groups were strong believers in the communal way of life, and that com-
monality caused them to make a supreme effort to get along. It took five
years before an Argentinean married a local, and Julio was one of the
first. Later groups intermarried freely, with kibbutz-born children and

with members of the youth movement and army groups spending time at the kibbutz.

Julio works in the planning department of Netafim. He was due to travel to Portugal the following week, meeting another member of the Netafim team who was coming over from Slovenia. Together they would spend an intensive week out in the fields with the Portuguese farmers, dealing with specific problems on the spot. He is always on the road. If he is not abroad, he is traveling in Israel, in the Jordan Valley or the Judaean hills, solving the problems of farmers there.

"I think our follow-up service is even more important than our product," Julio says. "You would be amazed at the relationships I have with some of our customers. It is almost like family."

Julio is a traditionalist when it comes to kibbutz life. He does not deny that technical adjustments should be made but is against anything that would detract from the essential values of equality and cooperation.

"Unlike lots of kibbutzniks, I do not have a love affair with capitalism," he says. "The secret of Hatzerim is the strength of togetherness, and I believe in it more every day!"

He understands the desire of members—particularly the youngsters—for freedom, agreeing that they must be allowed to work where they wish, but he does not favor absolving the community for responsibility for the members' livelihood. He gladly puts in his shift on the factory production line, managing seventy computerized machines that inject plastic. In other countries, he has seen the same machines manned by individual workers and admits that this approach might be cheaper. He is a strong believer in automation, though, particularly when it enables the kibbutz to function without outside workers.

Julio feels strongly that the kibbutzim have failed in that that they did not manage to pass on their ideals to the young. As a consequence, a whole generation of kibbutz children love their kibbutzim as places but have no understanding of their way of life. Their main concern seems to be that they do not want anyone to tell them where to travel or what to study.

"I understand the young people's demand for freedom," Julio repeats. "My quarrel is with their egotism. When I was their age, I wanted to change the world. I gave up my medical studies and became a farmer. I don't expect prizes for that, but I would like to see today's youngsters showing interest in society—not just in their own aspirations."

The veterans of Hatzerim were, by all accounts, an amazing group. Abie Ron has already been mentioned as one of the members who found the right formula for combining socialist idealism with financial prudence. Another was Zvi Keren, whose published memoir of the kibbutz supplied much of the background for this chapter. The best-known member, however, is Aharon Yadlin, still an active kibbutz movement leader at seventy-three.

The gray-haired, bespectacled Yadlin was a member of the Knesset, the Israeli parliament, for three decades. For two years he was the general secretary of the ruling Labor Party, and he served as minister of education for three years. In 1980, he resigned from parliament and returned to the kibbutz, but 1985 saw him back in public life as joint secretary of the United Kibbutz Movement, just before the financial collapse.

Like the other founders of Hatzerim, Yadlin was a member of the Israeli Scouts, who participated in the celebrated campaign in the fall of 1946 to establish eleven new kibbutzim in the Negev Desert, only Yadlin originally went to Beeri, another kibbutz some fifteen miles to the northwest of Hatzerim. In 1950, a year before the historic split in Kibbutz Hameuhad, he and some of his fellow members were already quarreling with their fellows about Marxism and socialist ideology. Realizing that a split was inevitable and that they would be in the minority at Beeri, they decided to join Hatzerim. Beeri is also an economically successful kibbutz, and Yadlin explains the secret of the success of both kibbutzim as resulting from financial caution. Other kibbutzim took loans in the 1970s and 1980s that they were later unable to pay back.

"We closed down unprofitable branches and checked everything a thousand times," he says. "We never took a loan that we couldn't repay, and when we borrowed money it was for productive projects."

The terms of the first recovery plan for the kibbutzim required Hatzerim, Beeri, and other financially responsible kibbutzim to help pay back part of the accumulated kibbutz debt. In a sense, they were penalized for their good behavior, and the payments stopped only after they had handed over millions of dollars.

Like many of his colleagues, Yadlin does not believe that Hatzerim can survive as a classical kibbutz in splendid isolation. Consequently, he is organizing an association of like-minded kibbutzim, including Hatzerim, Beeri, and others from all the movements, to preserve the values of cooperation and equality. He sees this as a bulwark, which will resist the momentum for change that he admits is sweeping the kibbutz movement and presents an alternative to the waverers.

Hatzerim is impressive. It has kept the faith and proved that the kibbutz system can work. After a visit to Hatzerim, one might conclude that the kibbutzim are, after all, in pretty good shape, but only half a dozen kibbutzim are as prosperous as Hatzerim, and about another forty are in a reasonably good financial situation. The remaining two hundred or so are struggling to pay their way.

Until the mid-1980s, the kibbutz movement was a powerful organization, with some 270 kibbutzim, most of them successful. It had ideological strength, political influence, and financial muscle. So why did the majority of the kibbutzim fail economically?

The next section of the book will endeavor to answer this question.

PART II

WHAT WENT WRONG?

6

מפולת

THE COLLAPSE OF 1985

When Aharon Yadlin, the former education minister, was released by Kibbutz Hatzerim in June 1985 to reenter public life as general secretary of the United Kibbutz Movement (UKM), his predecessors informed him that he was taking over the strongest enterprise in the State of Israel. The UKM was a union of Kibbutz Meuhad and the Ihud, which took place in 1980. With 167 settlements, it represented two-thirds of the country's kibbutzim. It was, they assured him, bigger, better, and more solid than any other business—even the banks.

Ten days later the movement's treasurers came to him in a panic, blurting out the fateful words "Balas cannot pay back our money."

They were referring to David Balas, an investment adviser, to whom the movement's "UKM Fund" had entrusted $100 million.

It was a time of soaring inflation, and those in charge of the finances of the UKM felt obliged to safeguard their funds against a loss in value, but they manifestly went too far. It is one thing to insure money against inflation. It is quite another to seek unrealistic profits on the fringes of legality in what was dubbed as the "gray market." It emerged that the investments had started on a small scale, but, when the welcome returns started coming in, the volume was increased.

His predecessor Eli Zamir of Maagan Michael (a kibbutz comparable to Hatzerim that we will visit in due course) remembers it differently.

"Maybe it was ten days before Aharon *knew* about Balas," he says. "It had been going on for six months, and we had already turned to the police. Anyway, we eventually got back over 80 percent of the money we invested through Balas."

It is legitimate to ask why the UKM was borrowing large sums of money in the first place. Zamir explains this issue in terms of the coming to power of the Likud right-wing government in 1977. This development was the culmination of a significant change in national values and priorities, he believes, although the kibbutz leaders did not realize it at the time. They thought that the Likud's election victory was a historical accident and that it would not last for long. Meanwhile, the kibbutzim had to go on growing and developing, and for that they needed money. The UKM Fund for the development of kibbutzim started borrowing on an unprecedented scale. Although the money was usually channeled at once to kibbutzim and kibbutz regional factories and corporations, there were sometimes interim periods when the loans had been secured, but the investments were not yet needed.

Zamir relates how the UKM simply did not know how to protect this money against inflation. None of the banks were helpful. Even Bank Hapoalim (the Workers' Bank, which at that time belonged to the Histadrut Labor Federation) only offered to guarantee the money against inflation—not against devaluation. The leaders of the UKM turned to Balas in desperation, hoping he would be their bulwark against both inflation and a possible devaluation.

Only two years earlier the kibbutz movement lost money through unwise and unethical speculation. Several kibbutzim and their financial institutions had incurred losses when the shares of Israel's major banks, which had been artificially manipulated, crashed. On that occasion, the government rescued them, as it saved thousands of individual Israeli citizens, by assuming ownership of the banks in question.

At the time it was not so much the failure of the investments that was condemned but the fact that kibbutzim were investing in the stock exchange at all. An additional cause for concern was that the kibbutz money managers had made the investments without proper authorization. Now, with the "Balas affair," it became clear that the financial officers had not even learned their lesson but had carried on with their questionable practices.

Nevertheless, although many kibbutz members were shocked when they learned what had happened, the Balas affair and the bank share losses were only the tip of the iceberg. If the money lost in these speculations had been the problem, it could have been solved relatively easily. The ventures were, however, symptomatic of something much more serious: the kibbutz movements—Kibbutz Artzi as well as the UKM, and many individual kibbutzim—had been borrowing money on a huge scale, without any guarantee that they could pay it back.

Initially, the loans taken by the kibbutzim and their corporations such as the UKM Fund were unlinked, and, as the rate of inflation increased, it was easy to repay them. However, the habit became addictive, and, even when the loans were linked to the cost-of-living index, the kibbutzim, their funds, regional factories, and corporations went on borrowing. Nothing was intrinsically wrong in this. If they had invested in new farming branches, factories, and businesses that earned money and enabled them to pay back what they had borrowed, it would have been perfectly acceptable behavior. Unfortunately, most of the money was invested in measures to improve the living standards of the kibbutz members. In the 1970s, many kibbutzim were bringing their children to sleep at home, and a large proportion of the borrowed money was spent on enlarging the individual apartments of the members to facilitate this move. Other expenditures were on dining halls, swimming pools, gymnasia, theaters, ball fields, and libraries.

In the early 1980s, inflation in Israel passed 400 percent and threatened to escalate even higher. In 1985, the government resolved on drastic action to bring it under control. This it achieved by implementing a one-time 15 percent devaluation of the Israeli currency and introducing a freeze on wages and prices, while leaving interest rates excessively high. Although the tactic worked and the inflation rate plummeted, hundreds of businesses went bankrupt.

The first reaction of the kibbutz movements compounded their basic mistakes: they asked the banks to reschedule the loans. This request would have made sense if they possessed the means to pay them back over the longer period, but for the most part, these means did not exist. Furthermore, as interest rates were sky-high, the collective kibbutz debt quickly escalated to between $5 and $6 billion. There was no way it could ever be paid back.

The kibbutzim were not alone in this situation. The cooperative *moshav* villages and the private farmers were facing similar problems, along with hundreds of small businesses around the country, but the kibbutzim were particularly vulnerable, as they were capital-intensive and had no equity. The entire kibbutz enterprise was based on credit. Many private concerns were able to survive the crisis because the wage freeze meant an effective cut of their payrolls, but kibbutzim do not have payrolls in the normal sense of the word. Devaluation sharply increased

Figure 6.1.   Uncompleted dining hall at a kibbutz in the center of the country.

Source: (Daniel Gavron)

their members' living expenses, which meant that the standard of living of many kibbutzim had to be sharply reduced.

The kibbutz movements did have two things going for them: the government did not want a mass collapse of the kibbutzim (or of the *moshavim* and private farmers, for that matter), and the banks had nothing to gain by seizing unprofitable assets. What would a bank do with a dairy that operated at a loss, a partly built dining hall, or a factory in the red? Furthermore, the banks shared responsibility for what happened. If the kibbutzim had behaved with incredible stupidity, their obtuseness was more than matched by that of the banks. The kibbutzim had gone on taking the loans; the banks had continued extending them. Consequently, it became clear that the only way out of the mess had to be a three-way deal, involving the government, the banks, and the kibbutzim.

Dr. Shimon Ravid, today a joint managing director of Bank Hapoalim, Israel's largest bank, was chief financial officer of the Jewish Agency, responsible for farming settlement in Israel, when the scale of the crisis of the kibbutzim (and the other settlements) became evident. Shimon

Peres was prime minister of Israel at the head of the National Unity Government, which had forced through the economic package that broke the inflation, and he appointed Ravid as his special adviser for an agricultural-sector recovery program.

In 1986, the crisis was still in its infancy, and only the *moshav* cooperatives and thirty-six kibbutzim were faced with impossible debts. Ravid worked out a package that combined a considerable debt write-off and a rescheduling of the balance. Under the terms of the "Ravid Plan," the government would supply the banks with the necessary credit but would not assume a direct financial obligation. By the time Ravid presented his proposals, an election had been held naming Yizhak Shamir of the right-wing Likud Party as prime minister, but he and his finance minister went along with the scheme. Unfortunately for the kibbutzim, a number of his party colleagues did not.

Although the government, the banks, the kibbutzim, and the *moshavim* agreed to the package, a group of Likud members of the Knesset, Israel's parliament, torpedoed the Ravid Plan in the Knesset Finance Committee. Despite the government's approval, several committee members made it plain to Ravid that they had no interest in bailing out the settlements, which they regarded as part of the Labor Party establishment.

As a result, the Ravid Plan became history, necessitating a far more ambitious rescue plan three years later. Ravid remains convinced that his plan would have worked and that the cost at that time would have been relatively modest. It was sabotaged, he maintains, for petty political reasons. When a rescue plan was finally implemented, it cost the nation far more.

Dr. Ariel Halperin, the man currently in charge of implementing the later recovery plan, the 1989 Kibbutz Arrangement, takes a more philosophical view. Noting that the arrangement has had to be amended twice—in 1996 and 1999—he suggests that the crisis was so large and so complex that it took time for the government, the banks, and the kibbutzim themselves to understand its dimensions. It was, in his opinion, a problem that had to be solved in stages.

The *moshav* debt problem had meanwhile been resolved by parliamentary legislation, but the kibbutz debt was both larger and more complicated. It was agreed (as Ravid had earlier suggested) to solve the problem by means of a voluntary agreement among the government, the banks, and the kibbutzim. By then, however, the problem was far more difficult to solve. The collective debt had escalated, and many more kibbutzim were affected.

An independent Kibbutz Arrangement Board was established by the government, the banks, and the kibbutzim to act as the trustee of the agreements, supported by a nonrofit company, with a team of economists, accountants, and lawyers. It was this team that worked out the Kibbutz Arrangement of 1989, which by now involved all the country's kibbutzim—not just thirty-six of them. The Kibbutz Arrangement was a framework within which hundreds of other agreements were worked out. The board was responsible for the economic parameters, the various financial transactions, and the individual recovery programs of the different kibbutzim. It also served as the arbiter when differences arose between the three parties.

Both Ravid and Halperin emphasize that the complexity of the problem was a result of the unprecedented system of mutual guarantees that governed the economic activities of the kibbutzim. The system goes back to the 1920s and 1930s, when the Jewish economy was largely built up by the labor movement in Palestine.

In 1920, the Histadrut Federation of Jewish Labor was formed by all the labor parties and groups existing at that time, including representatives of the kibbutzim, to establish a "Jewish Workers' Community" in Palestine. Initially a coordinating body of workers' councils and labor unions, it soon branched out with its own youth movement, sports clubs, immigrant absorption branch, and labor exchanges. Before long the Histadrut was dealing with social security, taking under its wing the Kupat Holim sick fund, originally founded by the agricultural workers, as well as setting up funds for pensions, the unemployed, invalids, widows, and orphans.

At its second convention in 1923, the Histadrut established Hevrat Ovdim (the Workers' Company) to organize the economic activity of the workers' community on the basis of mutual aid and responsibility. Every member of the Histadrut was also a member of Hevrat Ovdim, which owned all the financial and cooperative institutions of the Histadrut.

Among its enterprises were Bank Hapoalim (the Workers' Bank); the Solely Boneh construction company, which set up Koor Industries for its factories; the Shikun Ovdim housing company; the Sneh insurance company; the Tnuva marketing association; and the Hamashbir purchasing cooperative. Public transportation was run by the Dan, Egged, and Mekasher bus cooperatives.

All the unionized agricultural workers, including the kibbutz members, were members of the Hevrat Ovdim subsidiary, Nir Shitufi, which aimed to foster cooperative farming, modernize agriculture, train new workers, and extend financial aid to farmers. In due course, Nir Shitufi became a holding company, representing the kibbutzim and *moshavim* in land leases and loans, obviating the need for individual agreements. Over the years, the Histadrut and its enterprises became the dominant economic power in the emerging Jewish state.

Although the financial arms of the Zionist movement—the Jewish Agency for Palestine, the Jewish National Fund, and the Foundation Fund—were not part of the Histadrut, they worked in cooperation with it and increasingly came to be staffed by the same personnel. The Histadrut general secretary, David Ben-Gurion, was in due course elected chairman of the Jewish Agency and became the first prime minister of Israel. Thus, the Jewish Agency and the Histadrut were the entwined embryos from which the state emerged, although they continued to exist after it was established. As a result, Israel was ruled for its first three decades by coalitions led by Ben-Gurion's Mapai Labor Party.

The State of Israel was dominated by a labor economy, with a strong cooperative bent. Although the kibbutzim were always a small minority of the society, most of the time about 3 percent of the population as a whole, they operated in an exceptionally favorable environment. For this reason they flourished; for this reason they were assisted whenever problems did emerge; for this reason the election of 1977 was a shock to the kibbutz movement.

In all fairness, it must be stressed that 1977 turned out to be the culmination of a process in Israeli society, which confirmed the change in its social and economic norms and values. The process was started by the Labor Party itself in the 1960s, when it fostered industrialization and encouraged private investment. When that party subsequently returned to power, whether as part of a national unity coalition or on its own, it was as a party dedicated to the "free market" and only marginally more inclined to help the kibbutzim than the Likud. It was no longer an axiom that cooperation was a good thing. The kibbutzim couldn't appeal to ideological sentiments, and the Kibbutz Arrangement Board dealt with the crisis on strictly business terms.

The board's first priority was to confront the system of mutual guarantees, which was inappropriate to the 1980s and in many ways harked back to the 1930s. All the United Kibbutz Movement kibbutzim were members of the UKM Fund. The Kibbutz Artzi movement had its own fund. In addition, there were regional kibbutz corporations, including factories, slaughter houses, freezing plants, food-processing enterprises, and warehouses. The national and regional corporations were connected to each other and to each individual kibbutz by an interlocking system of guarantees, meaning that, in addition to its own debts, every kibbutz was liable for the huge collective debt.

The board went to work to disentangle this "octopus," enabling each kibbutz to deal with its own economic problems. By the time this was achieved, it was clear that the 1989 arrangement could not be implemented. One hundred thirty kibbutzim—almost half—were simply incapable of paying pack the rescheduled debts. In 1996, a Supplementary Kibbutz Arrangement was negotiated, and in 1999 an amendment to it was formulated.

The later agreements factor the land question into the arrangement, taking advantage of the fact that fifty-five kibbutzim are sitting on valuable land in the center of the country. It enables further write-offs for the outlying kibbutzim, balanced by requiring those in the central area to "sell back" part of their land to the government, which in turn will compensate the banks.

The land arrangement has caused considerable controversy in Israel, because the kibbutzim are for the most part lessees of national land, and their rental agreement stipulates that if they do not need the land for farming or industry, they are supposed to return it to the nation. There have been numerous media features about the "plunder of national land." The board, however, denies that its proposals are too favorable to the kibbutzim. It has merely decided to recognize the rights of the kibbutzim, which have been occupying the land for periods of between forty and sixty years, and worked out a compromise. It might be interesting if the matter were brought to court to see whether the occupancy of the kibbutzim would not be recognized as giving them rights, but so far none of the accusers has decided to test the matter.

It should also be pointed out that several kibbutzim and *moshavim*—including Givat Brenner in our sample—purchased land with their own money before the State of Israel was established and subsequently donated the land to the Jewish National Fund. This land later became the national land of the state. In the case of Givat Brenner, certainly, the word *plunder* appears grotesque.

Although it would be exaggerating to describe the kibbutz debt crisis as over, we can say that, following the agreements of 1989, 1996, and 1999, it has been brought under control. Some kibbutzim still have serious financial problems, but it is clear that they will be solved in the course of time. Nevertheless, the trauma of the past fifteen years has shattered the kibbutz way of life, possibly beyond repair. In many kibbutzim, the trust between the kibbutz and the individual member has almost totally broken down. Even without the crisis, the kibbutzim would almost certainly by now be in a process of change, but the crisis attached a supercharger to the process, accelerating it almost out of control and causing grave doubts about the survival of the kibbutz as an institution.

In the kibbutzim and in the nation at large, a fierce debate has raged. There are those who are convinced that the kibbutzim have been the victims of Israel's economic problems. They argue that it was the extremely harsh policy implemented to put the brakes on the runaway inflation of 1985 that broke the kibbutzim. There are even those who describe at least part of the kibbutz debt crisis as a "fiction," resulting from banking irregularities involving illegally high interest rates. This point has certainly not been proved, and even if there is any truth in the allegations, the kibbutzim must take responsibility for failing to notice such occurrences at the time. At the very least they are guilty of sloppy accounting.

For Aharon Yadlin, the former cabinet minister and member of a flourishing kibbutz, the answer is simple: the kibbutz money men are to blame for bringing a majority of kibbutzim to the verge of collapse. Although Yadlin has no pretensions to being an economic expert, he cites the example of his own kibbutz, Hatzerim, which remained faithful to its egalitarian principles, never took loans, never hired outside labor, and expected its members to work hard. Hatzerim, he maintains, is proof positive that the kibbutz system works.

At the other extreme is Israel Oz, a senior official of the finance ministry during the relevant period who dealt with the Kibbutz Arrangement on behalf of the government. Oz describes the kibbutz as "an economic fantasy" that could only survive as long as it was supported. As soon as the kibbutzim had to exist in the real world, he maintains, 80 to 90 percent of them could not pay their way. He is full of scorn for those who believe, like Yadlin, that the traditional kibbutz can survive and flourish.

"How many Hatzerims are there?" he demands. "Not even a dozen!"

The system was based on dependence, Oz declares. The kibbutz members were totally dependent on their kibbutz. They did not even look after their own children. They did not take responsibility for their daily life and make their own decisions like everyone else. Everything was done for them by the kibbutz institutions. Although Oz concedes that every society must subsidize its agriculture, he distinguishes between supporting an individual farmer and "paying for a children's house and a communal dining hall, which costs 'mythical sums' just to heat in winter or air-condition in summer."

The kibbutz was a useful instrument for pioneering, settling the borders, and building up a new nation, Oz says, but it was never a viable way of life in normal conditions. He is currently a consultant, advising kibbutzim on radical changes in their economic structure, involving allocation of assets to the members and a wage structure that will recognize the principle of "reward for effort."

The facts indicate that both Yadlin and Oz are exaggerating. While very few kibbutzim are as wealthy as Hatzerim, some fifty relatively successful kibbutzim prove that the system *can* work. At the same time, more than two hundred kibbutzim in varying degrees of crisis prove that something *is* seriously wrong. Most thoughtful kibbutzniks acknowledge that the kibbutz, which came into existence in another era, has to change considerably if it is to survive in the modern world.

Banker Shimon Ravid is not prepared to write off the kibbutz as a system of economic organization. He agrees that the original idea of Kibbutz Hameuhad in the 1920s to create the new Jewish nation as one large kibbutz was unrealistic, because the kibbutz way of life is not suitable for the majority. This does not mean, he says, that minority units based on the communal principle cannot survive. The kibbutz worked very well for more than half a century. It was the most efficient farming sector in Israel and operated above average in industry, too.

In Ravid's view, the kibbutz structure is ideally suited to high technology, but the movement had the bad luck to reach its peak in the "era of plastic" in the 1960s. By the time the high-tech period came along in the 1980s, most kibbutzim no longer had the energy and resources to take advantage of it. The crisis of the 1980s caused a lack of confidence among kibbutz members and damaged what had hitherto been a notable talent for adaptation. Ravid agrees that serious changes in the system would have been necessary anyway, but without the economic crisis, they could have been implemented in a much more orderly manner.

Answering charges that the kibbutzim had always been propped up by the settlement organizations and the government, Ravid notes that every nation has to subsidize the countryside: The United States grants millions of dollars in farm subsidies; the Norwegian government pumps money into its northern regions; the Germans support the vineyards along the Rhine, even though they will never be competitive.

"The basic question," says Ravid, "is, do you want to have only towns with an abandoned periphery, or do you want to maintain a healthy countryside that gives all of us a better quality of life?" If the kibbutzim do not survive in some form, he says, it will cost the national exchequer more in the long run, and Israeli society as a whole will suffer.

Ariel Halperin has been deeply immersed in the problem since he became chairman of the Kibbutz Arrangement Board in 1992. Initially, Halperin, who was himself born and brought up in a kibbutz, was convinced that, with relatively minor adjustments and sensible economic recovery plans, the kibbutz way of life could survive more or less intact. He has since come to the conclusion that the problem is far deeper and that fundamental changes are needed.

Halperin points out several ways in which most kibbutzim are failing, even if their debt problem is solved. Taken as a whole, the kibbutz economy has been stagnating, and this was so even during periods when the Israeli economy grew quite fast. Production per individual kibbutz member is lower than average, resulting in lower living standards. The kibbutz population has been declining in absolute terms since the late 1980s. Above all, the work system has broken down.

As we have seen, the kibbutzim have been using outside workers for many years, but, until comparatively recently, this practice was mainly confined to the factories. The principle of self-labor was largely preserved in the services and many of the agricultural branches. Today, however, hired workers can be found in every branch of the kibbutz, where they have replaced the members who prefer to work in outside jobs. Outsiders work in the children's houses, the kindergartens and schools, the kitchens, the cow sheds, chicken houses, orchards, and fields. Most significantly, they often serve as senior managers in the kibbutz factories, sometimes earning very large salaries. We have seen an example of this in Givat Brenner, with its paid general manager.

Although these developments may have caused the kibbutz founders to spin in their graves, they are not necessarily harmful. Indeed, one of the ideas of the New Kibbutz put forward by Yehuda Harel was to make the kibbutz more attractive by giving members the freedom to choose their own work. Making members responsible for earning their own living can increase productivity, as we have seen in the case of Hasolelim. But Halperin has found that, at the present time, the overall picture is that the members working outside earn less than it costs the kibbutz to replace them. The balance is negative. There are senior managers earning around $100,000 annually from the kibbutzim where they work; few kibbutzniks bring in that sort of money.

Halperin believes that the most important task facing the kibbutzim is to find a mechanism for restoring the trust between the kibbutz members and their kibbutz. This shift necessitates a fundamental structural change, because in the classical kibbutz, members had nothing except the promise that the kibbutz would always look after them and their families. On the other hand, although members were supposed to work where the community decided they should work, there was no way of compelling them to do so. The commune had no actual power over members or legal claims on them.

The entire system was based on trust, and it worked because both sides kept their promises. With very few exceptions, members performed whatever task the kibbutz assigned to them; the kibbutz looked after every facet of members' lives from cradle to grave. The kibbutz in turn was supported by the kibbutz movements, which was supported by the Jewish Agency Settlement Department, which was supported by the Israeli government, in a generally favorable social atmosphere.

For this reason, in previous economic crises somebody was always available to pick up the tab. The first crisis was as early as the 1920s. Others followed in the 1930s, 1950s, and 1960s, but the movement was always bailed out by "the system," because the settlements—both kibbutzim and *moshavim*—were regarded as vital to the success of the Zionist enterprise.

Why was the agricultural sector in the prestate Jewish community in Palestine and later in the State of Israel in need of constant bailouts? Part of the answer, as Ravid points out, is that the countryside in all modern nations has to be subsidized, but others have noted serious flaws in the economic performance of the kibbutzim. Strangely, as noted by Dr. Amir Helman, these were the opposite of those expected by the professional economists.

Helman was born at Kibbutz Afikim in the Jordan Valley. He has taught economics and management—including "alternative economics"—at the Ruppin College for the past twenty-one years. He also lectures at several universities, sits on a number of boards, and conducts research in Israel and abroad. He notes that in the 1920s, the professional economists were sure that without the usual material incentives, kibbutz members would produce less and consume more than those in private concerns. They were wrong: the kibbutz members were diligent, and they volunteered for—and even competed for—the most difficult jobs, without material rewards. This was true, as we have seen, in the early idealistic days of Degania, for example, when the pioneers found satisfaction in creating something new and in serving their fellow members, without the need for personal rewards.

Another interesting development, diametrically opposed to the forecasts of the economic experts, concerned overinvestment, which, as we have seen in the case of Givat Brenner, was a problem as early as the 1930s. The economists said that the collective structure would lead to an avoidance of effort and a lack of initiative. In fact, the opposite was the case: the kibbutz was a productive society, in which investments were high. The kibbutz managers were on the whole too enterprising, both because the overall aim of Zionism was expansion and growth and because the system of mutual guarantees removed any real risk. Another problem was the democratic kibbutz system of rotating managers, which meant that, like politicians or any elected officers, they wanted to prove themselves as quickly as possible. At the same time, the structure of the kibbutz meant that the manager was not answerable to a board of directors. He was, it is true, responsible to the general meeting of the kibbutz, but this was a nonexpert body, and the manager was not *personally* liable to dismissal if he failed. His position as a member of the kibbutz was guaranteed, even if his stewardship of a kibbutz venture ended in a fiasco. If we add to this the fact that every kibbutz was supported by the kibbutz movement, the Jewish Agency, and the government, it is clear that the system encouraged enterprise to the point of irresponsibility.

The kibbutz structure has other built-in weaknesses, which can be summed up in one word: duplication. There is more than a grain of truth in the charge of Israel Oz that communal dining halls, children's houses, laundries, and clothing stores—not to mention swimming pools, theaters, and gymnasia—are extravagances. Although the communal dining hall personifies kibbutz life, it makes less sense when every home has a kitchenette and dining corner, and the members eat many of their meals at home. The children's houses are unnecessarily large now that the kibbutz children sleep at home. Likewise, the communal laundry (unless it becomes a commercial business) is a luxury when every house has a washing machine.

In addition, many of the kibbutz members continued to enjoy a middle-class standard of living while engaging in working-class occupations. Ideologically correct, this did not always make economic sense. Very often the kibbutznik lived at the level of the top deciles of Israeli society, while earning the wages of the lower deciles. Furthermore, Helman pointed out, the standard of living on all the kibbutzim in Israel was very similar, regardless of the actual economic health of the kibbutz. Thus, whereas the rich kibbutzim were able to save and invest, the poor kibbutzim were moving deeper and deeper into debt. The kibbutz system was working for some but not for others.

This almost surrealistic situation prevailed until the 1980s because, as we have seen, the government, Jewish Agency, and kibbutz movements saw the kibbutzim as vitally important and provided support when necessary. However, when the crisis of 1985 hit, the system collapsed. The protective circles of the government, the Jewish Agency, the kibbutz movements, and the individual kibbutz imploded on the hapless kibbutznik. This time the government was not prepared to guarantee the settlements; the Jewish Agency was unwilling to support them; the kibbutz movements no longer had the resources; the individual kibbutz in many cases could not fulfill its promises.

Suddenly kibbutz members, who had regarded themselves as partners in a more or less flourishing enterprise, discovered that in reality they had nothing. They had no old age pension, no social security, no house, no property of any kind, no rights of bequest—and in most cases not very much to bequeath. Kibbutzniks, who had felt themselves to be the most secure individuals on the planet, instead found themselves abandoned, naked, and buffeted by a savage storm. The trauma was extreme; the loss of confidence, crippling.

Halperin is confident that, with the right methods, the situation can be retrieved. He favors a basic change in the system to replace the trust of individual members in their kibbutz. The kibbutz must legally acknowledge members' rights to its resources. The kibbutz factories and farming branches must finance members' health care, pension, and social welfare. They must pay for the education of their children. The members must own their houses and be entitled to bequeath their share of the kibbutz property to their descendants.

Each kibbutz will adopt its own model, suggests Halperin, but an allocation of assets to the members, guaranteed by law, is the bottom line of any reorganization plan. The question of differential payments, reward for effort, overtime pay, and privatization of budgets are all supplementary. Once basic trust is restored and members recover their sense of security, the rest will follow.

Whether Halperin is right or not, only time will tell. We have seen in the previous chapter how five kibbutzim are endeavoring to cope with the new situation. Later we will visit another group of settlements that indicate alternative options for the future, including solutions along the lines advocated by Halperin.

However, before we look ahead, it will be instructive to take one more glance backward to examine more fully the educational system of the kibbutz. We have seen that both external and internal reasons accounted for the economic collapse of 1985. It may be unfair to pass an entirely negative verdict on the kibbutz money managers, as many businesses have failed, particularly in times of general economic crisis. But the kibbutz treasurers and accountants did not only act imprudently from a business point of view; they also behaved in a manner inconsistent with kibbutz values.

Why did kibbutz education fail to pass on these values?

The collective sense of responsibility, so strong in the founding generation of the kibbutzim, transmitted itself to the second generation, but by the third and fourth generations on the kibbutz, the original thesis of the economists was coming true. Many of the members were not always contributing to the best of their ability; increasingly, the kibbutz found itself unable to satisfy its members' needs.

It is perfectly true that the kibbutz survived for seven decades, but it was in some ways an optical illusion. On the material level, the system was not always working, although the economic failure of many kibbutzim was hidden from view. Ideologically, too, all was not as it seemed: although the third and fourth generations seemed to go along with the doctrine, their belief in it was limited, and they became increasingly skeptical. When the system faced its first real crisis, an economic meltdown that left it on its own to face the world, it almost collapsed, and its survival is still uncertain.

In the early days of Degania, Yosef Bussel wrote, in a passage already quoted in this book:

> For people to think and feel as they should in a life of complete equality and complete partnership, they have to be born into it, and for that to happen generations will have to pass. Many things that we cannot achieve today will be achieved by comrades who have grown up in the new environment of the *kvutza*.

Subsequent to Bussel, kibbutz ideologues and educators openly proclaimed their intention of creating a "new human being," a person liberated from the bourgeois values of personal ambition and materialism. For seventy years, the kibbutz as an institution exerted unprecedented influence over its members. No totalitarian regime ever exercised such absolute control over its citizens as the free, voluntary, democratic kibbutz exercised over its members. Israel Oz was right in pointing out that it organized every facet of their lives: their accommodations, their work, their health, their leisure, their culture, their food, their clothing, their vacations, their hobbies, and—above all—the education and upbringing of their children.

Despite these optimal conditions, Bussel's prediction was wrong. The "comrades who grew up in the new environment of the *kvutza*" were not imbued with communal and egalitarian values. In the next chapter we will try to discover why.

7

חינוך

THE LIMITS OF EDUCATION

The fact that the kibbutz money managers were speculating on the Tel Aviv Stock Exchange is in itself a sign of a flaw in the kibbutz educational system. The founders would never have dreamed of such behavior. Even the most pragmatic among them could not have imagined making money without earning it. Even the most ruthless would not have made a decision about investing the resources of the community without bringing it to the kibbutz general meeting.

Although some kibbutz members of the third and fourth generations remain committed to the ethical imperatives of communal life, large numbers, particularly at the managerial level, confine their loyalty to their own kibbutzim. Their aim is to develop and improve their kibbutz, without too much regard for kibbutz principles. Many of them studied economics and business management at universities in Israel and abroad and were far more impressed by the ideas of competition and efficient administration than they were by the ideals of equality and mutual help. Even the Ruppin College of the kibbutz movement, where many promising managers were sent by their kibbutzim, taught modern business methods, with only an optional course in cooperative economics. These managers returned home to run a farming branch, or a factory, or maybe the entire kibbutz, strongly influenced by the concepts of profits, efficiency, balance sheets, cost accounting, and marketing strategy.

There are those who dispute this thesis, arguing that the kibbutzim were not sufficiently influenced by these ideas and continued running themselves in outdated, old-fashioned, communal, and egalitarian ways.

The bank shares and Balas crises, however, are proof that a significant proportion of the economic leadership of the kibbutz movements has abandoned traditional ideals and principles. While the kibbutzim in an increasingly capitalist environment must obviously work with banks and other capitalist institutions, that is a long way from investing borrowed money in unauthorized speculation of a questionable nature.

In a general way, kibbutz education can be regarded as a qualified success story, with only minor shortcomings. Although juvenile delinquency has existed in kibbutzim for many years, and a drug problem among kibbutz teenagers goes back more than three decades, kibbutz children are not on the whole problem youth. There have been murders of kibbutz members by their fellows and cases of child abuse, including sexual abuse of daughters by fathers, and even one case of gang rape, but the kibbutz crime rate is well below the national average. From the outset, the kibbutzim have conducted their affairs almost without the need for police intervention. Although in recent years more cases of the police being called have occurred, the kibbutzim are still remarkably harmonious and law-abiding.

Nor is the record praiseworthy only for the absence of negative behavior. Kibbutz children are for the most part friendly, helpful, constructive, hardworking, patriotic, and to a certain extent idealistic. Many of them spend an extra year prior to their army service as youth leaders in small towns and poor neighborhoods up and down the country. They can often be found at demonstrations in favor of peace with Israel's neighbors, campaigning for civil rights or lobbying for environmental causes. They still volunteer to be army officers and air force pilots and to serve in the elite combat units of the Israel Defense Forces in numbers out of all proportion to their relative strength in society. On a general scale, kibbutz education must surely rate at least a B-plus.

Nevertheless, despite decades of this education—some would say indoctrination—few kibbutz-raised children today really believe in kibbutz principles. Measured against the declared aim of creating a new type of human being through education to communal values, kibbutz education does not even rate a passing grade.

Until now the left-wing Kibbutz Artzi movement has been neglected in this account. Its origins were outlined in the chapter about Givat Brenner, but the five kibbutzim visited so far are all members of the United Kibbutz Movement (UKM). There is a reason for this: although the process of change sweeping through the kibbutz movement is also

Figure 7.1.   Kibbutz children celebrating the Shavuot harvest festival at Ein Dor in the 1960s.

Source: (Yehoshua Zamir)

affecting Kibbutz Artzi, that movement's kibbutzim are, for the most part, half a step behind the UKM, which means that their kibbutzim are less illustrative of the current transformation. However, now that we come to consider kibbutz education, Kibbutz Artzi moves to center stage, for it was this movement above all others that carried out education toward the values of equality and cooperation. It is therefore interesting to see how even Kibbutz Artzi failed to instill communal and egalitarian values in its children.

The origins of Kibbutz Artzi are to be found in "Our Community," that "monastic order without God" founded by members of the Hashomer Hatzair youth movement. At the end of 1922, those members of Our Community who remained with the group moved from their hilltop over Lake Kinneret to their permanent settlement of Beit Alpha in the Jezreel plain.

The members of Degania, as we have seen, saw the *kvutza* as a way of life that was not suitable for everybody, or even for a majority. Kibbutz Meuhad, of which Givat Brenner was originally a part, saw itself as the nucleus of one huge kibbutz that would eventually absorb the

entire Jewish community in Palestine. Kibbutz Artzi regarded its kibbutzim as revolutionary cells. These cells would at first cooperate with
other Zionist elements (including "bourgeois" groups) to create a Jewish nation, but, at the appropriate time, they were to be the spearhead of
a revolution that would establish a classless society in Palestine. As
such, they saw themselves as prototypes of the society-on-the-way and
strove to create new patterns of life, including new-style relations
between men and women and new concepts of family.

There are conflicting reports about the personal relations between
the members of the early kibbutzim. Some accounts describe a repressed
and puritanical atmosphere; others mention a period of "free love." On
the evidence of contemporary accounts, it seems that the members of the
first kibbutzim were not too promiscuous. At Beit Alpha, for example,
there was a brief period when the partitions in the living huts were taken
down, so that couples and single members slept in one common room,
but the partitions were restored after a few months.

In the kibbutzim of all the movements, the institution of the
"primus" is well documented. During the period when the members
slept in tents, it was common to have a couple together in the tent with
a third comrade (called the primus), but this was purely functional, a
result of shortage of accommodation. There is not the slightest hint of
group sex. Possibly, despite their revolt against the world of their parents, the pioneers were still influenced in their personal lives by the
traditions of the Jewish communities of Eastern Europe, where they
grew up.

As in all kibbutzim, the arrival of the first children in Beit Alpha
confirmed the existence of the nuclear family. The members of Degania
accepted the family unit as natural, although they also saw the *kvutza* as
an enlarged family. In Givat Brenner, Enzo Sereni stated clearly that the
large kibbutz should be "a community of families." In Kibbutz Artzi the
acceptance of the nuclear family unit was somewhat reluctant. The
"bourgeois family" was reviled, and attempts were made to weaken its
importance. For example, in most kibbutzim during the early years, it
was considered bad taste for husbands and wives to sit together in the
communal dining hall, and meeting a group of children, a parent would
make a point of greeting his or her own child last.

The more revolutionary approach of Kibbutz Artzi was a result of
its link with its Hashomer Hatzair youth movement. The Zionist youth
movements, which emerged in Europe in the 1920s, were in the tradition of the German youth movements, while at the same time directing

their gaze toward the early kibbutzim in Palestine. The young members camped out under the stars, hiked in the hills and forests, engaged in night-long discussions, sang folk songs, and danced folk dances. They believed in simplicity, equality, and comradeship and sought to build a better world, if necessary on the ashes of the old one.

Kibbutz Artzi and Hashomer Hatzair represented the kibbutz idea carried to the extreme. The kibbutz and the youth movement were entwined and symbiotic, so that when children were born in the kibbutzim, the educational system was greatly influenced by the youth movement. As more settlements of Kibbutz Artzi were founded and the movement grew, the influence tended to go in the other direction, with the kibbutz setting the tone, but the kibbutzim never forgot that they were the embodiment of the youth movement and its values.

Kibbutz members, and in particular Kibbutz Artzi, aimed to liberate the woman from what they called her "biological tragedy," the obligation of the woman to bear and raise the children, which gave her little time for anything else. Although the kibbutz could not liberate the woman from bearing children, it did endeavor to free her from the chores of raising them. The collective was responsible for this. It also absolved the woman from economic dependence on her husband. She was an equal member of the kibbutz, no different from her husband in her economic status. To this day, a Kibbutz Artzi veteran will refer to her husband as *ishi* (my man) instead of *ba'ali* (my husband, which also means my master in Hebrew).

From birth, the children were brought up in separate houses and cared for by trained child care workers. Their mothers would visit them to suckle them at regular intervals. After being weaned, the children would visit with their parents for two hours in the afternoons. In the evenings, the children were returned to their children's houses and put to bed by the child care workers. The child-parent link was deliberately downgraded. The children were not regarded as the exclusive property of their biological parents; they belonged to the whole community. Almost contradicting this thesis was the idea that parents and children could enjoy a better relationship within the communal framework. Parents could give their children love, uninhibited by the need to enforce discipline, which was the task of the child care workers and nurses and later also of the teachers.

In the Kibbutz Artzi movement, the idea evolved of creating a separate "Society of Children," in the form of a boarding school called a Mossad Hinuchi, for children from the age of twelve. The first Mossad was founded at Mishmar Haemek in the Jezreel plain, and others followed. The Mossad always served several kibbutzim, which meant that the older children lived some distance away from their parents.

The Mossad's educational program endeavored to integrate the ideas of John Dewey, Karl Marx, and Sigmund Freud, together with those of A. D. Gordon, the "prophet of labor" from Degania, and Ber Borochov, a Russian socialist-Zionist thinker. The professed aim of the Society of Children was to eliminate the "harmful influence" of the older generation and in particular to abolish "the authoritarian role of the father."

One of the early educators of Kibbutz Artzi, Shmuel Gollan, listed the characteristics of the new "kibbutz man." He had to be a hard worker, educated, sensitive, ethical, active, and loyal to the collective. The peer group, rather than the "biological family," was the center of the child's life; the collective was more important than the individual. Intellectual achievement was downgraded; ideological, social, ethical, and aesthetic values were thought to be more important than "technical proficiency." Group achievement was preferred to individual attainment; cooperation was valued above competition. Written projects were favored over examinations. Helping the weaker members of the group was more important than fostering excellence.

In place of the "authoritarian" teacher imparting knowledge, the kibbutz sought to create an environment in which the educator was a two-way channel between the child and the community. The Society of Children was ostensibly autonomous and gave the children freedom and responsibility; in reality, the (hidden) adult influence was directed toward teaching the future kibbutz members how to run their kibbutz.

In his contribution to the book *Education in the Changing Kibbutz* (which he also edited), Yeheskel Dar points out that reproduction and creation are contradictory aims in education. The transmission of a cultural and social direction from the older generation to the younger contradicts the desire to develop creative thinking and values. There was also a contradiction between the collective aspiration and the strong humanist message, which espoused individual freedom and self-expression.

In the words of an early Kibbutz Artzi authority, the aim of kibbutz education was

> to raise a generation which will perceive as its vision the fortification, perfection, and glorification of the commune, and which will be prepared to dedicate its life to the continuation of the work of the founders.

"What is our goal?" asked a member of Beit Alpha. "That our children should follow in our way . . . every other utopia has failed, and maybe here too there will be changes, but we shall succeed if we can train our children to follow in our way."

Many different influences were at work in the early Mossad boarding school, which was at its strongest and most influential in the 1940s and 1950s: the lack of authoritarianism and the project system from progressive education; the centrality of physical labor from Gordon and Borochov; the concept that all children were much the same except for differences caused by the capitalist system from Marx; the importance of liberating children from the Oedipus complex from Freud.

An educational document of the time stated:

> We have succeeded in winning the struggle against family living quarters, the dangers of which, according to modern psychological ideas, are so obvious. Separate living quarters for children are a guarantee of correct sex education:
> 1. The children are distanced from the traumatic effect of parental sex.
> 2. The Oedipus Complex, the root of most neuroses, is lessened.
> 3. Parents can give their love untainted by demands, building a more harmonious relationship between parents and children.

This rationalization of communal sleeping in the children's house seems, in retrospect, almost grotesque, as do these words of Shmuel Gollan:

> Parental love can be exaggerated. It is more the need of the parent than the child. It can lead to trauma and Oedipal complexes. Just as we distanced the children from intimate parental relations, we must lessen and control love from parents to children. We do not approve of uninhibited hugging, kissing, and caressing.

Even if these theories of child raising were correct—and in light of what is generally accepted today they were not—the practice all too often turned out to be defective. There were many reasons for a continuous changeover of the regular teachers and child care workers. Sickness, pregnancy, studies, and alternative work assignments frequently took the teachers, nurses, and child care workers away from their group.

All too often, unsuitable temporary workers were put into the children's houses. As a consequence, the results of kibbutz education were not always what they might have been.

Kibbutz educators were put on the defensive by American anthropologist Melford E. Spiro in his *Children of the Kibbutz,* published in 1958, and psychologist Bruno Bettelheim in his *Children of the Dream* (1969). Each of them concluded, in slightly different ways, that as a result of insufficient bonding with their parents—particularly their mothers—kibbutz children were often conformist, insecure, and emotionally shallow and found it difficult to create serious relationships as adults. "Real intimacy finds no fertile ground in the kibbutz," concluded Bettelheim.

He also pointed to the lack of ambition and personal achievement among kibbutz-raised children. "They will not express themselves," he pronounced. "They will not be leaders or philosophers, will not achieve anything in science or art."

However, in a recent newspaper article titled "Return to the Children of the Dream," a journalist visiting Ramat Yohanan discovered that the class examined by Bettelheim three decades earlier had a fine record of achievement. A member of that class goes through his classmates name by name, listing an industrial manager, an artist and poet, a composer who just received the prime minister's prize for classical music, a geologist, a mathematics professor, an astrophysicist with an international reputation, two sales directors of large companies, the manager of a high-tech company, a former pilot who is today a successful children's author, as well as former secretaries, treasurers, and farm managers of the kibbutz.

"Bettelheim got it totally wrong," he concludes, with a large measure of justification.

It is probably coincidental that Spiro chose Beit Alpha for his study, and Bettelheim went to Ramat Yohanan. In 1939 these two kibbutzim had implemented a partial population exchange between them, following a dispute about membership of Kibbutz Artzi. Thus, both researchers were dealing with the descendants of that quintessential commune, Our Community. Although both authors disguised the names of their kibbutzim, no secret lasts for long in Israel, and the identities of the two kibbutzim soon became common knowledge.

Bettelheim, who only spent six weeks at Kibbutz Ramat Yohanan, was dismissed by kibbutz educators as superficial, but Spiro, who spent almost a year at Beit Alpha, with his wife as assistant researcher, returning subsequently for shorter periods, was more difficult to disregard. His observations were taken seriously at least in part because he was generally positive about the kibbutz. After a visit in 1974, he concluded, "With all the stresses and strains, the community persists as a kibbutz. This is the measure of things, and here, if the founders could appreciate it, is the measure of *their* success. . . . There can be no doubt about the [children's] commitment to the perpetuation of the kibbutz." His final verdict on the kibbutz-raised person is that he is "a warm, sensitive, gracious human being."

Despite Spiro's generally positive conclusions, many young kibbutzniks are now saying that kibbutz educates toward mediocrity, and studies by Israeli researchers, many of them kibbutz members, tend to confirm the earlier findings of the two Americans. Summing up seventy years of communal education in an essay in *Education in the Changing Kibbutz,* Ora Aviezer concludes that not only has the kibbutz failed to produce a "new human being," but research has proven that the kibbutz-raised child is hardly different from other Israeli children. Furthermore, the communal sleeping system proved an unsuitable framework for raising children, having an adverse effect on the emotional development of the kibbutz child.

There can be little doubt that communal sleeping in the children's house affected half of the kibbutz population more than the other half. Both as mothers and as daughters, it was the women who were harmed by a system that was primarily designed by men. This is illustrated in *Shirat Hadeshe* (Song of the Lawn, 1991) by the late Nurit Leshem, a kibbutz psychologist and herself a first-generation kibbutz daughter. The book is a series of interviews with fifteen members of the first generation of women brought up on kibbutzim, mostly from Kibbutz Artzi. All but two of the women have remained kibbutz members. Leshem pointed out that her book is not a scientific research study.

"I am weak on statistics," she admitted, "but good at listening to human stories."

What her book demonstrates above all is that the kibbutz, a society aspiring to create absolute equality, failed when it came to sexual equality. On this topic Kibbutz Artzi had early on proclaimed:

> We have given [the woman] equal rights; we have emancipated her
> from the economic yoke; we have emancipated her from the burden of
> rearing children; we have emancipated her from the feeling of "belonging" to her husband, the provider and the one who commands; we have
> given her a new society; we broke the shackles that chained her hands.

This might be literally true; but in forcing the woman kibbutz member into an artificial parity with her male counterpart, the kibbutz system trampled on the most sensitive feelings of motherhood, femininity, and female self-expression.

In her introduction, Leshem wrote:

Allowed to suckle every four hours, left to cry and develop our lungs, we grew up without the basic security needed for survival. Sitting on the potty at regular intervals next to other children doing the same, we were educated to be the same; but we were, for all that, different. We tried to obliterate the difference, to learn to appear the same: same clothes, shoes, food, desires. We disguised our pain behind high walls.

At night the grownups leave and turn off all the lights. You know you will wet the bed because it is too frightening to go to the lavatory. . . . The child hides her pajamas, the child care worker finds them and slaps the child. . . . Heroes of the Land of Israel do not cry, so she runs behind the building to cry where no one can see her.

Woman after woman describes her deprivation. Deganit recalls, "No hugging, or kissing, or physical warmth." Ziva remembers a cast-iron rule: "Never cry. Like a chick that shows blood: show it and you are finished. Never ask for help, never stand out . . . it doesn't matter what you do—only what 'they' say about what you do."

"It was forbidden to waste food," relates Hannah. "If you vomited, you had to eat your vomit. When I had jaundice I was sick in the lavatory. The nurse slapped me. I knew my parents would never interfere."

Esty recalls how she wanted to study and brought her request to the kibbutz general meeting only to have it turned down. Her mother did not even attend the general meeting. Ahuva describes her mother as "strong and ruthless, trampling on everyone to get what she wanted, but always for the community—never for herself or her family." Hagit testifies, "Today, when my own children are leaving home, I have a fear of being abandoned."

Carmela writes:

Childhood was a continuous physical torture. There was no love. . . . I needed love desperately, but I wasn't allowed to have it. My feminine side was repressed. . . . I grew up like an orphan. My parents never kissed me until I was thirty!

My parents were not the dominant figures, nor my teachers. Film stars, despite the fact that we were told they were "decadent." I wanted to be like English and Americans, despite the fact that my teachers despised them.

This account from Efrat:

Once my mother heard me crying. She stood for a whole hour outside the baby house, not daring to interfere. It turned out that I had been forgotten and left in the yard. I almost suffered dehydration. And yet they still say that parents are not as qualified to bring up children as trained child care workers.

Efrat also recalled how she visited a "real family" in a *moshav*. She told her parents that it was "like paradise."

And, finally, this moving description:

One day, when all the children are playing in the yard, a little girl remains in the building. She goes to the dolls' corner. She knows that she must not take a doll. Only the child care worker is allowed to do that, but she picks up the doll and hugs her and kisses her. She opens her blouse and suckles the doll at her flat breast, pouring into her ear all the words that she wished she heard herself. She hugs and caresses and loves the doll. She does not hear the child care worker, who creeps up and slaps her face: "Whore, licentious woman, never, never, never do that again!"

These are just a few extracts from the interviews, translated from the Hebrew original. Leshem's book caused a sensation. The author received a cascade of letters, many of them adding their testimonies to the ones she recorded. Some wrote "choked with tears." More than one confessed that she had thought herself unique until she read the book.

A dramatized version of *Shirat Hadeshe* was presented in 1992, climaxing with the poignant incident of the doll. It was followed by a discussion at a kibbutz, with the participation of members from there and from many other kibbutzim. One participant, herself a kibbutz member of that generation, demanded to know why she and her contemporaries had kept silent for so long, why they had kept it all bottled up inside. Several denied the truth of Leshem's picture, insisting that they had discussed it with members of their generation and none of them recalled such grief and suffering. It is surely significant that all these speakers were male, and one of them admitted, "The kibbutz was supposed to provide solutions for men and women, but the chief sufferers were the women. In this the kibbutz has failed."

Subsequent correspondents pointed out that the 1940s were a time of hardship for many in the Jewish community in Palestine, with Spartan conditions, and a shortage of material goods. This was true for many children in the towns and villages of Israel, not just the kibbutz children.

One writer admitted that there had been fear but that her memories were for the most part happy: "I loved the children's house, being put to bed in a group. It was great fun together."

Another (a male) wrote nostalgically of the warm togetherness of the group, the feeling of companionship and purpose, of the hikes, the camps, the singing and dancing, the nights of fun and jokes and laughter.

One woman wrote that Leshem's book illustrated the triumph of the human spirit over ideologies, the victory of human feelings and natural creativity, which no institution can conquer: "Above the suffering, suppression, loneliness, you have shown in your book strong women, with strong inner forces, who just needed to be shown that they possessed them. You have been privileged."

Leshem's book dealt with a specific period of deprivation and sacrifice for the common cause that was not limited to the kibbutzim but was evident in all parts of the Jewish community in Palestine. Later generations, who lived in easier times, have happier memories. In many conversations, in Degania, Givat Brenner, Hasolelim, Neve Yam, Hatzerim, and several other kibbutzim not specifically mentioned, members who grew up with communal sleeping were adamant that the experience was overwhelmingly positive. While almost unanimously insisting that they wanted their own children at home, they maintained that they themselves had a great childhood and that, in living at home, their children were missing out on something very wonderful that they had experienced.

Aviva Zamir of Maagan Michael has also carried out a study of kibbutz women, *Mothers and Daughters,* published in 1986. Her interviews, which were confined to one kibbutz, were more focused on the question of women's work and the concept of sex equality in the kibbutz than on the problems of motherhood and communal sleeping. Furthermore, they were conducted at a time when the kibbutz in question was in the process of changing to home sleeping. Consequently, they tend to be much lower key on the question of communal child rearing, but some of the testimonies echo those in Leshem's book. Sarah, a fifty-six-year-old kibbutz mother recalls, "I so much wanted my children with me. When I couldn't stand it anymore, I used to take them and go to my mother in town. I derived deep satisfaction from having the children sleep with me for a few nights."

And later, "When Orit was little, I was not allowed to put her to bed, my own little girl. The child care worker told me that I could watch through the window." Yael, a mother of twenty-three, says, "Communal sleeping is very artificial, but I did not suffer as a child. It is as a mother that I am dying to have my baby sleep at home."

On the other hand, Hannah, a veteran member, insists, "Communal sleeping is a fantastically healthy arrangement. I enjoyed being alone with my husband. I had time for all sorts of activities. Our daughters don't know what they have let themselves in for!"

In an interview conducted shortly after the children came home, Hagit, a young mother in her twenties, says, "We are so much more relaxed now that the children are sleeping at home. We no longer run to the children's houses all day to gain every available minute with our kids."

Interviewed herself at her own kibbutz, Zamir agreed that the kibbutz woman was often frustrated as a mother.

> I was typical of my generation in that I pushed the problem aside. I believed in the kibbutz on the whole, so I accepted this aberration. Still, I remember running half a mile at night in the winter to feed my daughter, repeating to myself all the way, "This is the last generation of slavery!" And it was. Our daughters' generation was much more open and less self-sacrificing, and they changed it.

After speaking to Yeheskel Dar in Degania and reading *Education in the Changing Kibbutz,* I sought him out for a follow-up conversation in his office at the Hebrew University in Jerusalem. Dar, a professor of the sociology of education, noted that many of the women interviewed in *Shirat Hadeshe* were undergoing psychological treatment.

"I don't know how much it was the system and how much the individuals," he says. "Undoubtedly there was an interaction, but I don't think kibbutz education was generally harmful. It adversely affected some sensitive children, but the damage was not for the most part extreme."

I asked Dar why four generations of kibbutz education had not managed to pass on communal values in the way that Yosef Bussel predicted. He answered that the kibbutz education system—even that of Kibbutz Artzi—was based essentially on example.

"They thought that living it was enough," he says. "They did not really teach kibbutz life with texts about equality and community, in the way that religious educators instill religion with biblical and talmudic texts. They definitely overestimated the influence of the social structure."

He thinks, too, that Bussel enormously underestimated the importance of the personal revolution that he and his comrades carried out. The experience of rebelling against one's environment, of being an outsider, yet reinforced by the company of a group of friends with the same values, was extremely powerful. The kibbutz founders chose to join the group and to create a way of life built on ethics that were different from those with which they grew up. Those born in the kibbutz arrived there by chance. Consequently, the opposite of what Bussel wrote was true: those who made the revolutionary choice were able to live a communal life; those brought up as communards turned out to be less capable of living in a commune.

Another important reason that kibbutz education "failed" was the change in the general environment. Society did not stand still, points out Dar; the collective ethos of the Jewish community in Palestine was increasingly replaced by a more individualistic approach in the State of Israel. He does not think that the kibbutz would have succeeded more if it had cut itself off from society. It was the surrounding society that gave the kibbutz its sense of importance. It also granted the kibbutz resources that maintained its relatively high standard of living. Although he agrees that the kibbutz schools have become much more like other schools, he still hopes that the democratic tradition and something of the project system will be maintained.

The whole question of kibbutz education spotlights the ambivalence of the kibbutz movement in its relations with the outside society. As we have observed, the kibbutz rejected the traditional commune approach of withdrawal from society, rather aiming to lead and inspire it. Nevertheless, initially kibbutz schools maintained a policy of exclusivity. Although they admitted children from outside the kibbutz, educational control was maintained by the kibbutz, and an overwhelming majority of the teachers were kibbutz members.

In the 1970s, when the social gap between veteran Israelis and new immigrants—particularly those from Middle Eastern countries—was seen to have persisted from the 1950s, the education ministry introduced a policy of integration that obliged schools to accept all the children in their geographic area without regard to their social and economic backgrounds. The kibbutzim managed to obtain exemption from this policy on the grounds that they were educating specifically to kibbutz values. This was certainly one of the reasons for resentment against the kibbutzim among large sectors of the Israeli public. The kibbutzim may have seen it as their right to inculcate their values; many Israelis derided it as snobbish elitism.

Today, however, with the current opening up of the kibbutz to outside society, kibbutz schools are enormously popular with the public at large. Indeed, a major selling point of the new neighborhoods being constructed by some kibbutzim, such as Givat Brenner and Hasolelim, is the prospect of education for the children at a kibbutz school.

Although it retained its policy of exclusivity longer than the other kibbutz movements, the Kibbutz Artzi school system has also opened itself to the outside. For the past three years, the Shikma Mossad in the western Negev Desert has had children coming daily from the local towns and *moshavim,* as well as boarders from three kibbutzim and several immigrant youth groups. Situated at Kibbutz Yad Mordechai, some six miles south of the coastal town of Ashkelon, the Mossad has its own campus at the edge of the kibbutz.

One of the reasons that Shikma has become a regional school is financial: the kibbutzim could not afford to maintain a school for their members only. Even with 100 day students out of 260, the classes remain relatively small, with 22 to 23 students per class. The citizens of Ofakim, Sderot, and Netivot, towns populated mainly by oriental immigrants of the 1950s, are pleased to send their children to Shikma, and today the kibbutz school is happy to receive them.

Shikma is not really a kibbutz school anymore, let alone a classic Kibbutz Artzi Mossad. It follows the program of the Ministry of Education, it draws its teaching staff from both the kibbutzim and outside, most teaching is by the conventional frontal method, and all the children take the national matriculation examinations. Nonetheless, traces of the Society of Children remain.

Ronnie Bassin, a friendly, energetic man in his forties, is a member of Zikkim, one of the kibbutzim sending children to Shikma. He teaches literature and citizenship at the school but also instructs the students in how to carry out personal study projects—how to use computer databases, books, and other materials. The personal study project is in the spirit of the old Mossad, involving personal and group activities outside the classroom structure. There is also a less formal relationship between teachers and pupils than in town schools, he maintains, but he notes that the old-style ideological education is finished. There is no tendency to hold back outstanding students, and personal achievement is as much an aim in Shikma as in any other school.

Veteran teacher Hanoch Lekach has been a member of Karmiya, another of the kibbutzim sending children to Shikma, for forty-five years. With his sad, dark eyes, undisciplined sparse gray hair, gray mustache, gentle voice, and precise speech, Lekach is the prototype of the kibbutz veteran. He came to Mossad Shikma in the 1960s, when the classical Kibbutz Artzi–Hashomer Hatzair values were still dominant.

"We had a holistic organic approach," he recalls. "We educated by topics, seeing education and society as part of a whole."

An hour and a half of intensive work on a study project was the central part of the school day. The pupils returned home in the afternoons to their kibbutzim to work in the farming branches before returning to the Mossad in the evening. The students still go home to their parents in the afternoons, but nowadays they only work about once a week. The study program was produced by the education department of Kibbutz Artzi. The department still exists, but it has very little influence. Today the teaching is conducted according to the Ministry of Education program.

"In my opinion," says Lekach, "our ideological education was weakened after the Twentieth Congress of the Soviet Communist Party, the one where Nikita Khruschev denounced Stalin's reign of terror. After that it was very important to the teachers to prove that they were open-minded."

As more university-trained teachers entered the Mossad, they also had a profound effect. The Mossad became "academized." The difference with the religious education was that, whereas Kibbutz Artzi gradually relinquished control to the Ministry of Education, the religious sector maintained their separate program.

Lekach concedes that he and his colleagues were wrong about a lot of things. They were excessively naive, yet on the whole the system worked pretty well. Although he believed totally in kibbutz values and tried to educate his students to serve others while developing themselves, he insists that he never imagined it would be possible to create a "new human being."

At his kibbutz, Karmiya, the Society of Children was maintained right into the 1970s. Until 1974, the child care workers and teachers put the children to bed, and even after parents took over that role, it was several years before the younger children started sleeping at home. The Mossad children who are over the age of twelve still sleep at the boarding school. Lekach and his wife never saw anything wrong in communal sleeping. At the same time, looking back, Lekach sees that the parental influence on the children was always far stronger than that of the teacher or child care worker. Even when the system was totally communal, the parents' home was the major influence.

His emphatic tone reminded me of an earlier conversation with another teacher, Ruth Dotan, of Ayelet Hashahar in Upper Galilee. Ruth has spent her whole life in kibbutz education, although not in Kibbutz Artzi.

"A home where parents read produces children who read," she declares. "Television and computers do not stop reading in a home where there are books. And it is the same with values. It doesn't matter how strong the collective framework is; if the parents don't support it, it isn't going to work."

She angrily rejects the allegation that the kibbutz school educated to mediocrity. The kibbutz was years ahead of its time in recognizing the different needs of children with special talents. She herself used to take bored children out of the classroom and direct them to self-study projects in the library.

"Every child must get the maximum assistance suitable to his individual talents," she insists.

I always worked on that principle. There are always elites and they cannot be abolished. The question is, will the bright person serve society, or just look out for himself? One of my students was brilliant. He was interested in botany, how things grew, how much water they needed. Later he was one of the people who established Israel's national water company.

Ruth refuses to see kibbutz education—or indeed the kibbutz as a whole—as a failure. "It is falling apart now," she conceded, "but for nearly a hundred years we have proved that people do not have to live on the principle of 'dog eat dog.' History is circular. The kibbutz idea will come around again one day, although probably in a different form."

Hanoch Lekach describes himself as "in exile from my dream." If he has any regrets, it is that he did not realize that the kibbutz idea was already on the way out when he became a kibbutz member in the 1950s. Looking back, he feels that the kibbutz system was breaking down long before anyone realized it. Despite this, his life as a teacher has given him profound satisfaction. He acknowledges that many children growing up in kibbutzim have said that they were unhappy in the exaggeratedly communal framework that did not give them a chance for individual development but says he always tried to consider each child as an individual and help the student appropriately.

"We did not achieve everything we hoped for," he concedes, "but on the whole the system produced good results. I still try to instill the values of freedom, humanism, and tolerance."

A group of high school students from Shikma sprawl on the lawn outside the classrooms. They are dressed like teenagers anywhere: jeans, T-shirts, sneakers or bare feet. Two have earrings; one smokes. They are all from Zikkim, a smallish kibbutz a few miles north of the Mossad, but only one is a child of the kibbutz. Two are immigrants from Russia, with parents in development towns; one is from Tel Aviv. The three outside students have been adopted by families in Zikkim, whom they visit every afternoon. They see their own families every two weeks.

"Are you the 'new human being'?" I challenge Jonathan, a lanky young man with glasses, the child of immigrants from Argentina.

"I'm a normal person," he replies with a smile, "who loves his home and his way of life. That's all."

"He is different from a town kid," remarks Yaron. Long haired and swarthy, he is the one from Tel Aviv. His grandparents came to Israel from Iraq.

"Yaron is right," affirms Max, who was born in Moscow. He has a flat, good-natured face, wears an earring, and is distinctly heavier than the others. "What's more, I'm different now also. We are less spoiled than town kids. If we go on a field trip, all we need is a sleeping bag and some coffee. We don't demand air-conditioned rooms; we are happy to sleep outside."

"He started going barefoot last summer," says Yaron with a laugh. "He'll be a kibbutznik yet."

None of the boys are prepared to say that they will definitely remain at Zikkim. Max says he likes the place but does not want to be a kibbutz member. If Zikkim became an ordinary village, that would make him more likely to remain. He hopes to study psychology after his army service.

Nicolai, who comes from near Moscow, thinks he might make a career of the army. Yaron looks forward to studying architecture and would definitely like to travel. Max is keen to visit Russia to see what has happened there.

All of them are entirely positive about Shikma. Yaron appreciates that the relationship with the teachers is much less formal than at his Tel Aviv school. You might find yourself playing football against one teacher, he points out, and sitting next to another in the communal dining hall. Nicolai and Max go much further, confessing that when they first came to Shikma, they were in shock. In Russia, the teacher had absolute authority. The pupils remained quiet in class. If they wanted to say anything, they put up their hand and waited for permission. In Russia, they were afraid of the teachers, and they were astounded at the lack of formal discipline at the Mossad.

There is no political education in the school, but in the evenings the Hashomer Hatzair youth movement has its activities. They say that the movement encourages cooperation and liberal humanism but doesn't specifically educate toward kibbutz life. All of them express themselves as political doves on the Palestinian question. They say that Israel should withdraw from more territory and agree to the establishment of a Palestinian state in the West Bank and Gaza. They concede that they are probably influenced by the environment at Shikma, although Yaron maintained he was far more influenced by his own home in Tel Aviv. It should be pointed out that they expressed these attitudes while Israel still had a nationalist right-wing government that strongly opposed a Palestinian state.

Jonathan, born at Zikkim, strongly believes in the values of equality and cooperation but wants to try out other ways of life before deciding where to settle down. He is planning to spend a "year of service" as a youth leader in one of the towns before joining the army. He is sure that change must come to his kibbutz. It is happening slowly, but there is no alternative. The kibbutz will continue to exist, but it will be more private, less collective. If he stays in Zikkim, it will be because of the quality of life. He does not approve of what he has seen of life in the towns so far. "Money, money, money," he says dismissively. "I don't go for that." On the other hand, he also declares, "Ideology is bullshit!"

He and Max are in agreement that one of the most annoying things about the kibbutz is the fact that some members work so hard, whereas others allow the kibbutz to carry them. They both express themselves forcibly on that. Max adds the objection that "everybody knows where you are sleeping, and with whom!"

Possibly the most encouraging thing about the conversation was the manifest atmosphere of easy camaraderie between boys of such different origins. In this, at least, the kibbutz continues to make a valuable contribution.

In a society where example plays such a significant role in education, mention should be made of two groups of outsiders who have made their presence felt: the Nahal and the volunteers. Thousands of foreign volunteers have spent time living and working on kibbutzim all over Israel; Nahal army units are stationed at kibbutzim for several months of their army service.

Although visitors were attracted to experience communal life at first hand since the earliest days of the kibbutzim, outsiders only started coming in large numbers after the Six Day War of 1967. During the months before the war, when Israel's reserve army was mobilized for a lengthy period, volunteers—mainly Jewish volunteers—came in large numbers to replace the men who had been called up. At first only some of the volunteers stayed at kibbutzim; others worked at *moshavim;* a number worked in hospitals or at archeological digs. It quickly became evident, though, that the kibbutz structure was uniquely suitable for accommodating them.

The possibility of living and working on a kibbutz seems to have got around by word of mouth, as initially the kibbutz movements did nothing to encourage it. But in due course the volunteer movement became organized, and "kibbutz desks" were opened in many Western countries. Although many of the volunteers limited their stay to a few months, it became fashionable for youngsters to spend the year between school and university working on a kibbutz. In time, the proportion of Jews among the volunteers decreased to around 15 percent. The overwhelming majority came from Western Europe, with less than 10 percent coming from the United States and a similar proportion from South Africa, Australia, and South America. At its peak, the volunteer movement numbered fifty thousand per year, and in the two decades after 1967 some half a million youngsters enjoyed the kibbutz experience. In fact, "enjoyed" is accurate, as over 70 percent regularly responded to questionnaires and expressed themselves as satisfied or very satisfied, and a similar proportion were complimentary about the kibbutz way of life. They lived and worked on the kibbutzim; received accommodation, food, pocket money of some $70 per month; attended lectures and in some cases even week-long study courses at kibbutz colleges; toured the country; and generally had a good time.

The visitors mostly wanted to work in the farming branches, and initially about half of them did, notably in seasonal work such as fruit picking, but as Israeli agriculture became more mechanized, increasing numbers of volunteers found themselves in the service branches, such as the communal kitchens and dining halls. Some kibbutz members felt guilty that they were exploiting the visitors. As mentioned earlier, however, the overwhelming majority of kibbutz volunteers enjoyed their experience. A few of them even made efforts to start communes or cooperatives of their own when they returned home.

On the Internet, a former volunteer had this to say:

> You can divide your typical day into three main periods:
> Morning and Early Afternoon, which is the time you spend at work.
> Late Afternoon, when most people relax by the pool or take a nap. Perhaps you want to take a trip to town to get your pictures developed, or just sit outside and socialize with the others. You might want to go and play tennis or relax with a book you found in the kibbutz library.
> Evening and who knows how late at night, when it's fun time. Evenings can be rather wild as well as rather quiet. Sometimes with a lot of drinking and dancing, some other times with a guitar and bonfire.

He added this tip:

> Drinking among volunteers is commonly accepted within reasonable limits. You are there to have fun after all, but excessive drinking will get you a one-way ticket to the nearest town. If you smoke a joint keep it discreet, and forget everything about heavy drugs. That will get you a one-way ticket to the nearest police station, and possibly out of the country.

The flow of volunteers began to ebb in the 1980s, as Israel's image suffered from the Intifada, the Palestinian uprising. At the same time, the kibbutzim found less need of the visitors, were less able to afford them, and started to have ambivalent feelings about them. Although the kibbutz had always been an open society, the volunteers represented the outside world breaking in with a vengeance. The kibbutz children in particular were thrown into intimate social contact with enormous numbers of liberated, easy-going, hedonistic youth from the Western nations.

It would be unfair to blame the volunteers for the juvenile delinquency and drug problems that emerged among kibbutz-raised young people, but the Internet passage quoted here indicates that there was a connection. Furthermore, the foreign kids turned up, just when it was becoming fashionable for the kibbutz children to follow their army service with a lengthy trip abroad.

There were two primary reasons for this trend: the growing prosperity of the kibbutz, and of Israeli society in general, which permitted them to earn the money for such a vacation, and the increasingly active role that the young soldiers were required to fulfill in the aftermath of the Six Day War. There were battles with infiltrators on the borders, artillery wars along the Jordan and the Suez Canal, leading up to the Yom Kippur War of 1973. Subsequently, there was the prolonged fighting in Lebanon and the Intifada. Many Israeli youngsters, particularly those who served in combat units, took part in these wars and campaigns. They felt a strong need to escape after the tension and discipline of their military service.

The ex-soldiers went mainly to Asia and North and South America. Although most of them only spent a few months abroad, many stayed for longer periods. Thus, the foreign volunteers replaced the kibbutz-raised young men and women in more than one sense. They replaced them as workers, and, in a society that educated mainly by example, the volunteers became the role models for the kibbutz children, whose older siblings left them for foreign parts.

Of course, romances and marriages took place between the two groups. In some cases, the volunteer joined the kibbutz; in others, the kibbutz child followed the volunteer back to his or her country of origin. Undoubtedly, intermarriage caused concern, and it was one of the reasons the kibbutzim became less receptive to volunteers, but the phenomenon was marginal. Far more important was the general influence of the volunteers and the atmosphere they created. Their presence in the kibbutzim for two decades definitely helped erode traditional kibbutz values among the young generation of the kibbutz.

In theory, the Nahal unit of the Israel Defense Forces should have exerted a counterinfluence. The Nahal (the Hebrew acronym for "Fighting and Working Youth") was founded in 1949 as a division of the Israel Defense Forces. It looked back to the tradition of the Palmah, the prestate commando force based largely in the kibbutzim. The idea was to mobilize members of the Israeli youth movements into the army as groups, which would settle the border areas and spend part of their army service working in agriculture.

Before founding their own kibbutz, the youngsters spent several months training on existing kibbutzim. Although the Nahal was a success story, establishing more than a hundred new kibbutzim, by the

1970s the youth movements were weakening, and ideology was becoming less and less important in the kibbutzim and in Israel as a whole. The Nahal groups became smaller, and only a tiny minority remained kibbutz members after their military service. By the time the volunteers arrived, the weakened Nahal groups did little to counter the powerful effect of the volunteers. If anything, they themselves also came under the volunteers' cultural influence.

It was not, however, the volunteer influx that most worried the older generation of the kibbutz. They were far more concerned about the flow in the opposite direction, which was only marginally connected with the volunteers. Only a few dozen kibbutz children who married volunteers left the country, but several thousand others remained abroad after their postarmy trips.

In the case of India, Thailand, or Venezuela, the children usually came home after a few months or, in extreme cases, after a few years, but those who went to Western Europe, and especially North America, often settled permanently. The West Coast of the United States was a particular attraction. So many kibbutz children settled in Los Angeles that they became the subject of a study by Tel Aviv sociologist Naama Sabar, *Kibbutz L.A.*

It is a slim volume, but an important one, because apart from the economic collapse described in the previous chapter, the main danger facing the kibbutzim today is their failure to hang on to their latest generation. Even Hatzerim, a prosperous and successful kibbutz, keeps less than half of its young people. *Kibbutz L.A.*, based on interviews with Israelis from their midtwenties to their midforties, most of them living in the San Fernando valley in the late 1980s, tells us a great deal about why many youngsters left their kibbutzim—and left Israel altogether.

Obviously, all exiles have their own personal story, but certain themes recur. Their parents were cool and distant or, alternatively, suffocatingly close. The communal life was too intense; there was too little privacy and no encouragement of individual striving for attainment. Many were acutely aware of their parents' frustration with kibbutz life, and a number felt that they were indirectly encouraged to leave by their parents. They themselves also felt limited by the communal structure. More than one described being able to act decisively and make decisions during their military service, only to be foiled by the plethora of kibbutz committees when they returned home.

"I loved kibbutz life," said one, "but I was going in a different direction. I could see two steps ahead and I was annoyed that others did not. I was irritated by the apathy."

Settling down in Los Angeles proved relatively easy for many kibbutzniks, as they were met at the airport by former fellow members who at once fixed them up with jobs and accommodation. Ironically, the success of the kibbutz in educating its children to work hard is one of the factors making for swift absorption in their new environment. Outside the kibbutz, some of them had found Israeli society too harsh, too intrusive, too critical. America, and in particular Los Angeles, was free, open, undemanding. No one was looking over their shoulders. There was room to breathe.

It must be emphasized that these were, for the most part, bright, talented, energetic, and healthy young people. For them the United States was the land of infinite possibilities. It was not so much the prosperity that many of them manifestly achieved that gave them satisfaction as the feeling that they had attained it in their own way by means of their own hard work and ability.

"It's a different atmosphere here," said a former member who once ran the main farming branch of his kibbutz. "There are no obligations. I meet whoever I want to meet. I have privacy, freedom, and above all independence."

One girl, who left her kibbutz after being denied her wish to train as a sports instructor, came to Los Angeles for a few months and found her social life revolutionized.

"I was shy and lonely in Israel," she testified. "Here my phone never stopped ringing."

Shortly after reading *Kibbutz L.A.,* I spoke to Avery Glick in his first-floor apartment surrounded by trees and lawns in a pleasant Los Angeles suburb. He gives massage and treatment with the Feldenkreis method that he studied in Israel and in Los Angeles. His German-born wife, Moopie, whom he met in Los Angeles, has a small business partnership with a friend making decorated lampshades.

As we talk on his veranda, Joey, his chubby, eight-month baby dribbles all over his shirt. Avery concedes that he could have practiced Feldenkreis therapy at his kibbutz (which paid for his initial course of study) but says his mind was on other things. He wanted to make his own way in the world.

"On the kibbutz you have to conform to the rules," he explains.

"Outside you set your own rules. I like the fact that I can decide when to work and with whom."

He lived in Tel Aviv for six months but found his annual military service almost unbearable. It was, of course, bad for business, but the worst thing was that he was serving in the occupied territories during the Palestinian Intifada.

"My regular job as a therapist was to help people, to cure them," he notes. "In the army I was harming people. They actually encouraged us to beat rioters whom we caught. I couldn't stand it."

Avery is thirty-seven. He has a younger brother and two sisters, all of whom left their Galilee kibbutz. One sister spent several years in India before returning to Israel and to Judaism. She now lives in an orthodox community in Galilee. Avery is in contact with his family by E-mail, receives the kibbutz monthly journal, and generally keeps in touch. His parents came to Israel from England, he notes, and created a wonderful community. They aimed to build a new society with new values, and their dream came true in many ways. They sincerely thought they were building the best possible environment for their children, and they are manifestly disappointed that their offspring have decided to live elsewhere.

"My great-grandparents came to England from Russia," remarks Avery. My parents left England to live in Israel. I have come to Los Angeles. Where will Joey end up? I don't know."

His parents and their generation were naive and, in some respects, a little blind, he thinks. The kibbutz was relevant when it was founded, but it failed to adapt quickly enough to the general development of Israeli society.

"When changes were proposed at our kibbutz, the founding generation blocked them," he recalls. "If they had permitted change, a lot of the young people who left would have remained."

Avery believes that the kibbutz must move in a more capitalist direction, not just because it is inevitable but because it also makes sense. Equality is a nice idea, he thinks, but it can never be achieved.

"I don't know how to balance the ideas of equality and mutual support against private enterprise and initiative," he admits. "It's tough on the kibbutz, which was the only pure communism in the world."

Avery and Moopie do not plan to return to Israel. Moopie says that she would be prepared to spend a year at Avery's kibbutz, but she does not want to bring up her children there.

"We haven't found the right place to bring up our children," she admits. "We are looking for a small community where neighbors spend time with each other, where they really help one another, where the children can ride their bikes or run around barefoot without danger. Maybe a small town somewhere in California."

"Do you realize that you are looking for your kibbutz?" I ask them. Avery replies without hesitation.

Of course! I *loved* growing up on a kibbutz. It was the best possible environment. I want something like a kibbutz, but with more potential for individual achievement. My grandparents still live on our kibbutz, and they love it. The kibbutz is wonderful for old people and children. In between it is a problem, because it doesn't give enough opportunity for people to find their own way.

Nir Pearlson works as an architect in Eugene, Oregon, but came back to his kibbutz for six months. He and his American wife, Mimi, want the children to learn Hebrew and be linked to the kibbutz, but they don't want to live there.

"I haven't rejected it totally," he says, "but spending time here makes it clear to me that this is not the place I want to live. There is a strong loser mentality, which is tragic, because there is much good also."

Nir feels that some of the best members have been carrying the kibbutz on their shoulders for the past two decades, but now they are burned out and looking for interesting jobs outside the kibbutz. He senses a stagnation in the kibbutz, a certain inertia. In Eugene, he and Mimi decided where they wanted to live, and they socialize with whom they want, whereas in the kibbutz people are forced on each other.

"Perhaps the problem with the kibbutz is that the parents could not transmit their values to their children like DNA," says Nir. "It is not always so easy to pass on values by education."

For Mimi, her husband's kibbutz is her "favorite place in the world," but she would not live there permanently. She senses a certain sterility. "It reminds me of an Indian reservation in the United States," she says. "It is an 'idealism reservation,' with the idealism all in the past."

When we come to consider the relative failure of the kibbutz to perpetuate its values among its progeny, the matter of the woman member must be addressed. Many of the young people who left their kibbutzim (including, as we have seen, those in Los Angeles) were aware of their parents' dissatisfaction with the way of life but particularly felt the unhappiness of their mothers. This is significant when we realize that it was the women members, as mothers, child care workers, teachers, and nurses, who bore the brunt of kibbutz education. The child care workers and nurses were almost all female, and a majority of the teachers, particularly of the younger children, were women. The failure of the kibbutz to provide a satisfactory life for the *havera* (female kibbutz member) is well known and also well documented.

By far the most comprehensive study is by Lionel Tiger and Joseph Shepher, *Women in the Kibbutz*. The researchers found that the kibbutz succeeded in its economic, social, ideological, and political aims—the book was published in 1975—but in the division of labor, the failure was "pervasive and overwhelming."

> As social scientists, we have claimed the kibbutz to be what its founders and citizens as utopians claim it to be: an experiment that affirms possibilities for radical change in social forms and in people's commitments to one another. We have found that the aspect of the experiment involving major changes in women's lives was substantially less successful than the others.

Their wide-ranging study, which involved several thousand kibbutz women, found that in the early kibbutzim more than half of the women worked in production for a considerable time; this was followed by a gradual but continuous polarization, until only some 20 percent of kibbutz women were employed in productive occupations. There was the paradox of women working in child care but caring for other women's children. Working in the communal kitchen and dining hall, in the laundry and the clothing store, and running these services for the entire community, they were nonetheless deprived of their traditional role as homemakers for their own families.

Moreover, despite the formal equality, women were far less involved in running the kibbutz. They were less active in the kibbutz general meetings. Although they were overrepresented in the committees dealing with social and cultural matters, they were seriously underrepresented in committees dealing with economy, work, security, and general policy. Despite the fact that the women members had slightly more years of education than their male counterparts, only 14 percent held the highest leadership positions. This position was voluntary, the authors point out. There was no male conspiracy to keep women out of the top jobs—quite the reverse. The men wanted to elect women; the women often refused to stand for election and frequently stood down soon after being appointed to top posts.

The authors also note, however, that historically the male members, who were dominant in the kibbutz, strongly influenced basic child care policy. Had women been more involved, the severance of the mother-child link might have been less extreme, they suggest.

Aviva Zamir has spent much of her life examining the question of sex equality on the kibbutz. In her *Mothers and Daughters,* she quotes with approval some of the points made by Nava, a woman kibbutz member. Nava notes that the original concept of equality was expressed by an identity of tasks—that is, by women working at the same jobs as men. This did not last very long, and in any case it was a mistaken concept. Real equality, according to Nava, is "equality within diversity, an equal right to self-realization within the collective egalitarian framework of the kibbutz." Nava is confident that kibbutz education today is directed "toward sexual equivalence and mutual respect." But, she notes, "there is still a long way to go to change basic norms. If the principle of the kibbutz is 'from each according to his ability, to each according to his needs,' then eventually we shall find out what the real needs are—the natural needs as well as those directed by society."

Although Zamir has pointed out that very few central economic and executive kibbutz positions are held by women, even today, Nava's concept of equality might indicate that the kibbutz is getting nearer to what she calls "equivalence of the sexes," if not equality.

However, the breakthrough—if indeed it is a breakthrough—has come too late. The male leaders of the kibbutz movement may have had the best intentions, but they went too far too fast and tried to achieve too much. They set their sights too high and shut their minds to many human feelings. In carrying out their revolution, they were too ready to decide what was good for others. Above all, they continued over many years to show a gross insensitivity toward the feelings of their women comrades.

It is hardly surprising, therefore, that the educators (most of whom were women) largely failed to pass on the message that communal life was superior to other ways of living. Nor is it surprising that, when the crisis came, the female half of the kibbutz population wept fewer tears than the male half over the existential crisis of the society that proved so unresponsive to their needs. More than one of those advising the kibbutzim on the process of change report that the women members are "much more open than the men" to the changes. This reaction, too, should not occasion surprise.

Brought up in peer groups, encouraged in cooperative endeavors, urged to foster the group and assist its weaker members, taught to work and take on responsibility, the children of the kibbutz have on the whole emerged as hardworking, enterprising, responsible, and constructive citizens. But they have not for the most part imbibed the ideals of their parents. If anything, their experience of group life has turned them away from the group and encouraged them to value individual attainment. They find equality and cooperation boring; they are much more excited by personal achievement.

Although possessing a humane attitude toward their fellow humans, kibbutz-educated people also tend to be suspicious of them. While they have no desire to create a society based on rampant materialism, they firmly reject the concept that every member of society should be—as they put it—"the height of the lawn." They want more scope for private initiative and also greater rewards for it. They are contemptuous of the "*metapelet* complex," the exaggerated dependence of the individual on the group or community. They are also very hard on "parasites," members who do not pull their full weight.

It is difficult to pinpoint the reasons for the failure to inculcate kibbutz values in the young generation. It cannot be ascribed only—or even chiefly—to the shortcomings described in this chapter. An exaggerated dependence on theory, a lack of humanity, arrogance, exclusivity, suppression of the individual, and a failure to address the real needs of the female half of the kibbutz population have all been noted and criticized. But it seems probable that, even without these faults, the kibbutz educational system would have failed by the yardstick of its own aspirations.

Ultimately, the kibbutz was too weak to stand up to the environment in which it existed. The influence of the society outside the kibbutz, which permeated kibbutz life through economic activities, social contacts, books, newspapers, radio, television, and movies, was just too strong. On the one hand, the kibbutz children carried out their own revolt against their parents; on the other, with only a few exceptions, they conformed remarkably tamely to the values of Israeli society, which in turn was increasingly dominated by the culture and values of Europe and North America.

"Education is not the panacea we once thought it was," admits Aharon Yadlin sadly. "Its potential is limited. Whatever education it receives, every young generation needs to revolt in its own way."

"The new human being did not emerge," observes Amir Helman

with a smile. "People are egoists. Apparently we need a few more million years of evolution for different genes to be created."

Our visits to five kibbutzim, our account of the economic crisis triggered in 1985, and our review of various aspects of kibbutz education indicate that all is not well in the kibbutz household. There is a serious questioning of basic assumptions, and some very radical changes are being made. At the same time, as we have seen, this is not the first time there have been such developments. The kibbutzim have been undergoing change throughout the nine decades of their existence. Are the current changes in the kibbutz simply more of the same, similar to the adaptations that have been going on for ninety years? Or are we seeing something much more radical that means the end of the kibbutz as we know it?

Continuing our search for the answer, we will visit a further five settlements and try to map out the future face—or faces—of the kibbutz.

PART III
FACES OF THE FUTURE

8

מעגן מיכאל

MAAGAN MICHAEL
DIVORCE SETTLEMENT

On the Mediterranean coast, a mere ten miles south of Neve Yam, lies Kibbutz Maagan Michael. Although the environment is strikingly similar, the contrast between the two villages could not be more extreme. Neve Yam, as we have seen, suffered economic collapse and is no longer a kibbutz; Maagan Michael is a successful kibbutz, with a community of some 1,300, half of them members. If everything Neve Yam tried seemed to go wrong, almost everything Maagan Michael did went right.

The possessors of a sophisticated plastics factory, with an annual turnover nearing $100 million, flourishing agriculture, and a vigorous communal life, Maagan Michael is more like Hatzerim in the Negev Desert than its neighbor to the north, but the two successful kibbutzim differ in their approach to preserving their communal way of life. Whereas Hatzerim is practicing benign neglect regarding its structure, Maagan Michael has embarked on preventive medication.

Hatzerim has raised its standard of living so high that there is little incentive for change. Although Maagan Michael also lives well, it has taken out an insurance policy. Its members have projected themselves into the future and asked the question "What if . . . ?" Maagan Michael's initiative is regarded by some as a "virtual" exercise. The kibbutz members themselves prefer the term "divorce settlement."

Basically, they have determined the rules of the game and laid out what will happen if Maagan Michael stops being a kibbutz.

"We don't live in isolation," explains a member involved in drawing up the new agreement. "A few of the younger members started to

191

Figure 8.1.   Maagan Michael in 1949.

Source: (Yad Tabenkin Archives)

talk about the differentials being introduced in other kibbutzim; a veteran countered, 'OK, you want to earn more because of the valuable tasks you perform. That's fine, but what about my fifty years' hard work building this place?' "

The reply is "Yam Carmel" (the Carmel Sea—the kibbutz is situated between Mount Carmel and the sea), a cooperative owning all the productive assets of the kibbutz. Every member of Maagan Michael is also a member of Yam Carmel, with the percentage of ownership determined by seniority.

For the time being, the arrangement is "dormant." In the event of the kibbutz ceasing to be a kibbutz, it will be activated. If Maagan Michael goes bankrupt—a most unlikely occurrence—what is left will be allocated according to the aforementioned agreement. If the members simply decide that they do not want to live on a kibbutz, the assets will be distributed using the agreed formula.

Whatever happens, the rules of the game have been determined, and that seems to have given the members—particularly the veterans—a sense of security. Maagan Michael is now free to continue as a traditional kibbutz, but with a psychological safety net.

Does this exercise point to an underlying sense of insecurity, or is it evidence that the members of Maagan Michael have an extraordinary talent for looking ahead? Maybe a bit of both. Even in kibbutz terms the members of Maagan Michael are a remarkable bunch. Their future is difficult to predict, but their past is interesting and unusual. Today's prosperous seaside village was established fifty years ago as a collection of huts and tents on an empty stretch of sand and scrub. In that it resembles many other kibbutzim, but, unlike the others, it started out as an illegal underground arms factory, some fifty miles south of its present location.

The initial settlement group was formed in 1942 and consisted of members of the scouting youth movement from Jerusalem, Haifa, and Tel Aviv. After agricultural training on several kibbutzim, they were joined by young German immigrants, smuggled out of Europe through Youth Aliya, who were located at Kibbutz Ein Gev on the shores of Lake Kinneret opposite Degania. In 1945 the combined group was sent to a site near Rehovot, fifteen miles south of Tel Aviv, called the "Hill of the Kibbutzim," to become part of the illegal arms manufacturing enterprise of the Hagana Jewish defense force. This was not what they wanted. They were determined to become a fishing village, particularly as some of their members had trained as fishermen in Lake Kinneret, but, as World War

II ended and the Jewish-Arab struggle for Palestine began, waging war—not fishing and farming—was the imperative of the hour.

Beneath the huts and tents of the new kibbutz, a workshop measuring twenty-four by one hundred feet was dug out some twenty feet below ground level. On top of it a bakery and a laundry were established. Entrance to the munitions factory was via a large rotating washing machine and a ten-ton oven that moved on rails. The bakery's smokestack was the munitions plant's air vent; the laundry washed the linen of a local hospital and the uniforms of the British soldiers stationed at a nearby camp, who would certainly have taken drastic action had they known what lay underneath it.

Working in shifts, thirty young men and women of the so-called Ayalon Institute lived a double life. Together with Hagana experts, they labored at their dangerous, unhealthy task. They could only enter and leave the plant at night or early in the morning. They developed a pallor, quite inconsistent with their alleged occupation as farmers, and had to be made up with artificial tans. They had to clean carefully any traces of oil and metal filings on their clothes and disguise the oily smell. The high consumption of electricity was attributed to the ovens and washing machines.

Above ground their colleagues established, in addition to the laundry and bakery, a dairy, poultry branch, carpentry shop, and metal workshop (which provided an alibi for the metal filings and machine oil found on some members). Only people vetted by Hagana intelligence could become members of the kibbutz, and even then new members were only admitted to the secret of the underground plant on a need-to-know basis, when they were required to work shifts.

The main produce of the factory was ammunition for the "Sten" submachine gun, the Hagana's main weapon, which was illegally manufactured at another secret factory. By the time the British army left Palestine in 1948, the new State of Israel was declared, and the war with the local Arab irregulars and the surrounding Arab states began, the plant had manufactured over two million bullets.

The enterprise was almost discovered late in 1947 when the dissident Stern Group blew up a British train within yards of the kibbutz. Only the genuine efforts of the kibbutzniks to assist the British wounded prevented the soldiers who had been rushed to the scene from conducting a thorough search of their village, which was the nearest Jewish settlement. Had they taken a really close look, the troops would surely have discovered the secret plant.

Figure 8.2.   The Plasson factory of Maagan Michael in the 1990s.

Source: (Factory brochure)

During the following year, work was stepped up in the factory, and other members of the kibbutz served in the various Hagana units and then in the new Israel Defense Forces. When the British left and secrecy was no longer essential, the factory was transferred to a new site, becoming the basis of Taas (the Israel Military Industries). The site of the factory reverted to the Weizmann Institute of Science nearby, which established some laboratories there. Today it has been restored as a museum.

In August 1949 the members established Maagan Michael (Michael's Harbor) at its present site on the Mediterranean coast, one of the last settlements on the land of PICA, the Jewish Colonization Association of the Barons Hirsh and Rothschild. In its early years, the kibbutz subsisted on its fish ponds, fruit trees, dairy, poultry, and the wages of its members who still worked for the military industry. Fulfilling its original dream, the kibbutz acquired fishing boats, which were based in Haifa, but here their experience was similar to that of Neve Yam, and they got rid of the vessels in 1960.

In 1964, the Plasson plastics factory was established. The members who worked in the poultry branch and who had to load table birds into the heavy metal cages, which were both heavy and hard on the hands, proposed making plastic cages for the chickens. They also produced automatic drinking troughs for poultry. These were the first products, but the factory swiftly developed into a modern export-based concern, famous for the high quality of its products. Its plastic pipe fittings are used in agriculture, industry, mines, municipal water systems, and gas distribution. With an annual turnover nearing $100 million, an enterprising R & D section, and a highly trained workforce, Plasson has played a role at Maagan Michael similar to that of Netafim at Hatzerim. A decade or so later, the kibbutz established another workshop for the manufacture of printed circuits; today the second factory makes delicate metal equipment for the medical profession and other specialized customers.

For a time, the kibbutz managed without outside labor at Plasson, although the factory worked in three shifts around the clock. Today, though, it has about one hundred hired workers. Nevertheless, each male member of Maagan Michael is required to contribute a week per year, either a night shift on the Plasson production line or guard duty. The women members do not have this obligation, on the assumption that "someone has to be with the children." In addition, members are required to contribute special work days.

Veteran Moshe Berechman, well past retirement age but still working at Plasson, "in ways in which I can make a contribution without treading on the toes of the younger managers," headed the team that produced the "Agreement for Resolving Each Member's Share in the Assets of the Kibbutz." A soft-voiced, gray-haired man who still strides energetically around the kibbutz in a light summer shirt and shorts, Berechman invited me to lunch in the airy dining hall overlooking the Mediterranean.

"We don't have magnetic cards or payment for meals," he told me. "If I hadn't invited you today, there would have been two more slices of turkey breast left over—*so what?*" Moshe sees no point in what other kibbutzim call the "privatization" of the dining hall. Most of the expenses are fixed ones, he notes: labor, air conditioning, lighting, and maintenance. The actual food represents a relatively small proportion of the costs.

Afterward, we sit in the shade on the terrace, overlooking the Mediterranean as he explains the reasons that prompted Maagan Michael to establish a formal link between the members and their ownership of the assets of the kibbutz. Maagan Michael has the reputation of being a conservative kibbutz, he tells me, but in fact it was always open to change. It was among the first kibbutzim to introduce self-service in the dining hall, one of the first to bring the children to sleep at home, and it moved energetically in the direction of rationalizing personal allowances of members.

Although Maagan Michael was not affected by the collapse of 1985, the crisis in the kibbutz movement obviously had its effect. Some members began to talk about differential salaries; others wondered aloud whether the Kibbutz should go on absorbing new members. As a successful community in an idyllic setting, Maagan Michael has a large number of candidates waiting in line to become members, and the kibbutz, which is always short of manpower, notably for Plasson, admits two new families every year.

"There was a lack of logic in the traditional kibbutz system," concedes Moshe. "Before we introduced our new system, a person could apply to join Maagan Michael, go through a year's trial, become a member, and at once he was an owner of our assets on equal terms with somebody who had worked here for fifty years."

Many members did not see why the kibbutz should be so generous about distributing their wealth, but Maagan Michael needs new members. Despite its manifest success, it only keeps around 40 percent of its children—some say as little as a third. So absorption is vital to the future of the kibbutz, and that is one of the reasons for the new ownership formula.

Moshe and his colleagues hope that the new system will also enhance the personal commitment of the members. Although Maagan Michael is a successful kibbutz, with a high work ethic, he thinks that only between 15 and 20 percent of the members really feel complete identity with the kibbutz. The others, for the most part, do their jobs and fulfill their duties, but in a routine manner. Moshe sought a way to make the members realize they were property owners and shore up their feeling of responsibility to the enterprise.

Then, as mentioned, there was the matter of differential salaries. A large majority of the members reject this. Among the veterans, opposition nears 100 percent, but there was talk about how other kibbutzim had introduced it and about how the incentive of higher earnings had increased motivation. The veterans felt that if this idea was even being talked about, it was imperative to factor in the seniority element. The members who had worked up to fifty years creating the wealth were surely entitled to benefit from their labor, before any question of differentials came up.

As we have seen, the model adopted by Maagan Michael was to create the Yam Carmel cooperative, including every member of the kibbutz, with his percentage of ownership relating to his seniority. Veterans, with more than thirty years of membership, have the maximum, a 100 percent share; newcomers start with 3 1/3 percent at the end of their first year of membership, getting an additional 3 1/3 percent for every year of membership, until they, too, reach 100 percent. Members who have been there less than thirty years own a percentage that reflects the number of years they have been members. This way, all the members will eventually become equal owners with the veterans, but the former system, whereby the newcomer at once became a full partner with those who had built up the enterprise for years, has been rationalized. Under the new arrangement, the children of the kibbutz who apply for membership will start with a five-year bonus in recognition of their army service and the years of part-time work on the kibbutz during their schooling.

Under the system introduced at Maagan Michael, the assets have been attributed but not distributed. Everyone knows what they are worth, but for the time being there is no question of a member cashing in his or her share. On the other hand, it is not merely theoretical: the arrangement is in place, waiting to be activated if and when it becomes necessary.

Few kibbutz members are familiar with their constitutions, and not many know of the existence of paragraph 125, which states that if the kibbutz breaks up, any assets remaining after the debts are paid will be transferred to Nir Shitufi, the cooperative of the Agriculture Workers Union. Founded in 1924 within the framework of the Histadrut, Nir Shitufi is an organization to which all kibbutz members belong. It is doubtful whether most kibbutzniks know that they are members of Nir Shitufi—or have even heard of it—but this is the organization that, according to paragraph 125, will inherit their property if their commune disintegrates. Paragraph 125 further stipulates that Nir Shitufi will take care of the needy members of the former kibbutz, such as the minors, the disabled, and the orphans, but after doing this, it will utilize the remaining assets as it sees fit.

In the early days, not all kibbutzim had constitutions, and those that did had ones that were not too carefully phrased. Most kibbutzim acquired formal constitutions in the 1970s based on a standard document drawn up by the kibbutz movements and the Registrar of Cooperative Societies. Every kibbutz accepted the general formulation, and the constitutions of individual kibbutzim are almost identical. Very few kibbutzniks have in the past paid much attention to their constitutions, and certainly not to the paragraphs dealing with what happens if they break up, but in the current situation, the constitution has become relevant. Maagan Michael has amended paragraph 125 so that, in the event of the kibbutz ceasing to be a kibbutz, the assets will not revert to Nir Shitufi but will be distributed to the kibbutz members according to the constitution of the Yam Carmel Cooperative.

Although the model Moshe Berechman and his colleagues have worked out for Maagan Michael clearly separates the kibbutz income from its assets, Moshe scorns the idea of the New Kibbutz to separate business from community.

"What nonsense!" he declares. "When the president of the United States saved Chrysler, did he do it for Chrysler or for the workers of Detroit? All over the world, the barriers between business and community are breaking down. Many businesses are involving themselves in social projects. Why should the kibbutz move in the opposite direction?"

The suggestion that separating the business from the community prevents the community from consuming the assets of its productive branches elicits further scorn. There are foolish people who consume their assets, he notes, and there are wise people who do not. It has nothing to do with the kibbutz as such.

The idea of differential incomes, which was at one time being aired at Maagan Michael and which was one of the incentives for working out the attribution of assets through the Yam Carmel Cooperative, has for the time being dropped out of sight. The income will continue to be distributed on an egalitarian basis, but Moshe Berechman suggests a new formula for this: "Not 'from each according to his ability, to each according to his needs' but 'from each according to his ability, to each according to his *preferences.*'"

This relates more realistically to the modern era, he thinks. In a situation of relative prosperity, it is almost impossible to define needs, but anyone can say what he or she prefers to have, and the kibbutz will endeavor to supply it within the limits of its economic situation.

The home of Aviva and Eli Zamir, an impressive veteran couple, is near the communal dining hall. In most kibbutzim, even the prosperous ones, the usual drink is what Israelis call *botz* (mud). It is crudely ground coffee onto which boiling water is poured, and the result is indeed somewhat muddy although tasty enough. Here, however, sitting in a comfortable armchair, in front of a glass-topped table, I am offered properly brewed coffee. We have already met Eli, a former general secretary of the UKM, in the chapter on the collapse of 1985, and Aviva, a well-known sociologist, in the chapter on education.

With regard to what is happening in Maagan Michael, Eli offers the interpretation that the attribution of assets via Yam Carmel was constructed as a barrier against the collapse of the system. If all members know what they are "worth," he suggests, their anxiety is lessened and they feel less impelled to make radical changes. The young members will be less likely to push for differential salaries, which may bring them personal advantage, if they know that this will be accompanied by an allocation of assets, from which they will not benefit very much.

Looking at the big picture, Eli posits that the kibbutzim failed because there were too many of them, and consequently most of them were too small. Even at Maagan Michael, with its six hundred members, not enough able leaders are available. There are more senior administrative posts than the members can fill. The kibbutzim were placed around the borders of the Jewish community of Palestine and then of the State of Israel to defend them, he notes. Maagan Michael, for example, was established to defend the sea coast. As a result, most kibbutzim have between one hundred and two hundred members, and some had even fewer. They have no chance of succeeding, because there are not enough first-class people in a community of that size. Although he acknowledges that some small kibbutzim succeeded and some large ones failed, he sees size as a very crucial factor.

Another important element was the attitude to the individual. Today the rights of the individual members are recognized in all kibbutzim, but in the past there was a "brutal ideology of sacrifice" in many settlements. Kibbutz leaders stated baldly that the individual must be prepared to suffer for the common cause. Eli recounts an incident in the early days of the Maagan Michael group, before they settled at their present site. A musically talented member won a scholarship to study in Jerusalem, at the only academy in the country at that time. The matter was brought to the general meeting, where, after a long and lively discussion, the vote was in favor of his studying. He was also allocated living expenses, although the group had very little money at the time.

"Kibbutz Meuhad sent a special delegation to ask us if we had gone out of our minds," recalls Eli with a laugh.

Aviva adds an anecdote about the first member of Maagan Michael to receive a radio as a present:

"We arranged that the set would be rotated among our members; another kibbutz 'solved' the same problem by putting the radio in the store under lock and key."

Although these stories may seem trivial, Eli and Aviva are both convinced that those kibbutzim that gave due consideration to the needs of the individual member were the more successful. At the same time, Aviva, who has conducted many interviews with kibbutz members in the course of her work, also believes that today the most contented members are found in those kibbutzim that preserve the traditional framework.

"I'm not an ideologue," she emphasizes. "All my children have left Maagan Michael, and I don't regard that as a tragedy, but I think a kibbutz should be a kibbutz. In kibbutzim which have made too many changes, there is uncertainty, frustration, and disappointment."

She adds an interesting comment about the income differentials being introduced in other kibbutzim: if the members' salaries are being evaluated by outside experts "according to the market," this must discriminate against the women members. Not only do Israeli women get paid less for performing the same tasks as men, but many of the jobs traditionally performed by women—cooking, cleaning, sewing, typing, nursing, teaching , psychology, and social work—earn less than "male" occupations. If a kibbutz introduces differential pay according to the market value of the jobs, its women members will suffer.

Irit Sherman is the coordinator for human resources of Maagan Michael. There was no such position in the traditional kibbutz, but many kibbutzim, including those faithful to the classical structure, have introduced the position in the past decade. It represents a further tilt in the balance toward considering the needs of the individual and away from emphasizing the good of the community. Irit is the first incumbent at Maagan Michael, and she spent the first two years working out what her actual job was. A year ago, the relevant committee reached its conclusion, and now she hopes she will "survive" another three years in the job.

Irit was born during the Rehovot period, when the group was manufacturing illegal arms, and she came to Maagan Michael as an infant. She has two history degrees and has been a teacher for most of her career, later specializing in enrichment courses. She also worked for a time at the Holocaust Museum at Lohamei Hagettaot, a kibbutz founded by survivors from the wartime ghettoes of Europe.

The main task of the coordinator for human resources is to find suitable places of work for the members of Maagan Michael, taking into consideration the needs of the kibbutz. Formerly, the work coordinator (a position now abolished) assigned jobs on the basis of need, only considering the wishes of the individual member as a secondary factor. After many discussions, the Human Resources Committee came up with a formulation that "the member of Maagan Michael is responsible for his work." She stresses the word *avoda* (work) as opposed to *parnassa* (living or livelihood), which has been adopted by many kibbutzim. Maagan Michael, she explains, is still responsible for the livelihood of its members.

Members are supposed to find their own work, but Irit will help them. Some members still treat her as a labor exchange, but most appreciate the nature of her role. The needs of the kibbutz are important, and clearly sometimes compromises are made, but the emphasis is on making sure that the individual has satisfying and rewarding work. In addition to the human resources coordinator, there is a manpower coordinator, and the two of them sit on a four-member committee with the kibbutz general manager and the coordinator of services. It is this committee that has to give formal permission to a member to take up work outside the kibbutz.

"In the old days, people worked where they were assigned," notes Irit. "Today in many kibbutzim they work wherever they wish. At Maagan Michael we are trying to find a 'golden mean.' We neither encourage nor discourage members to work outside, but we are always short of manpower, particularly at Plasson, so if a member wants to work outside he has to get permission from our committee. In fact, we almost never turn anyone down."

Irit regrets missing "by about five years" the experience of traveling the world, which later became almost universal for kibbutz youth after their army service, but in her day it was not the done thing. After her military service, she wanted to study, and the only sure way at that time was to agree to become a teacher. As it turned out, she enjoyed teaching. Satisfied in her work, she has never felt frustrated as a woman or as a mother. She accepted communal sleeping and the change to family sleeping, but it was never a big issue for her. She has good memories of her childhood and does not think she has more complexes than a child who slept at home.

According to Irit, Maagan Michael is a very conservative society. Changes do happen but take a long time, and it is extremely difficult to get things approved at the general meeting. After the introduction of individual pensions for the members was approved by the kibbutz general meeting, a proposal for an extra savings fund, to enable members to assist their children who have left, was turned down. In due course, it was brought back to the general meeting in a more modest format and approved.

Irit supports the action taken on the attribution of assets because "if we do break up, there won't be a general scramble for the property." She thinks a collapse is unlikely but cannot totally rule it out. Her impression is that most of the young people at Maagan Michael want to maintain the kibbutz system, although along with that they demand more personal responsibility for their lives. She freely admits that she herself is less certain about the kibbutz way of life than her parents and their generation are.

"I don't think that the kibbutz is a natural way of life," she confesses. "I am not sure it is possible in today's world. I have many question marks. Outside the kibbutz you are dependent on money; inside you are dependent on people. You don't make all your own decisions, and you have to identify strongly with the way of life."

Many people have joined the kibbutz over the years for various reasons. They were attracted to the quality of life, or they were running away from the rat race, but those reasons are not ideological. The members should ask themselves whether the kibbutz has any added value. In the past, Maagan Michael sometimes showed a disregard for personal rights. In any society there is a conflict of interests between the individual and the community; but in a kibbutz it is more extreme. At the same time, there is the feeling of being part of something bigger than yourself.

"Everything that exists in human society exists on the kibbutz. Maybe we have managed to live with less violence and crime." She smiles and knocks on the wooden table. "But the positive and the negative are always with you."

Irit served on the Team for Change and feels that Maagan Michael may not stop with the current dormant attribution of assets. Despite its inherent conservatism, she does not discount the possibility that the kibbutz will go further in altering its structure.

When Ada Gross was a toddler, she repeatedly ran home from the children's house, until her mother defied kibbutz custom and took her home to sleep. That did not happen at Maagan Michael but at Sarid, a settlement of the left-wing Kibbutz Artzi movement, where the rules were even stricter.

Ada left her own kibbutz after army service. She traveled the world, spent some years in a very radical kibbutz called Kerem Shalom, which subsequently collapsed, lived with her husband in Europe, came back to Israel, settled in Haifa, and then decided to return to kibbutz life.

"My mother never accepted communal sleeping," says Ada, with a touch of defiance. "And nor do I. I would have returned to Sarid fifteen years ago; but I was not prepared to put my daughter into the children's house. No way!"

So she and her husband Yair came to Maagan Michael, where they had friends and where their skills were needed. She works as head of quality control at the Plasson factory; Yair is a production engineer there.

She thinks that communal sleeping is very harmful and that those who grew up that way simply don't realize how much harm it did them. Or possibly, she suggests, they do not want to know, locking away their memories in a corner. She is convinced that strengthening the family also strengthens the group.

"People should not be too much in each other's pockets," she says. "We need a strong community, but a community of families, with autonomy and privacy. It is more natural that way."

She opposes the introduction of differential incomes, believing that it only happens in failing kibbutzim, where the few strong members take advantage of their weaker comrades. Nevertheless, she thinks that Maagan Michael would survive it.

"The kibbutz will carry on, even if there are differentials," she asserts. "It won't destroy it any more than the electric kettle or family sleeping destroyed it."

Regarding the attribution of assets, she shrugs her shoulders. "I always say that, if we get to the stage of breaking up, it will be debts that we distribute—not assets!"

Ada's children, damp haired from a pool party, come in as we talk, taking snacks from the refrigerator. She would like her children to live at Maagan Michael when they grow up but only after a period living away from the kibbutz, as she herself did. She does not want them simply to stay on. It must be a conscious decision.

One the whole, she thinks that Maagan Michael has achieved the right balance between family and community, but, like Irit, she complains about the conservatism of the kibbutz. She is pushing hard for a flexible working week and is extremely frustrated that she cannot get it through the general meeting. Some years ago, magnetic cards were introduced at Plasson and subsequently at every workplace in the kibbutz, so everyone's hours are recorded. She cannot understand why members should not be free to work a five-day week, provided they put in the requisite hours.

Yuval Tzur is also worrying about the organizational structure of Maagan Michael; but from a different angle. He wants to utilize technology to make sure that the members receive accurate information about what is going on at the kibbutz. He acknowledges that the old methods worked in the past—office holders making decisions, committee discussions, the general meeting—but thinks that something else is needed today. He has no wish to tamper with the egalitarian and communal nature of the kibbutz; he simply wants to bring it up-to-date.

Large, crop haired, dressed in a tank top and shorts, Yuval does not look like a computer whiz kid. He does look like the manager of the kibbutz banana plantation, a job he has held for the past three years, expanding it and doubling its income. He is already late for a meeting of his Structural Reorganization Committee, but he takes the time to talk about Maagan Michael as he sees it.

"Generally speaking, there is no better place than a kibbutz, and particularly this kibbutz, for living a balanced and dynamic life," he proclaims. "If there is a better division between work, family, and social life, I haven't found it."

Yuval left Maagan Michael after his army service and supported himself through his studies in agriculture and economics at the Hebrew University, although the kibbutz did pay his tuition fees. He married, ran a small gardening business, and started raising his children.

"I came back to the kibbutz because I did not want to spend fifteen years establishing myself and then have my daughter ask me who I was," he explains. "I have put the bananas on a sound footing. Now, if I want, I can become a schoolteacher, for example, without it affecting my standard of living in the tiniest respect. Where else in the world can you find a way of life that gives you that?"

Yuval is looking for modern methods of preserving the old kibbutz values and "liberating the energy" of the members. He wants to see a nonhierarchical cooperative structure, with the maximum participation of everyone. The kibbutz can be networked, with everyone having access to all possible information via computer.

"We are a huge business today," he points out. "It's difficult to mobilize everyone, to liberate the energy from below; but there is no reason why information cannot be made available in real time in a form that you don't have to be a genius to understand. Knowledge will lead to involvement."

Yuval is not opposed to increasing the money (or the leisure) at the disposal of the members. Like Ada, he is in favor of a flexible working week, and if someone wants to earn a little extra in his or her spare time, he sees nothing wrong with that. A counterargument is that the sick or disabled member cannot do this. Of course, the disadvantaged must be looked after, he says, but that does not mean "castrating" the rest of the membership. He supports the attribution of assets via the Yam Carmel cooperative, because it encourages the absorption of new members, which is vital for the kibbutz. Many kibbutz children leave, he notes, and the kibbutz cannot survive without new members joining.

"The bottom line is that everyone in Maagan Michael can live from cradle to grave with honor," he affirms. "There are no poor or neglected, as in other places. We have to preserve that basic reality."

He realizes that many members feel shackled by kibbutz life but believes this is largely psychological. The members of Maagan Michael are freer than they realize, he suggests; they just have to learn to take advantage of their freedom.

"If someone wants to start a business in town, doesn't he have to run to the bank with loan guarantors?" he demands. "So here he has to apply to the relevant committee—big deal!"

Moran Yahalom, some ten years younger than Yuval, does not agree.

"With all the advantages of kibbutz life, you are still not autonomous," she insists.

> Approval for studying my undergraduate degree was automatic, but I had to get permission to study for my second degree. I am not completely free to spend my allowance as I want. Even my food is decided for me by someone else. I am dependent on the general meeting.
>
> It is scary: twenty years down the line, if things go wrong, I could be left with nothing. I know that I can fail in town, but at least it depends on me. Today the members of Maagan Michael are a marvelous group, but in twenty years time I could be totally dependent on people I don't even respect!

Tanned, athletic, brimming with health, Moran is the quintessential kibbutz child. She is debating with herself and her boyfriend, Gil, whether to become a member. At present she lives at Maagan Michael, with the rights of a daughter of the kibbutz. She puts in an agreed number of hours work every week and studies for her second psychology degree at the expense of the kibbutz. Gil, as her companion, has the same conditions, except that he has to pay his own tuition fees at medical school.

Moran grew up in a group, with pressure on the members to prove that they were the best group. She was one of the prominent members, who took it on themselves to lead the group to maximum achievement.

"As a result, I've had enough of it," she declares. "I want to worry about myself. I am prepared to take on specific tasks, but I am not going to be responsible for other people's lives. I won't decide for them."

She admits that she would find it impossible to replicate elsewhere the standard of living and the quality of life she enjoys on the kibbutz, but she still hesitates about making the commitment.

"It's probably my fault that I haven't really learned about the attribution of assets," she admits, "but I would definitely like to see even more radical changes. If Maagan Michael were a normal village, I would stay without the slightest hesitation."

At the same time, she says, she grew up with socialism, and some of it has "stuck to me." She would like the community to maintain services for health and education and also have a fund to help the weaker members, but she does not see the point of the huge cooperative enterprise.

"Despite my views, I don't want to become a member and then fight to change things," she says.

"Why not? Are you in a minority?"

"No, I don't think so—at least not in my age group." She smiles, embarrassed. "I suppose it shows that I have got used to thinking that young people's opinions are not important. Maagan Michael is a small society, and the hierarchy of age is very important."

She is sure that the kibbutz will only change very slowly, and paradoxically she is glad of that. She does not want to see hasty decisions. Even if she does not stay, she emphasizes, she cares deeply about the kibbutz and wants it to prosper.

Moran is planning to marry her boyfriend next month. The two of them met at a friend's wedding. Gil had no previous experience of kibbutz life. He was not even in a youth movement. He admits to finding Maagan Michael very strange at first.

"I went to visit Moran when she was working at Plasson." he recalls. "It was Saturday morning, and suddenly all these kibbutzniks appeared on their bicycles to work for a *giyuss* [special shift]. I respect them for it. They realize that they have to work for what they have here. At the same time there are things I would like to see changed. There is still too much intrusion by the community into the private life of the individual."

Gil does not rule out the idea of applying for membership of Maagan Michael. He finds much that is admirable in the kibbutz, and not just the material things. He is impressed with the education of the children and the quality of life. As an outsider, he is conscious of the debate among the children of the kibbutz, and his impression is that even those who are in favor of preserving the basic kibbutz way of life want quite a few changes.

He has been accepted into Moran's group in a friendly way but admits he still finds some of the "codes and assumptions" difficult to understand. He is amazed at the vitality of their peer group. Gil spent a few hours every day with his classmates at school, and then it was over. Clearly the group was something much bigger for Moran and her contemporaries at the kibbutz than it was for him.

"The younger children are different though," says Gil. "My impression is that today's school kids at Maagan Michael are very like the ones I grew up with. The differences between town and kibbutz children have narrowed."

It is difficult to assess whether the attribution of assets at Maagan Michael, the kibbutz divorce settlement, will help the kibbutz maintain its communal egalitarian way of life. There are certainly many changes that the kibbutz can make without harming its basic values. Better information, a flexible working week, and even more personal autonomy— these changes do not have to sabotage the underlying ethic.

The members spent about four years discussing the attribution of assets through the Yam Carmel cooperative. They will probably need at least the same amount of time to absorb the implications of the new setup. After that, there could be changes even in this conservative community.

Will Maagan Michael one day actually allocate or distribute its assets, instead of merely attributing them? Only time will tell, but other experiments are taking place in the kibbutz movement. In our next chapter we will visit a kibbutz that has gone much further than Maagan Michael, distributing its assets and re-creating itself as a capitalist enterprise, with its members as shareholders.

9

כפר רופין

KFAR RUPPIN
CAPITALIST KIBBUTZ

"Capitalism is the exploitation of man by man; socialism is exactly the opposite!"

A visit to Kfar Ruppin, a sixty-two-year-old kibbutz in the Beit Shean Valley, puts one in mind of this old anarchist joke. The kibbutz has turned its industrial and agricultural branches into limited companies, established a holding company for them, and distributed shares to its members on the basis of seniority. As of January 1, 1999, the kibbutzniks of Kfar Ruppin are capitalists in every sense of the word, but to find any difference between their way of life yesterday and their way of life today, one would need a powerful magnifying glass. Tomorrow, of course, is another matter. In time, things may change considerably; then again, they may not.

Many other kibbutzim are watching Kfar Ruppin to see how it works out; some are already preparing to follow its example. More than one observer of the kibbutz scene predicts that Kfar Ruppin is the face of the kibbutz future. It is certainly *one* of the faces; there is no doubt that others will also try the capitalist option.

In fact, a capitalist commune is not a historical first. In 1932, the Amana commune, seven villages in Iowa in the United States, went through a remarkably similar process. Amana was a German Christian sect, the members of which settled in the United States in the previous century, led by inspirational charismatic leaders. Although there was no democracy and the elders ran the communities with an iron hand, the joint economy was organized like the kibbutz on communal egalitarian lines. Initially, the villages managed to keep themselves relatively iso-lated, but as the outside world burst in, the Amana villagers went through a process in the first three decades of the century comparable to that expe-rienced by the kibbutzniks in the past three decades. Barbara Yambura, who grew up in Amana, has recorded in *A Change and a Parting* the wan-ing influence of the elders, the growth of materialism, the feeling that many members were not pulling their weight, and the abandoning of the communal ethic. Following a referendum, the communal set up was reconstituted as the Amana Society, a modified stock corporation with class A (voting) stock for the adult members and prior distributive (own-ership) shares, allocated according to the number of years of service.

As we shall see, there are many similarities in the path adopted by Kfar Ruppin, so what the kibbutz has done is not unprecedented, but it is a revolution in Israeli terms: nothing remotely like it has ever been carried out by a kibbutz until now.

"It's strange," remarks veteran Rachel Noy. "Many of our founders were German Jews, and we were always known as 'the *Yekke* Kibbutz,' very conventional, never stepping out of line. Suddenly we find our-selves the innovators."

Not many people would have predicted that Kfar Ruppin would be the first to take such drastic action. The conventional wisdom is that in the current situation, the weak are the trailblazers; the kibbutzim in cri-sis are those leading the charge. But Kfar Ruppin does not fit this pat-tern. Not a financial giant, like Hatzerim or Maagan Michael, it is nev-ertheless economically healthy, with more than enough income to pay its relatively modest debts.

"We have a very good leadership cadre," explains David Glazner, a second-generation member of Kfar Ruppin and former schoolteacher. "We always had the capacity to look ahead and deal with problems before they emerged. The founders were from Germany and Czecho-slovakia. I like to say that they combined a German sense of order with a Slavic heart."

This may be so, but in the early years the two groups clashed in an explosive confrontation that almost blew the young kibbutz apart.

"**T**he Banativ Affair" is still traumatic for those who lived through it. For fifty years the subject was taboo, and, even ten years ago, when Rachel Noy wrote a paper on the event for her course as an archivist, many members still found it painful to talk about it. At the same time, it has been argued that it guaranteed the success of the kibbutz.

Figure 9.1.   Kfar Ruppin in 1939.

Source: (Israel Government Press Office)

The founders of Kfar Ruppin were young refugees from Germany and Austria who arrived in Palestine in 1933 and 1934. They initially lived near Herzliya, north of Tel Aviv, where they found work in the citrus orchards. Gradually, the young people coalesced into a group, which they called Massad (Foundation). In 1937, looking for a spot to establish a new settlement, they arrived in the Beit Shean valley, nearly a thousand feet below sea level, where the temperatures regularly reach over forty degrees centigrade in summer (with fifty-four degrees recorded one August!).

Massad was aligned with Hever Hakvutzot, the association of small kibbutzim, such as Degania, some fifteen miles to the north. Not content with choosing one of the most climatically hostile regions in the country, the youngsters of Massad insisted on a swampy site on the banks of the River Jordan, several miles from the nearest existing settlement point, and moved there in November 1938. In addition to the extreme heat and humidity, there were the mosquitoes, including the deadly malaria-causing anopheles. Most of the members caught malaria, all of them were affected by the heat, and their morale was not improved by reports of the persecution of the Jews coming out of Germany, where many of them still had families. Several joined the British army, feeling they had to do their bit against Hitler; others simply left, unable to bear the harsh conditions.

Dr. Arthur Ruppin, whose support had been so crucial to Massad (as well as to virtually all the settlement groups until then) died, and the members chose the name Kfar Ruppin (Ruppin's Village) in his memory. They established their *kvutza,* with the usual tents and huts, and even one permanent building, but their initial attempts at farming were not too successful. Their main problem was a shortage of members, and they repeatedly issued appeals to their movement, Hever Hakvutzot, to send them reinforcements. With many young people mobilized to the British army and most settlements sparsely populated, there was not much manpower available, but in due course, they were sent a Czech pioneer group called Banativ (On the Way).

Whereas the Massad youngsters came to Palestine on an individual basis and gradually developed into a settlement group, the kernel of Banativ was a strongly welded unit of the Young Maccabi youth movement, its members passionate believers in socialism and Zionism. The first group arrived in Palestine in 1938 "illegally," and they were followed by another "illegal" group that was detained by the British and sent to the Pacific island of Mauritius. Other youth movement graduates from Czechoslovakia and Germany, including some who managed to escape from Europe, joined Banativ, which gained a reputation as a hardworking, strongly motivated group, determined to found its own kibbutz.

In 1942, Banativ acceded to the urgings of Hever Hakvutzot to give up their ambition of founding their own settlement—at least temporarily—and come to the aid of Kfar Ruppin. Still in their twenties, they were not too pleased with some of their new comrades of the Massad group, who were ten years older than them and who behaved in a manner of which they disapproved. After several years in the blistering heat, the Massad members were tired. They guarded their privacy, sometimes ate in their rooms, hoarded food parcels, did not always turn up to general meetings, and—horror of horrors(!)—were known to play cards. Nevertheless, the Banativ members felt drawn to Kfar Ruppin and to the pioneering challenge of the location. They remained at the kibbutz but jealously guarded their independent group life, keeping themselves separate from the Massad people.

Then, with what today seems breathtaking arrogance, Banativ prepared a list of those members of Massad with whom they were not prepared to live. They announced that they would only remain if these "unsuitable" members were transferred to other kibbutzim. Although Hever Hakvutzot was unhappy about this "hit list," hours of fierce discussions did not manage to secure its abolition, only its reduction from eighteen to fifteen, and finally to nine. When it became clear that about half of the members of Massad wanted Banativ to join them despite this humiliating condition, the nine members remaining on the list announced that they would not stand in the way of the union of Massad and Banativ but would leave voluntarily. A further eleven, who were not on the list, said they would also leave, and in April 1943 the remaining twenty-nine members of Massad were formally joined by sixty members of Banativ.

In a letter written at the time, Aharon Zinger of the Massad group tried to explain to the soldier-members of Kfar Ruppin, who were serving away from the kibbutz, what had happened. The letter is replete with expressions of scorn for the young newcomers and outrage at their demand.

"Each individual is a decent likable youngster," wrote Zinger, "but as a collective they are fanatical, egotistic, really wild beasts. They see themselves as a chosen elite."

Yosef Baratz and Tanhum Tanpilov came from Degania to try to help with the problem, and Zinger described how they all sat and debated from eight in the evening until four the following morning, without reaching a conclusion. However, the Massad people were in a bind. They lacked confidence in their future, fearing inevitable decline without reinforcements. The chance of being strengthened by one of the most dynamic groups of young people in the country was difficult to forgo. Reluctantly they gave way.

"The Massad group has ceased to exist," wrote Zinger sadly. "We became what we are through weakness. We did not know how to build a strong group."

Members of both groups feel the trauma of what happened six decades ago to this day.

"We felt guilty about it for many years," a veteran of Massad told Rachel Noy when she composed her paper. "How did we agree to the Banativ conditions, and how did we agree to go on living with them? It is difficult for me to think about it. We were terribly insulted." Later he added, "To be fair, from the moment of the union, the Banativ people recognized us as the founders of the kibbutz and treated us with the utmost respect."

Another said that the list had not surprised the members of Massad. The people on it were marginal members who did not contribute to the group.

"We would never have got rid of them by ourselves, but Kfar Ruppin would not have achieved what it did if the decision had not been implemented."

The Banativ people also look back on the affair with mixed feelings.

"We were young," explained one of them. "We dreamed of an ideal society. We did not know then that it was impossible to achieve."

Another was unrepentant: "We had to do what we did in those circumstances. I would do the same today, although it was a difficult and ruthless decision."

"It was a demand that I am ashamed of, although I was one of the most emphatic of the demanders," said another veteran of Banativ. "Only fanatical youngsters without experience could have made such a demand."

It is, of course, impossible to say what would have happened if the Banativ Affair had not occurred. In any event, the unified group proved dynamic and successful. Kfar Ruppin became a prosperous kibbutz, overcoming the extreme harshness of its physical conditions, but the incident left its scars beneath the surface. A decade before the famous split in Kibbutz Hameuhad, Kfar Ruppin was born in the sin of its own minisplit. The idealistic presumption and intellectual fanaticism of Banativ presaged what was to happen in other kibbutzim ten years later.

Today Kfar Ruppin has the look and feel of a successful kibbutz. Well laid-out public buildings, including a pleasant, airy dining hall, are set in spectacular gardens. The heat and the plentiful water from the Jordan have combined to produce a sort of manicured jungle. There is a profusion of vegetation that exceeds even other veteran kibbutzim: more trees, more shrubs, more flowers, greener lawns. The heat is oppressive, even to an Israeli used to hot summers, but today the ubiquitous air conditioner alleviates the worst temperatures.

Like Degania, Kfar Ruppin and its Beit Shean valley neighbors had to fight Arab forces in 1948, but thereafter it experienced relative quiet until the Six Day War of 1967. In that war, Israeli forces captured the West Bank, which had been part of the Kingdom of Jordan. After it, the Palestinian Liberation Organization waged a War of Attrition from across the Jordan, and Kfar Ruppin was in the front line. The kibbutz children slept in the shelters for three years under intermittent shelling. High barbed-wire fences were erected and a patrol road was constructed

Figure 9.2.   Kfar Ruppin in the 1980s.

Source: (Yad Tabenkin Archives)

to prevent infiltration and mine laying. The dining hall was hit by a shell and had to be rebuilt.

At the same time the kibbutz continued to prosper with field crops, dates, citrus, dairy, poultry, and an extremely successful fish-farming branch, which today produces over nine hundred tons of carp, mullet, and St. Peter's fish per year. Kfar Ruppin's Palkar Plastics factory manufactures PVC components for roofs, fences, garden furniture, and educational toys, with annual exports worth $3.5 million. A relatively new branch is ornamental fish, which is also geared to exports. Unlike many other kibbutzim, Kfar Ruppin weathered the crisis of 1985 with little trouble, its debts manageable, its income more than adequate to cover them.

There was one perennial problem: as in its earliest days, the kibbutz suffered from a shortage of members. Paradoxically, the Massad-Banativ union was so successful that they were never reinforced with new members from the youth movements, as the movement's settlement groups were directed to "weaker" kibbutzim. Although several groups did undergo their training and army service at Kfar Ruppin, and some of them even expressed a strong desire to remain there, Hever Hakvutzot always sent them to other kibbutzim, where they were needed more urgently. In addition, Kfar Ruppin, relatively isolated and unbearably hot, found it difficult to attract newcomers on an individual basis.

Today 440 people live at Kfar Ruppin, of whom 240 are members, candidate-members, and children serving in the army. There are 170 children who have not yet reached military age. The rest are parents of members, new immigrants, and nonmember residents. The active membership must be calculated lower, as many of the soldiers will not return after their army service. Like all kibbutzim, Kfar Ruppin loses a large proportion of its children.

"Actual distance is not a factor anymore," explains a member. "Tel Aviv, Haifa, and Jerusalem are all within reach by car in a couple of hours, but there is still the *feeling* of being isolated. This has consolidated us as a community, but it has also driven many of the kids away."

The desire to hold on to more of its children—not the financial situation—is undoubtedly one of the main motivations behind the changes at Kfar Ruppin, which is reasonable.

"We are doing it from a position of strength," stresses Etan Yatziv, the kibbutz treasurer. "We have been able to ask ourselves the question 'What do we want?' rather than 'What can we do?' "

Etan means "strong, enduring" in Hebrew; Yatziv means "stable, solid." It is rare to find someone whose name suits him so well. In his forties, Etan Yatziv is a stocky gray-haired man, relaxed and confident, with an engaging sense of humor. He tells a joke about a newly independent colony that decides to celebrate its liberation from the British Empire by resolving to have its citizens drive on the right-hand side of the road, instead of the left. To give the citizens time to get used to the change, the government decides that in the first stage, only trucks will travel on the right.

"We think that introducing pay differentials without dealing with the question of assets is a 'trucks only' policy," he states. "We think it is liable to lead to dangerous accidents."

Reputedly less than enthusiastic about the changes, Etan proved to be an exceptionally articulate exponent of the process. The failure to keep their children at home was only one of the factors, he told me; there was also a loss of commitment and involvement. Many of the members had stopped feeling that Kfar Ruppin was theirs.

"The way of life our parents created sixty years ago was fine for the young," he remarks. "I don't think they realized that they were going to grow old one day. When you are young, everything belongs to everyone, and needs are very similar. Older people are more egotistic, more family centered."

The members sought a model that would continue with the positive features of communal life, that would foster identity between member and collective and increase motivation. They were determined to find an inclusive solution, one that dealt with all the aspects and that would work economically.

The question of differential incomes was tackled first, but it was implemented on a very moderate scale, and it was made clear that the question of personal ownership of the kibbutz assets would follow quickly on its heels. Unlike Hasolelim, where the members agreed to complete salary differentials, at Kfar Ruppin they resolved on four components of reward for effort: seniority, overtime, branch benefit, and salary evaluation. As the veterans were less likely to benefit from the other elements, seniority was the first to be factored into the equation. Every veteran receives a bonus according to his seniority. Overtime with pay was permitted, but only in a branch other than that where the member worked regularly.

"We didn't want people sleeping on the job and then putting in for overtime to complete it," cracked Etan with a chuckle.

The overtime work includes tasks hitherto performed by outside workers and special shifts for such tasks as loading a batch of meat poultry, filling extra orders from the factory, working additional nursing shifts, and giving private tuition to the schoolchildren.

The next element is connected to the branch where the member works. If the branch makes a profit, those who work there get a bonus. The fourth element relates to the value of the job performed. As in other kibbutzim, those working outside know exactly what they earn, and, as in other kibbutzim, a consultant was brought in to evaluate the jobs performed on the kibbutz. Those earning above the standard initially received an increment of 3 percent, later increased to 6 percent.

As 60 percent of the kibbutz spending is still collective, for health, education, housing, and community services, the marginal differentials listed earlier relate to only 40 percent of the budget. Consequently, Kfar Ruppin is still pretty egalitarian with regard to income. The document approving the changes states clearly that differentials must be limited, and every member must receive enough "to live with self-respect." With characteristic caution, the kibbutz first reduced the overall monthly allocation by 10 percent to finance the various increments. The rest was supposed to come from increased productivity, resulting from improved motivation.

"We found that production did in fact increase," remarks Etan. "If I suggested that this is because of the new system, some members would throw stones at me, so I don't. On the other hand, you can't argue with success."

Two years were required to pass the income adjustments through the various discussion groups, committees, and finally the kibbutz general meeting. The allocation of assets, which involved changing about fifty clauses in the constitution of the kibbutz, took two more years.

The earning branches of the kibbutz were divided into three: the factory, the fish farm, and the remaining agricultural branches. The factory and the fish farm became limited companies; the rest of the agriculture became a cooperative. The reason for the cooperative is that the dairy is an important and profitable branch, and, under the current Israeli farming regime, milk quotas cannot be transferred to limited companies. At the same time, a new agreement was reached with the kibbutz's banks, whereby the three companies have replaced the kibbutz as the official debtors.

A holding company was established for the three enterprises, and the shares were divided up according to the formula of 26 percent to the kibbutz as a collective, 74 percent to the members as individuals. In addition, each member was awarded one nontransferable voting share, and the kibbutz received twenty-six voting shares.

Before the share allocation was worked out, old debts to the members were taken care of. First, all members received an allocation for each of their children, to replace the severance pay currently given by the kibbutz to all leavers. Second, anyone who previously handed in assets to the kibbutz (in most cases German reparation payments for the families of Holocaust victims) was paid back, to the extent of three annual allocations, with any balance being given in the form of shares.

Once that was taken care of, the 74 percent of the shares were divided as follows: half on the basis of absolute equality, half on the basis of seniority. Here again, we see an equalization mechanism, because the veterans, who generally earn less, will own more property.

On June 25, 1998, the Team for the Allocation of Assets brought to the general meeting of Kfar Ruppin a proposal to approve in principle the establishment of the limited companies, the cooperative, and the holding company. The necessary changes in the kibbutz constitution were proposed at a later stage. Changing the constitution required a majority of 75 percent. The general meeting eventually approved the new model with a majority of over 90 percent, and on January 1, 1999, the members of Kfar Ruppin became its owners, with shares officially registered in their own names.

To allow the new system to begin smoothly, the whole arrangement is frozen for six years, although this period may be shortened by a decision of the general meeting. During the freeze, the shares are held for the members by a specially established trustee company. The members can bequeath their property shares, but not their voting shares. During the period of the freeze, heirs will not be able to sell their shares. They will be registered to them and held by the trustee. They will not, of course, inherit a voting share.

After the period of the freeze, the members will be able to trade a proportion of their property shares, but the kibbutz as a collective will have first preference, and the individual members second preference. Every member must hold a specified minimum of shares, and no member may acquire more than 13.5 percent of the total.

As noted, the voting shares are not transferable. The only way to acquire a voting share is to become a member. The procedure of attaining membership remains unchanged: a year's probation, followed by a vote of the general meeting, accepting the candidate as a member. Under the new system, however, the new member will have to buy into the kibbutz, acquiring 25 percent of the share allocation of the current members. This also applies to kibbutz children. New members who do not have sufficient resources to buy the shares will receive a loan from the kibbutz at a reasonable rate of interest, which they will have to pay back out of their monthly allocation and bonuses. If, in the future, Kfar Ruppin's holding company pays dividends, these can of course also be used to pay back the debt to the kibbutz.

Apart from the 74 percent of voting shares owned by the members, the kibbutz has 26 percent of the shares as a collective. These twenty-six votes are cast by the kibbutz secretary, with the authority of the management committee and ultimately of the general meeting. As the shares will be tradable, 74 percent of the ownership of the kibbutz can, in theory, be acquired by an outsider, but as the kibbutz and its members have the first option to purchase shares that become available, this is extremely unlikely. Moreover the outsider cannot acquire voting shares.

Today, members who decide to leave Kfar Ruppin receive severance pay according to a standard worked out by the kibbutz. After the freeze is over, departing members will relinquish their voting share and will be free to sell their property shares. As Kfar Ruppin is a successful economic concern, there is no reason that the shares will not be salable, but some members may be unwilling to go through the hassle of selling them, so the kibbutz guarantees to buy back these shares at 70 percent of their value, as assessed by an outside accountant.

A notable feature of the new system is that if children of the kibbutz leave, their parents can sell some of their shares, provided they keep the mandatory minimum, and give them the money to help them on their way. Kibbutz children are, of course, entitled to severance pay, which in the future will be in the form of a proportion of their parents' shares, but often this is insufficient. One of the big frustrations of kibbutz veterans in recent years has been their inability to assist their children who leave. They may be living at a relatively high standard but have very little ready cash. The new Kfar Ruppin model offers a solution to what has been an extremely painful problem. (It will be recalled that Maagan Michael established a special fund for the purpose of helping children who leave, and Hatzerim permits members to disburse a percentage of their inheritance to assist their children who live outside the kibbutz.)

The Registrar of Cooperative Societies is currently looking into the question of definitions. That office may decide the change the status of Kfar Ruppin from "kibbutz" to something else, in which case the basis for paying income tax will be changed. Kfar Ruppin's economic team has carried out a number of simulation exercises, concluding that there will not be a significant difference in the income tax paid if the basis of calculation is changed.

Like Hasolelim, Kfar Ruppin still regards itself as a kibbutz, albeit of a different type. It is clear that, even if it is now a capitalist enterprise, it is a community that continues to enjoy a large measure of equality. It should be mentioned that, along with the changes, a special committee has been established to ensure that the kibbutz continues to look after those of its children with special needs, including the setting up of a mutual fund for the purpose.

"Absolute equality was a utopian idea that never worked," maintains Etan. "We are trying to work this out as fairly as possible. We are lucky that we are in a reasonable economic position. We are able to allocate assets because we have them. If we were heavily in debt like many kibbutzim, we couldn't do it."

One thing missing from the allocation of assets is the house of the individual member. The reason is that at Kfar Ruppin, with its geographic and climatic disadvantages, the houses are not worth very much.

"We started with our most valuable assets, our productive branches," explains Etan. "Another kibbutz, situated near a large town, may be sitting on valuable land, and they may do it the other way around. Our process is suitable for the specific conditions of Kfar Ruppin."

Other items have not been included in the new economic structure at this stage. Income from renting homes to residents is still paid directly to the kibbutz, as is any income from admitting outside children to the school or kindergartens. Kfar Ruppin's growing tourism branch, which specializes in tourism for bird-watchers, also belongs to the community, not the companies. This could change in time. The kibbutz remains the lessee of the land from the state and rents it to the companies. It supplies water and manpower to the companies. The kibbutz derives its income from the rent and the salaries of its members.

The process of change started about ten years ago, with the transfer of items such as electricity consumption, laundry, food, and some of the cultural expenses to the individual member, says David Glazner, who is working on developing Kfar Ruppin's tourism enterprise. Even before that, the children were brought home to sleep, strengthening the family unit in relation to the community.

"I see the difference in the field trips I organize for the kibbutz," says Glazner. "The excursions used to be either for groups of members or for the children; today almost all trips are family outings."

The same generation as Etan Yatziv, Glazner was also born at Kfar Ruppin. A tall, burly man, with thick, dark hair and horn-rimmed glasses, dressed in jeans, checked shirt, and sandals, he has been a schoolteacher for most of his adult life, and it shows in his manner of speech, at once didactic and thoughtful. He has twice served as kibbutz secretary in between his periods of teaching. Now, after being headmaster of the regional school at a nearby kibbutz, he decided on a new career.

"My image of the old kibbutz is of several members sitting in the club room sharing a copy of *Davar,* the labor movement newspaper," he says. "Times change, and we have to adapt to them, but there is a constant struggle to preserve the link between the freedom of the individual and a caring society."

Glazner approves of the changes being made at Kfar Ruppin, but, unlike many kibbutzniks of his generation, he has not fallen in love with capitalism. He hopes that, in the striving for excellence, the concept of community, of the team working together, will not be lost. Many high-tech industries thrive on teamwork, he points out. While not opposed to the differentials and incentives that have been introduced, he is wary of the connection between income and motivation. Several studies have shown that as income rises it become less important, he notes.

"I came to work in the tourism enterprise because of the challenge," he emphasizes. "There is terrific potential here."

He goes on to talk about the special bird-watching tourism. Three hundred species of birds inhabit the Jordan and Beit Shean valleys, and many more migrate through the area. Storks, pelicans, cranes, and every type of raptor pass over Kfar Ruppin on their way from Europe to Africa in the fall and fly back in the spring.

"A bird-watcher from Europe can see more species in a week-long vacation here than in a whole year back home," enthuses Glazner.

The kibbutz earns an income from providing accommodation, meals, guiding, and other services. There is a bird-ringing station, which supplies the statistics, and viewing stations are under construction. As the site becomes better known, it will also be a venue where bird-watchers come to meet each other and compare notes.

Returning to the subject of the changes, Glazner is confident that the new system in Kfar Ruppin is proving itself. Members who wanted to build extensions to their homes have worked overtime to earn the necessary money.

"That is just what we wanted," he says. "The member is happy with the result. Today he feels he is being helped; before the changes, there were members who felt the kibbutz was exploiting them."

The old ethic of "from each according to his ability, to each according to his needs" was suitable for a small, young commune—not for a multigenerational community. "Needs" have become entirely different from member to member, he points out. A veteran might require around-the-clock care; a member in her thirties needs support to complete her doctorate; a third may want special training for his child.

"That doesn't mean that we should not preserve mutual assistance," he affirms. "The capitalists have taught us that a worker who feels secure and who identifies with his company is more productive."

As an educator, Glazner agrees that the kibbutz did not produce a "new human being," but he maintains that it was European educators at the turn of the century who put forward the idea. On the whole, kibbutz education produced positive citizens. He acknowledges that the kibbutznik may be a bit narrow-minded and not sufficiently competitive but insists that, on the whole, the system did a good job. He feels that his own kids are still growing up in a Society of Children, even if they spend more time at home. Today's system is suitable for today, he affirms.

"We should take advantage of the fact that in many ways the kibbutz is suited to the world of today," he concludes. "I don't think we have to dismantle collective life in order to rebuild it. We must preserve the worthwhile things, while adapting to the modern environment."

Rachel Noy also spent most of her life in teaching, but in earlier times. When she retired seventeen years ago, Rachel told the Kfar Ruppin journal that she had always regarded teaching as a "mission." She wanted to be an "educator" as well as a teacher. She always felt a great weight of responsibility, particularly with the youngest children. She knew that she was shaping them for the future. She tried to teach them behavior as well as knowledge—how to speak, how to *listen.*

"I tried to inculcate values," she recalled, "but should they be our society's values, the values of the child's parents, or my personal values?"

"Weren't they the same?" asked the interviewer.

"Not always," replied Rachel.

She went on to talk about the specific problems of being a kibbutz teacher, in which you are under scrutiny twenty-four hours a day and have to set a personal example all the time.

Coming back to the present, I ask her whether the kibbutz system educated to mediocrity. Rachel is less defensive than many other teachers. There is a measure of truth in the charge, she concedes. One looked for the average. From her own observation, she thinks the good teachers provided the bright children with adequate challenges. The bright child may have suffered with the average teacher. Toward the end of her career, she saw what was happening all over the country and started sending bright children to special classes that were available at a school in the region.

For many years, Rachel was editor of the Kfar Ruppin journal, which she admits to using as a mouthpiece for her views on education and everything else. She retired from the editorship because she felt that she no longer represented more than a minority view in the kibbutz. She was very much in favor of the children sleeping at home, and she accepted the "privatization" of many items in the personal allowance; but the latest developments are difficult to accept. She points out that immigrants from the former Soviet Union came to Kfar Ruppin on the "first home in Israel" scheme, and some of them became excellent members. She does not feel she can offer them membership today, when they will be required to buy shares.

"It was logical to introduce payment for meals in the dining hall," she admits. "Truck drivers and all sorts of outsiders were eating there for free, but it did not end there. I am not happy about the evaluation of work in terms of money. I realize that people want change, but it is not my kibbutz in the way it was for so many years. It is not my path."

Her husband, Yaacov, known most of his life as "Chech," is pragmatic. He feels that there is no choice if there is to be a chance to keep the third generation.

"Many of the second generation stayed," he says, "but the third generation goes to the Amazon or the Himalayas. When they come back, they don't want the old-style kibbutz. Maybe the new system will encourage them to stay. It's worth a try."

Chech is seventy-nine. Always physically active despite an early climbing accident that left him with a limp, operations on both knees now necessitate the use of an electric cart to get around. He retains a notable narrative skill and loves telling stories of the old days. He was one of those sent to Mauritius by the British. He utilized his time there to learn scouting and sports skills that stood him in good stead later on as a youth leader and sports instructor. For many years he served as military commander of the kibbutz, and he has a pension from the Border Police.

"To be frank with you, I still believe in the kibbutz system," he affirms, "but I also want to help my children outside the kibbutz. They all left and they all need money. That is the main reason that I accept the new system."

Like Chech, Anina Korati spent the war in Mauritius. She came back to Palestine in 1945, and, as she worked in a hospital on the British-ruled island, she took up residence in Afula and started studying nursing at the local hospital. In 1946, her boyfriend was demobilized from the British army, and she joined him at Kfar Ruppin.

"I was utterly thrilled with working on the land, although I was half-dead from the heat and the mosquitoes," she recalls. "I was terribly idealistic then."

She soon returned to nursing, however, and became interested in psychology, studying the subject by means of a British Council correspondence course. Although she never completed a formal degree in the subject, she participated in study days and enrichment courses and continues to work as a family psychologist in the local area, but not at her own kibbutz.

"I thought communism would save the world," she says with a sad smile. "Everyone helping each other, the strong supporting the weak. I believed totally in the 'new human being.' I still think that 'from each according to his ability, to each according to his needs' is the greatest idea that humanity has produced."

Nevertheless, it became clear to her that it could not be implemented. She received an electric kettle from her aunt, and she used it in her room. On the other hand, she and her late husband gave in all their German reparation money to the kibbutz.

"I think we really did give according to our abilities," she says. "Needs were another thing: I always needed more. I wanted twenty books—not one. I wanted the freedom to buy in a shop of my choice."

The new regime in Kfar Ruppin makes her "feel nostalgic" for the old days, but she has no regrets. She is sorry that people cannot live in partnership and equality, just as she is sorry they cannot live in peace. Regarding the reformers, she looks on what she calls "their discovery of the wheel" with some amusement, but she admires their energy and dedication.

Her friend Hannah Raz arrived in Kfar Ruppin in 1949. She was born in Czechoslovakia but sent out of Nazi-ruled Europe to refuge in England. She grew up there with a Christian family and took her first degree in Oxford. After World War II, she discovered that she and her sister were the only survivors of her family. Coming to Israel seemed to her "the only rational answer."

She established the English Department at the Oranim Kibbutz College, taught English and education, studied again in Oxford for her second degree, completed her doctorate in education and the methodology of foreign language teaching at the Hebrew University, edited the quarterly *English Teaching Guidance,* served on the education committee of her kibbutz, worked as a senior consultant, and generally managed to keep pretty busy. Now retired, she still works as a translator, notably for the English-language monthly *Kibbutz Trends.*

She was always opposed to the communal sleeping arrangements for children and says her first speech at the kibbutz general meeting ("as soon as I learned Hebrew well enough") was a trenchant criticism of the system. However, she accepted it as part of a package of communal education that she thought was basically right. She never missed the other aspects of homemaking. Except for the children's sleeping arrangements, communal life suited her very well. She was lucky to find work that she loved and that gave her tremendous satisfaction, so she never felt the frustration that some other women members felt.

"No, I did not go for that 'new human being' idea," she says. "We had the Society of Children and a measure of democracy in the school.

Our essential aim was to bring up a *mensch* [Yiddish for 'decent person']. We hoped the kids would return to Kfar Ruppin, and about half of them did for many years. Recently it has declined, of course; unfortunately, very few come back today."

She thinks that the desire to keep the children is a rationalization of the reason for the introduction of the new system at the kibbutz. In her view, there are fundamental psychological reasons why certain people pushed for change. She did not object to the early changes, but the introduction of differentials, albeit marginal, was a "red line" for her.

"I hope it won't go further," she says. "It will destroy the kibbutz way of life."

Hannah acknowledges that the majority for change was overwhelming, conceding that the process was thorough and democratic, but she maintains that the advocates of change came to the members "to explain their ideas—not to discuss them." She feels that enormous pressure was exerted by the proponents of change. A feeling of inevitability and an atmosphere of panic were created that stampeded the members. She thinks that Kfar Ruppin is still more of a kibbutz than many other kibbutzim, but she sees the recent decision as a regression rather than an advance. She is concerned about the new management style of the kibbutz branches, which is authoritarian rather than one of partnership.

"I suppose we were lucky in a way," she says. "The self-appointed committee that pushed through the changes were excellent people of the middle age group. They could have decided to leave, but instead they stayed and changed the kibbutz."

One of the people at whom the new system is directed is Haim Raviv. At lunch in the communal dining hall, on the eve of his flight back to New Zealand, the tanned, dark-haired, amiable youngster talked freely of his hopes and concerns. At the table across from where we sat, a young man planning to run a tourist hostel in Nepal sat eating his meal—another kibbutz child lost to the ambiance of the East.

"I am very proud of what this kibbutz has achieved," said Haim. "I congratulate the members. They have created a healthier society. Not a better one, but a healthier one. The old kibbutz was detached from reality. The kibbutz must stop quarreling with human nature, and Kfar Ruppin has done that."

Haim is back in Israel for a brief visit. He lives with his wife in Wellington, where she is undergoing conversion to Judaism. In eighteen months they plan to return to Kfar Ruppin for a trial period. He hopes it will end up with both of them becoming members.

His mother was a member of the Banativ group; his father was accepted as a boarder at the kibbutz school at the age of fourteen. Haim left school early and went to work on the sod farm that the kibbutz had at that time. After army service in South Lebanon, he returned to work on the kibbutz, studying half the week to complete his matriculation. Periods of work in town and abroad followed. At that time, the policy at Kfar Ruppin was to require the children to decide about membership by the age of twenty-eight.

"I decided not to mess around," he explains. "My girlfriend, who later became my wife, did not see her future here, so I told the kibbutz I was leaving. My severance pay is still in a savings account."

Haim and his girlfriend lived for a time in Tel Aviv, and then in England, before going to New Zealand, his wife's native country. There he works in construction, making a reasonable living, but he would like to return to his country of birth.

"I couldn't live in Tel Aviv," he insists. "I never liked it there. Kfar Ruppin may be hot and isolated, but it is a great place to bring up children. Look, I don't know about the details of the changes, as I haven't been here during the past four years, but my mother was very active in pushing for them, and I am very pleased with the general direction."

Haim grew up in the Society of Children at Kfar Ruppin but maintains that most of his fellow students do not believe in the classical kibbutz way of doing things. Basically, he thinks, human beings are egotistical. They are prepared to help each other up to a point, but in the final analysis they worry about themselves. He is not surprised that the kibbutz where he grew up was first with the changes.

"I saw the sparks in the field that started off the snowball," he says, with an outrageous mixture of metaphors. "Kfar Ruppin is like a country that can make peace because it has a strong army. We have a great second generation here. In many kibbutzim, this generation collapsed. With us they are the pillars of the kibbutz. They have adapted it to reality.

"I had an argument with a fellow Israeli in New Zealand who said that Kfar Ruppin is no longer a kibbutz. You don't live by definitions. Call it what the hell you want. If people live together and help each other, I think that's a kibbutz!"

It is difficult to predict whether the new setup at this kibbutz in the burning hot Beit Shean valley will attract new members or lure back its children who have left. Like many other kibbutzim, Kfar Ruppin is also planning a neighborhood attached to the kibbutz, but the members are the first to admit that the climate and isolated location place a huge question mark over the project.

What can be said is that the reformers of Kfar Ruppin have invested an enormous amount of imagination, thought, and energy in their experiment. They surely refute the thesis that kibbutz education produces mediocrity, and they deserve credit for their courage and ingenuity. Clearly the change at Kfar Ruppin is far more radical than that of Maagan Michael. There is nothing "virtual" about what they have done, nor is it in any way a "divorce settlement." The new structure will not be introduced "if the kibbutz breaks up." It is in place here and now, part of the new community that is Kfar Ruppin; the freeze is only temporary.

It is also fair to say that the change is also more basic than that introduced by Hasolelim—although Hasolelim is also working on an allocation of assets program. The Kfar Ruppin model implements the separation of the community from the business, as put forward in *The New Kibbutz* by Yehuda Harel, and goes much further. It is the most far-reaching attempt so far to replace the old system of trust with a legally guaranteed social contract, as proposed by Ariel Halperin. It remains a relatively egalitarian society, with a large measure of cooperation and mutual assistance.

Maybe, as Haim Raviv suggested, it does not really matter whether Kfar Ruppin is a kibbutz or not, but it is moving away from the kibbutz model. The differentials are likely to increase; the members will trade their shares; the new members must already buy into the business. If Kfar Ruppin is still a kibbutz today, the accent is on "still." Without in any way denigrating the Kfar Ruppin model or criticizing the choice of its members, the verdict must be that the kibbutz is in the process of evolving into something else.

10

עין צורים

EIN TZURIM
NO IMMUNITY

My original title for this chapter was "Guardians of the Flame." During my visits to the different kibbutzim, I was consistently told that the sixteen kibbutzim of Kibbutz Dati, the religious kibbutz movement, seemed to be immune to the winds of change sweeping through the rest of the movement. If Kibbutz Artzi was half a step behind the United Kibbutz Movement in implementing changes, Kibbutz Dati belonged to an entirely different era. A number of observers went on to point out that Christian religious communes had historically been more successful than their secular socialist counterparts, notably in the United States, and therefore a similar faithfulness to communal principles was to be expected from Israel's religious kibbutzim.

The statistics reinforced this thesis. The survey carried out by Haifa University's Institute for the Research of the Kibbutz and the Cooperative Idea, which supplied the facts and figures cited in the introduction to this book, presented a picture of a small sector faithfully maintaining traditional values. This is not to say that there were no changes: more than half of the religious kibbutzim now encourage their members to work outside, over 60 percent have hired top managers in their business sectors, and two-thirds have canceled the communal evening meal in the dining hall. On the other hand, no religious kibbutz has introduced payment for overtime or implemented a connection between members' work and the allowance they receive. A mere 8 percent permit the purchase of private vehicles or extension of private living quarters from personal resources. Thus, the changes do not for the most part touch on the principles of the kibbutz way of life; egalitarianism is being preserved.

Further investigation, however, shows this picture to be erroneous. My target kibbutz, Ein Tzurim, is in the throes of change, and this situation is far from unique in Kibbutz Dati. If Kibbutz Artzi is a half-step behind the UKM, then Kibbutz Dati is only one step behind Kibbutz Artzi. The parallel with religious communes abroad is fallacious. Kibbutz Dati is not a group of isolated fanatical communes, with charismatic leaders. Like their secular counterparts in Israel, the religious kibbutzim are democratic. They are also fully involved in Israeli society and therefore subject to its influences.

The members of Ein Tzurim, particularly the younger ones, are using exactly the same language as their fellows in the secular kibbutzim. Kibbutz Dati has no immunity from the overwhelming process of change that is sweeping the kibbutz movement.

Ein Tzurim was the first kibbutz of religious pioneers born in Palestine. While still in their teens, the members were involved in the famous "Biriya Incident" of 1946. The British were still ruling Palestine at that time, trying to hold the ring between the increasingly belligerent Jewish and Arab forces contending for control of the country. Biriya was a small settlement adjacent to the town of Safed, high up in the hills of Galilee. Safed, although one of the four cities holy to the Jews (the others are Tiberias, Hebron, and Jerusalem), does not date back to biblical times. It became famous as a center of the Kabbala (Jewish mysticism) in the late mediaeval period, and some Jews lived there ever since. In 1946 the population of Safed consisted of about twelve thousand Arabs and two thousand Jews. Biriya, built on land purchased by Baron Rothschild, was occupied by a religious unit of the Palmah, with the expressed object of defending Safed's Jewish community.

In the spring of 1946, British troops discovered a secret arms store in Biriya and arrested all its inhabitants. In response, thousands of Jewish settlers from all over Galilee marched up to the area and established "Biriya-B," which was also demolished by the British army. When the Jews obstinately set up "Biriya-C," the British authorities permitted twenty young religious pioneers to remain.

They occupied the site for some months before being offered alternative locations more suitable for farming settlement. That fall they moved to a site equidistant between Jerusalem and Hebron, which they called Ein Tzurim (the Spring of Rocks), after a nearby

Figure 10.1.   Ein Tzurim in 1946.

Source: (Israel Government Press Office)

spring. Ein Tzurim was one of four kibbutzim in the area, called "the Etzion Bloc."

Kibbutz veteran Gershon Shaffat remembers that they numbered about fifty, living in cramped conditions, six or seven to a small hut. Their water was brought from Jerusalem by tankers, escorted by British troops. They occupied themselves mainly in clearing rocks, building terraces, and planting trees for the Jewish National Fund.

Following the vote of the United Nations General Assembly in November 1947 in favor of partitioning Palestine between the Jews and the Arabs, pressure increased on the Etzion Bloc, which guarded the southern approaches to Jerusalem, a prize to which both Jews and Arabs aspired above all. Only two weeks after the vote, a convoy of trucks coming from Jerusalem was ambushed on its way to the block, and ten of the twenty-six passengers were killed.

"During that period we lived in war conditions," recalls Shaffat. "We were in a siege situation."

In January 1948, the young children and their mothers were evacuated from the Etzion Bloc to Jerusalem, but there were no children in

Ein Tzurim, so their women members remained. Shortly afterward the members of the four kibbutzim beat back a concerted Arab attack, but a Hagana unit of thirty-five men, sent to reinforce them, was ambushed and wiped out.

Shaffat, an Orthodox Jew all his life, touches his knitted skullcap and smiles as he says, "I traveled on Shabbat more in those few months than in the rest of my life all together." Traveling on the Sabbath is forbidden by the Jewish religion, but the chief rabbi of Palestine sent the settlers a telegram:

> In everything you deem necessary for defense, go ahead. Build everything necessary and do not consider our Holy Sabbath. Not only is this permitted but it is incumbent upon you. May the Lord preserve you and hasten your salvation.

Shaffat does not remember particular problems about religious observance during the siege, but an account by Dov Kenoll, a member of neighboring Kfar Etzion, published in 1958, recalls a great deal of discussion about Sabbath observance. Three of the kibbutzim in the Etzion Bloc were religious; the fourth belonged to the left-wing Kibbutz Artzi movement. Traditionally, religious Jews turn to a rabbi to adjudicate problems of religious observance, but as they were cut off from Jerusalem, the three kibbutzim appointed their own religious committee.

A debate ensued between those who demanded that the members not actually serving in defense be prohibited from working on the Sabbath, and those who said that if Sabbath work were banned, the total workload would be increased, and the members standing guard would be less efficient because of fatigue. The debate was won by the pro-Sabbath work faction. Sabbath work approved by the committee included the laying of barbed wire, digging ditches, repairing weapons, building an airstrip, manufacturing and laying mines, and marking the location of the mines on a special map. Also authorized were farming chores connected with maintaining food supplies, such as attending to the livestock and cultivating the vegetable garden. In addition, there was a debate about military training on the Sabbath, and here the Jerusalem rabbinate came through with a ruling that approved training in the Etzion Bloc, which it noted was on the front line.

On the eve of the end of the British mandate and the establishment of the State of Israel in May 1948, Kfar Etzion was attacked by Arab irregulars and overwhelmed. Only six of its hundred defenders survived.

Not long afterward, the other three kibbutzim of the bloc managed to surrender to the Transjordanian Arab Legion, which was commanded by British officers, thus avoiding massacres similar to that of Kfar Etzion. The survivors were taken away to Transjordan. The women prisoners were returned to Israel after three weeks, but the men spent ten months at a prison camp in the Transjordanian desert.

Although it was burning hot during the day and extremely cold at night, Shaffat describes the treatment they received at the camp as "correct." There was one occasion when a soldier fired into the camp and killed a prisoner, but this was the only incident of its kind. The prisoners tried to keep fit playing soccer. They also spent many hours studying religious texts, and some time playing chess. "I was the chess champion of the camp," claims Shaffat.

In 1949, the prisoners were repatriated and reunited with their comrades, the released women prisoners, who were at a work camp, and those of the men who were away from Ein Tzurim at the time of the siege. The Etzion Bloc was now in Jordan (although it would be recaptured and resettled in 1967), so the group decided on an alternative site some twenty-five miles southeast of Tel Aviv and ten miles south of Givat Brenner.

By all accounts, the new Ein Tzurim was socially cohesive and also had some agricultural successes—notably with its dairy herd, which even today is the third most productive in the country, cow for cow—but it never took off economically, and its membership remained below 200. Today there are 170 members, which means a community of more than 400, as religious people tend to have large families.

Apart from the dairy there was a poultry branch, vineyards, and citrus groves. Quite early on, the kibbutz established a workshop for leather garments, which kept going until the 1980s, with reasonable success. Its other industrial venture, the Otzma factory for the manufacture of air conditioners, lost money for many years, but today it has turned the corner.

Ein Tzurim had debts, but not unmanageable ones. Its economic recovery was achieved in the past few years by a general improvement in efficiency and the construction of a residential neighborhood on kibbutz land. It was the first kibbutz to build a neighborhood, but, in contrast to the plans of other kibbutzim, it did not include it in its own municipal framework. The Etrog neighborhood became part of a nearby community settlement, and its only link to Ein Tzurim is that it purchases services from the kibbutz. It uses the swimming pool, the kindergartens, and other facilities. Two hundred fifty units have already been finished, and another forty are scheduled. The income from selling the houses has balanced Ein Tzurim's budget.

Although the impetus for change comes from the younger members, seventy-year-old Gershon Shaffat is the chairman of Ein Tzurim's Team for Change. The portly, genial Shaffat served as a member of the Knesset, Israel's parliament, for the right-wing Tehiya Party. Subsequently, he was involved in Ein Tzurim's economic management, including the construction of the Etrog neighborhood.

"We do not live in isolation," he explains, quoting an Aramaic maxim to the effect that what occurs in one place affects another. "Our members hear about what is happening in other kibbutzim. They read the kibbutz journals and are well aware of the debate going on in the movement."

Shaffat's Team for Change faces exactly the same demands voiced by members of other kibbutzim: they want more privacy; they would like to own their houses and other kibbutz assets; they insist on freedom to use their money as they wish. The kibbutz has partly unified the different allowances, as in other kibbutzim, using the same term: "privatization." Pensions have already been introduced, with special funds for the older members. The matters of the responsibility of the member for making a living and the link between work and income are under discussion.

"Today kibbutz members aren't prepared to work for ten or twelve hours a day without a direct reward," explains Shaffat. "The change is unstoppable. We are trying to organize things so that we can live together, but not in each other's pockets. We want to implement the changes with as much of a consensus as possible. We need a lot of patience. The youngsters must not be too hasty; we veterans must not see every change as a tragedy."

Despite the similarities between what is going on at Ein Tzurim and other kibbutzim, the question of religious influence remains intriguing. An early publication of Kibbutz Dati suggests that religion is virtually a requirement for someone seeking to lead a communal life: "Only a powerful transcendent force, such as religion, can lead a person to renounce all private possessions and conventional family life, and to shape his daily living in all its minutiae according to the precepts of the group." Another passage is even more specific:

Some members devote their free time to communal affairs—committee meetings or economic planning; others return to their rooms after the day's work, oblivious to all worries or responsibilities. Only the inner feeling that it is *sinful* to pursue comfort at the expense of one's duties can deter a person from such a course.

Asked whether religious people were better suited to communal living, Ein Tzurim veteran Avraham Kol chose to put it more modestly: "Religious people are accustomed to living within frameworks, compulsory frameworks. There are regulations. Possibly someone used to living his life within the limits imposed by religious observance finds it easier to observe other rules, such as those of the kibbutz."

Nevertheless, Kol makes it clear that the religious faith of the members has not prevented them from asking for the same sort of things demanded by members of other kibbutzim. Differential incomes seem wrong to him. He is worried that if the kibbutz introduces marginal differentials, they will eventually increase. His own hope is for less extreme changes, but he realizes that the younger members expect more radical developments, including differentials of one sort or another.

"We need more security and more autonomy for the members," he suggests, "but without harming the principle of mutual assistance. We should take care to preserve the essential features of kibbutz life."

Michal Chen is the kibbutz secretary, and, in this role, she is presiding over the current changes. She and her husband joined Ein Tzurim in 1974 after living at another kibbutz. Following a career as a teacher, ending up as headmistress of the regional kibbutz school at nearby Yavne for eight years, she was elected secretary. Prior to this position, she made her desire for change very clear, although she hesitates to say she has a mandate for it.

From her point of view, the main problem is that only just over a third of Ein Tzurim's children have decided to remain at the kibbutz. She says that the reasons for leaving are varied and very personal. A member might wish to leave the parental home, to abandon the intensive group life, to flee from gossip, or simply to strike out on his or her own. It is usually a combination of several reasons.

"With us there is another reason," she says sadly. "Some of our children move away from religion. It happens in the army, or sometimes afterward. They cannot live here permanently unless they are religiously observant."

Despite this, she thinks that the main reason the youngsters leave Ein Tzurim is that they have stopped believing in equality and cooperation. The basic axioms with which Michal grew up are not working any more. Increasing numbers of young people say that the kibbutz way is not for them:

"We don't want to pull this wagon, when so many are on board and so few are pulling it!"

Michal, who says that this represents her own attitude, hastens to add that she is not talking about the veterans. As a kibbutz and as a religious community, Ein Tzurim is totally committed to the welfare of its older members. Anything else is "unthinkable." Nevertheless, she is not willing to carry on with the old system. She is not prepared to stand in front of a committee and ask for things. She is determined to run her own personal life and make her own decisions.

The Team for Change is working with an adviser from the United Kibbutz Movement. It is discussing social security, privatization, work and livelihood, differential salaries, separation of business from community, and residency. The matter of differentials and the allocation of assets have proved complicated and been left for future discussion. The veterans are worried about the changes, allows Michal, particularly the ones whose children have left. Those with children at Ein Tzurim are inclined to vote with the children in favor of changes.

"The others don't seem to realize that their children have left because they disagreed with exactly the same things that we are trying to change," says Michal. "They show understanding for their own children who have left, but no understanding for the youngsters who have remained."

The changes are moving forward, but not too quickly. Privatization is proceeding gradually. Members now pay for food, clothing, recreation, and vacations, but they still don't pay for their own electricity. More significantly, a proposal to pay members extra money for overtime seemed to have everyone's approval, only to be voted down by a recent general meeting.

Raz Dior and Eli Daubey represent the generation of managers in their forties. Dior is the general manager of Ein Tzurim; Daubey runs the Otzma factory. They are pragmatic, outspoken, tough-minded. Dior is very much aware that he is operating in a different climate from that which prevailed at the time his parents ran the kibbutz.

"They could still get things from the government and other institutions," he explains. "Those days are past. Now we have to be professional businessmen. Our parents wanted to build the kibbutz and the nation; we have to be much more commercial."

He thinks that the changes are necessary and that they should be implemented quickly. He is one of those who has helped put Ein Tzurim on a sound economic footing; if the success is to continue, however, the rules must be changed. He is absolutely convinced that the members should be responsible for earning their own livings.

What about the argument that if Ein Tzurim is economically healthy, it means that the system is working, so why change it?

"That is not the point," he insists. "We have been telling each other stories for the last thirty years, and the time has come to ask ourselves what we really want: do we want to dance the hora in the dining hall, or do we want to add five hundred square feet to our rooms? Do we want our children to study at university or have them work in the orchards?"

His attitude is echoed by Daubey, who believes that the young generation no longer wants collective ownership. In the past people were more idealistic, he says. Today they want to own things personally; they also want careers and private lives.

"If a member is not responsible for earning his own living, it is corrupt," he says forthrightly. "It is a system that does not work. Maybe it did once, but it doesn't today."

Daubey has been running Otzma for three years, and today the factory is earning money. It has a board of directors with two outside members including the chairman, but so far no outside partners. Otzma has a labor force of eighty, half of them members of Ein Tzurim. It is run on strictly business lines, and, even before the formal separation of business and community, there was no question of "milking" the factory for the benefit of the kibbutz members. The old-style rotation of management is a thing of the past; he will remain manager of Otzma as long as the board wants him.

Daubey has heard about the allocation of assets at Kfar Ruppin and is confident that it is a move in the right direction. At Ein Tzurim, he would start with the houses and then move to the other assets. The matter is under discussion, although things are not moving fast enough. He understands the fears of the veterans but insists that they will not be pushed aside. They already have the equivalent of pensions, and, if the houses and other assets are allocated, they will be secure.

Although both Daubey and Dior have a no-nonsense approach toward kibbutz values, an attitude that rejects the mythology of the past, neither of them has the least inclination to revise his religious views.

Despite some snags, the winds of change are manifestly blowing through Ein Tzurim; interestingly, they do not affect religious observance. Some of the children of the kibbutz do abandon religion, but they are a small percentage. Youngsters who stop believing are free to remain at the kibbutz through their army service. They are not required to be observant—merely to respect the others who are. However, if they continue with their secular way of life, they are ultimately expected to make their home elsewhere. The Jewish religion is still the strong cement that binds Ein Tzurim together. Even the Etrog neighborhood, although it is not formally linked to the kibbutz, only accepts religious residents.

When the Zionist movement emerged toward the end of the nineteenth century, most religious Jews shunned it. Although two pious rabbis were among the first to propose a modern return to Zion, the majority of observant Jews believed that Zionism was an impudent attempt to anticipate the Messiah. This attitude is still prevalent among the ultra-Orthodox Jewish community in Israel.

Religious Zionists were a minority in their own community, and they were also a minority in the emerging Zionist entity in Palestine, which was aggressively secular. From the outset, the religious Zionists were determined to prove to the secular Zionists that they were capable of participating fully in the pioneering endeavors. They were no less concerned to prove to their religious critics that an independent modern Jewish nation could be run without breaching Jewish religious law.

Religious kibbutzim were at the forefront of this twin struggle. Clearly, all food served in the communal dining halls of religious kibbutzim is kosher—that is, in accordance with the requirements of Jewish law. Any meat must be from a permitted animal or bird and slaughtered according to Jewish tradition. Milk and milk products must be kept separate from meat, and no cooking is permitted on the Sabbath.

Other problems of Sabbath observance are more problematic. One of the most important principles of Jewish law is the prohibition of work on the Sabbath. The Bible tells us that God created the universe in six days and rested on the seventh; human beings are expected to behave likewise. In the Diaspora, it was customary for Jews to employ gentiles to perform necessary tasks on a Saturday, but the religious kibbutzim fiercely rejected this course. They maintained that if gentiles were required to perform vital tasks, the Jewish nation would not be truly independent. At the same time, they were totally committed to a strict observance of religious law.

We have already mentioned the matter of self-defense on the Sabbath. Since the time of the Hasmonean revolt of the second century B.C.E., the need to fight on the Sabbath to save one's life was accepted. The chief rabbi's telegram to the settlers of the Etzion Bloc, mentioned earlier, was only confirming this principle; other matters were more complicated.

As we have seen, many of the kibbutzim experienced Arab hostility in the years after their establishment; but this was not always in the form of direct military confrontation. Faced with hostile neighbors setting fire to crops or diverting the kibbutz water supply, the secular kibbutz members could take appropriate action at all times. What were the religious kibbutzniks to do if the actions occurred on Saturday? In almost every case, the rabbis ruled that it was legitimate to put out fires or restore the supply of water to the fields on the Sabbath, as this was ultimately a matter of saving lives.

Milking the cows was a more complex issue. Cows must be milked every day of the week to avoid their suffering. According to the Jewish tradition, animals must not be allowed to suffer, and therefore milking must be carried out even at the cost of violating the Sabbath. The question is, Can one benefit from this? Rabbinical tradition cites thirty-nine types of work prohibited on the Sabbath. Many of them concern farming, but milking is not one of them. Nevertheless, milking was defined as work, and it was forbidden to benefit from it directly. One religious kibbutz milked the cows straight onto the ground, letting the milk run away; other religious farmers adopted the practice of milking into buckets of rice or meal, holding that it was legitimate the eat the nonliquid "porridge," as the milk was not being used as milk. In the kibbutzim, the herds became too large for this porridge making to be practical, so they milked into a bucket containing chlorophyll, subsequently making (nonliquid) cheese from the milk.

Later, when electrical milking machines were introduced, the religious kibbutzim adapted them to pour away the first milk, since that was obtained as a result of putting the milking equipment onto the cow, while storing the milk obtained subsequently, which was usable on the grounds that it was obtained from an automatic operation.

Producing electricity on the Sabbath on a national scale was approved because hospitals and other institutions needed it for preserving life, which superseded the Sabbath. Nevertheless, in the early days some kibbutzim faced problems when their local generator broke down on the Sabbath.

Another problem is the collection of eggs, which is specifically mentioned as forbidden. The Talmud biblical commentary contains a ruling that children are permitted to carry on the Sabbath in a good cause, and a rabbi offered this as a justification for children collecting the eggs. In this case, Kibbutz Dati was more strict than the Talmud itself. The movement decided that making children work on the Sabbath was a bad educational example, and therefore the eggs laid on the Sabbath would be relinquished.

These are only some of the questions dealt with by the religious kibbutzim in their struggle to observe Judaism scrupulously in the context of an independent Jewish national life.

Zeev Shfaram is the coordinator of the Committee for Jewish Observance at Ein Tzurim. With the usual knitted skullcap of the religious kibbutznik, he wears a short-sleeved shirt, shorts, and sandals, a mode of dress that would be considered immodest by ultra-Orthodox circles in Israel. Shfaram is not quite a founder of Ein Tzurim, having arrived with a youth group from Switzerland in 1949. He worked at Otzma in machine maintenance for fifteen years, but, following two heart attacks, he now provides computer services for the factory from his home.

His committee works closely with the kibbutz rabbi, who was appointed five years ago. Rabbi Raphael Feuerstein was Ein Tzurim's first rabbi, and initially many members were doubtful about the idea. Historically, religious kibbutzim ran themselves without resident rabbis, only appealing to the nearest rabbinical authority for adjudication over questions of religious law. Today several kibbutzim have their own rabbis, and at Ein Tzurim there is universal appreciation for their rabbi's work. Feuerstein is the son of Professor Reuven Feuerstein, a psychologist and educator internationally renowned for his work with children with learning disabilities. His son is a psychologist as well as a rabbi, and apart from his ministry, he has been greatly valued as a counselor to the kibbutz members. Unfortunately, he is winding up his tour of duty as Ein Tzurim's rabbi, and the kibbutz is looking for a successor.

Feuerstein is a charismatic personality, says Shfaram, who can hold the attention of kindergarten children when he talks to them about Jewish subjects and also teach and discuss Judaism with adults to a profound level. Although the rabbi is the authority who rules on matters of Jewish religious law and observance, he only ruled directly on personal matters. When it came to general matters affecting the kibbutz, Feuerstein, although not himself a kibbutz member, always saw the importance of consulting with the kibbutzniks before making his rulings.

Among the questions put to the rabbi are those concerning the children of Ein Tzurim serving in the army. Although religious soldiers are supposed to be entirely at home in the Israel Defense Forces, which are staffed with army rabbis, matters come up with religious soldiers serving in isolated outposts under secular commanders. Then they can call their own rabbi to ask for guidance.

Another problem concerns the kibbutz guests. Like many secular kibbutzim, Ein Tzurim has established a tourism branch, renting kibbutz rooms and selling dining hall meals to visitors from the outside. The special appeal of Ein Tzurim is for weekend visitors, seeking to spend the weekend in a community that has the right atmosphere of Sabbath observance, peace, and piety. Some ultra-Orthodox guests are not satisfied with the kosher food provided at Ein Tzurim and want food certified by their own rabbis. The tourism branch manager then turns to the rabbi for his authorization.

Strangely enough, the old question of Sabbath milking has come up again at Ein Tzurim. Like many agricultural enterprises in Israel, the kibbutz has recently started employing workers from Thailand. As the Thais are around anyway, why not let them milk on Saturday and let the members enjoy their Sabbath peace? Most of the members of Ein Tzurim feel that a vital principle is at stake here: the idea that Jews can run the country, including the agriculture, by themselves. Therefore, they are resolutely opposed to employing the Thai workers for the purpose of ensuring Sabbath observance.

Apart from his work at Ein Tzurim, Feuerstein is active in an association of rabbis that performs Jewish weddings free of charge. Applications for his services come in from around the country, and the kibbutz phone exchange deals with the requests.

Then there is the question of *tzadaka* ("charity" based on the Hebrew word for "justice"). The Bible records the custom of leaving the remains of the crop at the edges of the field for the poor, and Jewish tradition has subsequently translated this into the obligation to give money to the needy. Yavne, which is a rich religious kibbutz, maintains a children's center in Ashdod and gives away a lot of money to good causes. Ein Tzurim has never been rich but has consistently given a percentage of each member's personal allowance to charity. Shfaram is concerned about the changes taking place at Ein Tzurim from both a social and a religious point of view. Jewish tradition considers cooperation and partnership as the finest form of charity, he explains.

"It is better than giving," he says. "Instead of receiving a handout, the recipient is invited to come and be a partner, standing on his own two feet with self-respect. That is real Judaism."

The rabbi is not asked to concern himself with the changes in the cooperative structure of the kibbutz. Kibbutz Dati has a tradition of not introducing religion where it does not belong. Shfaram thinks that it is legitimate to cite the Jewish tradition in support of cooperation and an egalitarian lifestyle but not right to appeal to a rabbinical authority for a religious legal ruling on that subject. He thinks this would be equivalent to mixing religion and politics, comparing it to the question of an Israeli withdrawal from the territories occupied in the Six Day War of 1967. Although he is against withdrawal for reasons of military security, he objects to the way some religious people have appealed to the rabbis and thus made it a matter of Jewish religious law.

Shfaram takes me to see the synagogue, decorated with mosaics showing the six days of creation. The work was carried out by a secular member of Givat Brenner. Adjoining the synagogue is the Beit Midrash (House of Learning), a spacious book-lined room with a large library of Judaica. It is used for study by children as well as adults. Every day, between afternoon and evening prayers, there is a *shiur* (a Talmud lesson), and there is also a weekly lesson conducted by a former member.

In addition, the rabbi conducts a seminar on the Rambam, Rabbi Moses Ben-Maimon (Maimonides), the medieval scholar whom many regard as the greatest Jewish religious authority of the postbiblical era. The rabbi also gives a talk on current events from the point of view of Jewish religious belief. All in all, there is a vibrant Jewish life at Ein Tzurim, which combines strict orthodoxy with a tolerant liberal approach. At Ein Tzurim, some married women wear scarves or hats in obedience to the obligation of modesty, but other women do not cover their heads. None wear wigs, which is regarded as hypocritical. Some wear trousers for work; others refrain from donning garments they regard as masculine and inappropriate for women. The kibbutz swimming pool is closed on Saturday, but during the week, there are hours for men only, hours for women only, and hours for mixed bathing. This practice, which is observed in all the settlements of Kibbutz Dati, has not been submitted for a rabbinical ruling.

Of course, the philosophy that rejects religious coercion has its price: four of Shfaram's six children are among the children of Ein Tzurim who have stopped being observant.

"We are an open society," he explains, "without compulsion, and yet I sometimes feel that, if I had shown greater wisdom, more of them might have remained religious."

Although some of the children of Ein Tzurim may abandon a religious way of life, the future of religious tradition seems assured there—at least in the immediate future. This is not the case with regard to the kibbutz tradition. Ein Tzurim may be going more slowly than a lot of other kibbutzim, but there is a clear move toward a less cooperative, less egalitarian, more individualistic way of life. The members of Ein Tzurim are indeed Guardians of the Flame, but they are preserving the religious flame—not the socialist one.

The religious kibbutzim on the whole are not in an economic crisis. Because they were more conservative than their secular counterparts, they were slower to invest in industries and therefore much less in need of capital. As a result, they took fewer bank loans, although it must be noted that they were also more cautious about borrowing money for other purposes, such as building homes or dining halls. Even their synagogues were built with outside donations, where they were not paid for by the kibbutzim themselves. Consequently, unlike many of the secular kibbutzim, they are not forced to make changes because of economic reasons, but, like the secular kibbutzim, they have a demographic problem. Like them, they are finding it difficult to hold their third and forth generations and for the same reason: a lessening of belief in cooperation and the egalitarian ethic.

In the religious kibbutzim, as in all kibbutzim, there is the phenomenon of the youngest generation leaving to pursue its own agenda. Even the tradition in religious families of the older generation aging within the family circle is not strong enough to prevent this. Consequently, several religious kibbutzim are contemplating the neighborhood solution, but they are thinking in terms of a neighborhood for their own children (and maybe other youngsters) linked to their kibbutzim, rather than the Ein Tzurim model of a neighborhood as a purely commercial enterprise.

Many in Kibbutz Dati are determined to maintain the classical kibbutz, but several others see a necessary loosening of doctrine—kibbutz doctrine, not religious doctrine. They see new neighborhoods linked to the kibbutzim, with the differences between neighborhood and kibbutz becoming increasingly blurred as time goes on. The important thing, say these members, is to preserve the settlements, but not necessarily in kibbutz form.

So despite the fact that the religious kibbutzim are moving more slowly, they are not immune to the winds of change blowing through the kibbutz movement. Ultimately they will go through the same process as the other kibbutzim. The religious kibbutzim cannot be considered separately. What the UKM is doing today and Kibbutz Artzi will do tomorrow, Kibbutz Dati will do the day after tomorrow. The process seems to be irreversible.

Can the classical kibbutz way of life find reinforcement from some of the new experiments being carried out on the fringes? Our next visit will be to an urban kibbutz, the members of which are striving to correct what they see as the mistakes of the classical kibbutz.

11

תמוז

TAMUZ
URBAN COMMUNE

None of the early attempts to create kibbutzim inside towns or cities were successful. As we have seen, the traditional kibbutz combined collective endeavor, communal living, and egalitarian principles with the ideal of pioneering, physical labor, and the redemption of the soil of the Jewish homeland. This fused into a compound that held together. In addition, it was clearly more feasible to maintain a communal group in comparative isolation. For these reasons, the urban communes in Israel were far less successful than the conventional rural kibbutzim.

Three urban kibbutzim in the suburbs of Jerusalem, Haifa, and Herzliya became ordinary kibbutzim that just happened to be located near towns (although two of them are now set to become urban suburbs again and make healthy profits in the bargain, as they are sitting on prime building land). A fourth was Efal, near Tel Aviv, and lasted until 1951, when its members went their own private ways. It has since become an education and research center of the United Kibbutz Movement. The latest urban experiment to disintegrate, Kvutzat Shaal, founded in 1968 by a group of eighteen graduates of the American Habonim movement in the new town of Carmiel, near Haifa, lasted less than four years before disbanding. However, four urban kibbutzim have now existed for periods of between ten and twenty years, which is a short time span in kibbutz terms but relatively long compared to communes in other times and places.

Because the new urban experiments are largely the creations of children of kibbutzim who have sought to correct what they see as flaws in the societies where they grew up, these urban experiments may have a better chance of success than the earlier ones. In any event, they are interesting as living critiques of the classical kibbutz. Reshit, which was founded in Jerusalem in 1979, today has a population of around one hundred; the other three are about half that size. Their members recall the earliest days of Degania and the small *kvutza*. Certainly they contend with the challenges of living together in harmony, cooperation, and democracy in ways that modern kibbutz members do not even contemplate. At the same time, today's urban kibbutzim are creations of their time, contemporary not only in their locations, occupations, and structures but also in their communal ethic.

Not for them the sacrifice for the common cause, the subservience of the individual to the group, the personal deprivation for the sake of the superior communal goal. Today's urban communards are almost obsessed with their individual autonomy, their personal freedom, and their civil rights. For them, the communal life is, more than anything else, a means to greater personal freedom and fulfillment. It is not that they are unaware of the society around them—quite the reverse: they are making supreme efforts to reach out to the populations of the towns where they live. Their involvement and interaction with Israeli society at large for the most part preceded similar attempts by the conventional kibbutzim, but where the traditional kibbutz aimed to lead the Zionist enterprise, the modern urban kibbutz aspires to create a superior quality of life for its members, while making a contribution to the quality of the surrounding society.

Kibbutz Tamuz was founded twelve years ago in Beit Shemesh, a small town near Jerusalem. Its name derives simply from the fact that the first group settled there in the Hebrew month of Tamuz, which usually corresponds to June or July. A brief explanation of the decision-making process at Tamuz, written by one of its members, Yiftah Goldman, throws considerable light on the purposes and aspirations of this comparatively new creation: "Tamuz is a new type of community," he writes. "The freedom of man must be expressed in every moment of communal life."

He goes on to discuss the inherent tension between the individual and society. Any social framework presents a problem for human freedom, he concedes, but a person cannot be free outside society, so he must strive to create his community as a free society. Democracy is not merely a question of the rights of the individual but involves his active participation in running the community. The "democracy of participation" does not cancel the rights of the individual, but it is not satisfied merely with those rights. Tamuz does not have a formal structure but makes decisions in various forums, almost never involving votes:

> In Tamuz we see the general meeting as a creative framework, during which the members express their views, discuss the views of others, and change their minds during the course of the dialogue. The test of the community is to what extent it can reduce confrontation in the general meeting and create partnership.
>
> At Tamuz the individual makes his own decisions about his personal life. In contrast to the traditional kibbutz, there are no committees making decisions for him. On the other hand, Tamuz does not adopt the classical liberal approach that an individual is free to do as he wants provided he does not harm others.

Quoting John Donne that "no man is an island," Goldman argues that every action that individuals take impacts on their fellow humans and that this is even more the case in a communal society like Tamuz than in society at large. The Tamuz principle states, "Everyone makes his own decisions about his private life, *despite* the fact that these decisions have a general effect."

Tamuz, as a community, does not try to evade the complexities of this situation. The fact that individuals make the final decision about their own lives does not absolve them from discussing the matter with their comrades, who are their colleagues, advisers, and partners in discussion:

> The system at Tamuz is based on mutual trust. It is axiomatic that every member wants what is best for the community, but it is also assumed that the community aims to benefit the individual member. The members believe that the two things are interdependent. This sort of trust is not something that be taken for granted but has to be worked for all the time.
>
> The commune has deliberately refrained from establishing control mechanisms, which are based on the assumption that people try to take advantage of each other and must be prevented from doing so. The Tamuz assumption is that, given the opportunity, people prefer a life based on trust and partnership, than one based on exploitation and deceit. In the absence of control mechanisms, continuous dialogue between the members is maintained.

The community holds weekly general meetings, both for practical decision making and for discussion of principles and general problems. Sometimes the general meeting is broken up into smaller discussion groups. Votes are almost never taken, but decisions are not made by consensus, either, which is regarded as a "relative majority." Instead, the members try to reach a sense of the feeling of the meeting.

Explaining why each voice is not necessarily equal, Goldman gives the example of a group of actors putting on William Shakespeare's *Macbeth*. The actress playing Lady Macbeth may ask her fellow actors whether she should play her as a victim or a monster, and although she may be influenced by their advice, she will make the ultimate decision, as she is the one who is going to have to face the audience. So there is nothing sacred about the majority. On the contrary, the opinion of the person responsible for carrying out the decision has more weight than the views of the other participants in the discussion.

There are also discussion groups on a range of topics, such as the celebration of festivals or the children's education. When personal problems are discussed, it is usually in these smaller frameworks. If, for example, a member wants to go abroad and needs financial assistance from the community, this will usually be discussed and approved by three or four members, without the need for confirmation by the general meeting.

In addition, Tamuz holds seminars every two months for longer discussions (up to ten hours) on general topics, such as Israeli society, culture and education in the community, and the connection between kibbutz and town. Apart from giving the members the time to discuss these more complex issues, the seminars are seen as a further opportunity for personal contact among the members.

Goldman acknowledges that the Tamuz system places extraordinary pressure on the members. In the absence of formal frameworks or control mechanisms, the responsibility lies with the individual. Members decide what tasks and duties to assume, and they are responsible for a host of daily decisions that affect their fellow members. Because of the pressure, it is accepted at Tamuz that a member may want to take "time out" from the community, withdraw for a limited period from all responsibilities, stop coming to meetings, and even avoid social contact with others.

The danger that the Tamuz system will break down is frankly laid out. Possibly they are trying for too much, admits Goldman. In an aggressive, competitive society, the attempt to live by the principles of partnership, trust, and responsibility may simply be unrealistic. Alternatively, the community might be maintained by strong ideological motives at the expense of the individual. Goldman warns:

> We have known communities where members have denied themselves for the good of the cause or the idea. The Tamuz principle cannot allow a solution of that sort. Our community must enlarge personal freedom, not limit it. It must makes our members' lives richer, more varied, more interesting, more satisfying. A life of asceticism, life based on self-denial for the sake of the ideal, is not a life of freedom.

Tamuz is not looking for harmony or permanence. It has to be a dynamic and developing society, always changing and aware of its weaknesses and problems. There are disagreements, grudges, feelings of anger and frustration, he admits, but they do not harm the essential solidarity.

Meeting Yiftah Goldman, one is at once struck by the contrast between the man and his writing. Not that he is not serious. Slight, sensitive, bespectacled, he takes life very seriously indeed, as befits a philosophy lecturer at Tel Aviv University; but his conversation is full of humor.

"I don't want you to get the false impression that everything is all sweetness and light," he tells me. "Last night at the general meeting one of the members annoyed me so much I could have happily strangled him, but this morning he asked me if I'd take his kids to school, and of course I agreed."

Yiftah grew up at Yotvata, a large, successful kibbutz in the Arava Valley in the far south of the country. Yotvata is a classical kibbutz in the tradition of Hatzerim and Maagan Michael. Yiftah says that he still loves and respects the kibbutz but feels something else is needed, "alongside Yotvata, not instead of it." In the old days, he notes, there were many forms: the *kvutza,* the large kibbutz, the Labor Battalion, the *moshav.* It was only later around the 1940s and 1950s that kibbutzim became uniform and institutionalized. He thinks that the diversity of the early days should be reproduced.

Yiftah had always assumed that he would return to Yotvata. However, between leaving school and the army, he joined a group of kibbutz-born youngsters working as youth leaders. They went into the army together and began to discuss a common future during their military service. Some members thought they should return to their own kibbutzim;

others thought they should found a new kibbutz; a majority began to consider linking up with an urban kibbutz. What attracted them to Tamuz (then just starting out) was its liberal ideology, and in particular its positive attitude toward the individual. Yiftah gradually realized that he had much more in common with his fellow soldiers than with his friends back at Yotvata.

"It wasn't just the people of my own year," he recalls, "but the whole young community at the kibbutz. I simply didn't have anything to talk to them about. We lacked a common language."

Shortly after completing their military service, Yiftah and his comrades joined Tamuz, which, starting with nine members in 1987, had grown to fifteen. At first the new group maintained its independence, pooling its members' money separately from Tamuz, but by the end of the year most of them had joined the kibbutz on an individual basis.

Eran joined Tamuz a few years later. He is a physical education instructor, who grew up at Ein Harod, the first large kibbutz. His wife Hila, a special education teacher, is from a *moshav*. Eran was very sure that he did not want to return to Ein Harod after his army service. In his view, any child born on a conventional kibbutz has to "find his own corner" if he wants to become a member; he did not find his. Initially, although Eran and Hila came to Tamuz for the prosaic reason that a former classmate of Eran's, who was living there, told them they could rent an apartment cheaply, they found the combination of urban kibbutz and development town fascinating.

"It was rather like going back to my prearmy days, when we lived as a group of youth leaders," says Eran. "It was strange at first, with general meetings called to discuss every small matter."

He finds it much more satisfying than the brand of communal life in which he grew up. At Ein Harod everything was clearly laid out. If he had returned home, he would have gone to work in one of the branches of the kibbutz, and maybe in time he would have become the head of that branch. The horizons were limited. In Tamuz he finds tremendous scope for being really involved, while at the same time maintaining his individuality. There is far more consideration of the needs of the individual than at Ein Harod.

Yiftah acknowledges that Tamuz can only work on a small scale. In his opinion, if Tamuz grows to one hundred members, it should split into two units of fifty, and he believes that even fifty might be too large. Currently, the kibbutz has thirty-three members, two families who may become candidates, and three resident students. The students are economically independent and can choose their own degree of involvement in the community's social and cultural life. Two of them participate very fully; the third is simply a tenant.

Tamuz owns no cooperative enterprises, and each member is responsible for his or her own work. Aside from that, Tamuz operates in traditional kibbutz economic format, with seven collectively owned cars; the pooling of salaries; the joint financing of education, health, transportation, and phones; a communal laundry service; and the distribution of allowances to members on the basis of family size. One member, a computer programmer, explained that he had taken employment in the private sector to earn a higher salary. Despite the fact that the earnings are pooled, there is still the desire on the part of some members to feel they are making an adequate financial contribution to the kibbutz.

Tamuz members maintain separate households but enjoy a communal Sabbath meal together every Friday night. They celebrate the Jewish festivals as a group, in the kibbutz secular tradition. On my first visit, I found the kibbutz in a run-down apartment block, which they rented. There was absolutely nothing that indicated the existence of a communal society. Two of the apartments were adapted as kindergarten and day care center, the shelter was refurbished as a communal dining hall and meeting place, but none of this is visible. Since then they have moved to a building specially designed for the kibbutz. The members have bought their new apartments on an individual basis, with the intention that if anyone leaves, that member will sell his or her apartment back to the kibbutz.

So far sixteen units have been constructed. The pleasantly proportioned cubes are positioned in a manner that allows more green areas than usual at the expense of parking lots. They own only seven cars among them, whereas a similar group of people living privately would have between sixteen and thirty vehicles.

Erez took over the project from his wife, Adriana, when she gave birth. He points to the public terraces, overlooking what will be shady green lawns. Each apartment also has its own private terrace, which interconnects with its neighbor. Sixteen apartments are not enough for the current members, bearing in mind that they also need to accommodate their communal dining hall, kindergarten, day care center, and communal laundry. So they have rented six more apartments in the vicinity. They have acquired more land for later stages. They intend to sell six apartments to people who want to be associated with the kibbutz

Figure 11.1.   New apartments of Kibbutz Tamuz in 1999.

Source: (Daniel Gavron)

without becoming full members. At a later stage they will construct an additional twelve apartments.

Ram Carmi, the architect who designed the Israeli Supreme Court building in Jerusalem, was struck with the concept of an urban kibbutz and volunteered his services at a greatly reduced fee. A former kibbutz member himself, Carmi sought to find a way of expressing the communal idea architecturally, something he thinks rural kibbutzim have not achieved. In any case, it was not practical to reproduce the rural kibbutz pattern in town. He looked to the medieval monastery for his inspiration, which in his view was the archetypal self-sufficient community. Although the basic concept is Carmi's, the actual plans were done by three young architects of the Stav Company who designed the individual apartments along a central "spine" that gives access to the communal activities. The idea was to find a compromise between the desire of the kibbutz to be part of its urban environment, while remaining a distinct community. The first impressions of the Tamuz members are mostly positive. Even the critics concede that they are happy in the pleasant apartments. On the theoretical level, though, there are dissenting voices. Some of the members say they would have been happier with a less ambitious, more functional design, with more emphasis on living space and less on esthetics. They are concerned that the striking buildings may not fit in to the local neighborhood and hope that the ostentatious exterior will not elicit envy from their fellow citizens. It should be pointed out that the communal building accommodating the central hall, classrooms, kindergartens, day care centers, and other facilities has not yet been built; the architects say it will not be possible to assess the success of their concept until it is complete.

Beit Shemesh is situated in the Judaean hills eighteen miles west of Jerusalem. It was established in 1950 as one of the two dozen "development towns" built in Israel to absorb the mass immigration after the establishment of the state. Not very successful in its early years, with a higher-than-average unemployment rate, it has nevertheless grown to a community of some thirty thousand. In recent years, many people who work in Jerusalem and the Tel Aviv area and cannot afford the rents in those cities have made their homes there.

Tamuz was located deliberately in Beit Shemesh, with the idea of making a contribution to the community there. From the outset, the kibbutz engaged in educational projects in the town and admitted their neighbors' children to their kindergartens and day care centers. The members also ran adult education projects in the town. Two years ago, Tamuz established an official nonprofit association, the Center for Cooperative Learning, to facilitate its educational work in the town. One of the members, Osnat (Ossie) Elnatan, works full-time at the center.

Ossie grew up in Tel Aviv and joined the Reform Judaism Movement, which is relatively new in Israel. She served in the Nahal army unit at Kibbutz Yahel in the Arava Valley in the south. At twenty-four she joined nearby Lotan, where she married Hanan, a son of Kibbutz Mishmar Hanagev. They lived at Lotan for twelve years, before leaving three years ago. They decided that, with only fifty members, the desert kibbutz did not have an assured future.

They looked for a way to preserve both their communal lifestyle and a practical expression of their Reform Judaism. They first considered Hatzerim but (surprisingly) came to the conclusion that even that notably successful enterprise did not have a future as a kibbutz.

"Only the founders really believe in the kibbutz way of life," she affirms. "I think that when the next generation takes over at Hatzerim, it will stop being a kibbutz. It will become privatized, and that will be the end of the story."

So Ossie and Hanan decided to try Tamuz, admittedly much smaller and less obviously secure than Hatzerim, but also "with fewer pretensions." It was quite difficult to become absorbed into Tamuz, she admits. They had been members of the founding group of Lotan, and Ossie was successively farm manager and the head of various agricultural branches, but in Tamuz they were newcomers and it was not easy. They had another child, which helped weld them to the group. Ossie also took an undergraduate degree in economics at Ruppin and began studying for her master's in Judaic studies at the Shechter College in Jerusalem.

They miss Lotan, she admits. Their eldest child goes back often, and children come from Lotan to spend vacations with them in Tamuz. She sees nothing strange in opting for Tamuz even if it will only last for one generation. It is worthwhile in itself. People tell her that they have taken the bad things from town and kibbutz: they have to give in their salaries and do not even gain the benefit of a green rural environment.

"I think it is the *best* of both worlds," she says defiantly. "We live communally and also play our part in Israeli society."

She is certain that Tamuz exerts an influence. She does not know how much, but it does impact on the town of Beit Shemesh. Its Center for Cooperative Learning has a twin focus she explains: pluralistic Jewish education and community service. Their Beit Midrash consists of adult classes one day per week from September to June. They teach Bible, Talmud, local geography, and Jewish history and culture from a non-Orthodox point of view. Most of the students are local teachers, with a sprinkling of older people. There were twenty-seven students in 1999 and forty registered for 2000. In addition, they organize adult evening classes and enrichment programs for children, including assistance with homework. There is also a group of children with special needs, who have sports activities, hobby groups, special classes, and are served meals.

"For me, the involvement in Beit Shemesh is no less important than the communal life," says Ossie. "We have founded a Women's Council in Beit Shemesh to advance the cause of women. At present, there is only one woman on the municipal council, and we aim to improve that. The Women's Council is a personal involvement of mine, not an official Tamuz initiative."

Hagar and Danny Elbaz, both in their forties, have purchased an apartment in the Tamuz complex but have no intention of joining the kibbutz. They are the first of an eventual six nonmember resident families, associated with Tamuz but not members.

Hagar was born on a kibbutz but grew up in Jerusalem. She is a textile designer. Danny, who was born in Morocco, serves in the police. They lived opposite Tamuz and sent their youngest daughter to the kibbutz day care center. Later they became involved in activities together with the Tamuz members: parents' committees, education, local politics, and citizens' empowerment. Hagar feels she has a lot in common with the members of Tamuz. She and her husband very much want to be part of the Tamuz community and continue to be involved in education and social activism in Beit Shemesh. She is attracted to the non-Orthodox Judaism of Tamuz and plans to study this year at the Beit Midrash. She does not, however, see herself as a kibbutznik. She feels that the era of economic sharing is in the past.

"Anyway, I can't start this intensive communal living at my time of life," she says emphatically. "I'm not going to start going to general meetings to discuss budgets and so on. At the same time, we feel very good with the Tamuz members. We'll celebrate the New Year with them, Shavuot, and Independence Day—that sort of thing."

Although she feels a strong affinity with Tamuz, Hagar, who has been living in Beit Shemesh for sixteen years, thinks they have failed to become an integral part of the local community. Despite their genuine efforts and the many good things they have introduced, they are still not accepted by the locals. She is irritated by the sometimes grotesque rumors that go around concerning the kibbutz members—one of the most recent is that they do not have their sons circumcised—but she also says they do not always have the right approach to the local citizens.

She gives a recent example: Tamuz is looking for an administrative secretary for its Beit Midrash. They held a long discussion about whether they should employ a local citizen in her late twenties or thirties, or whether they should look for a young woman just out of the army, to whom they could better explain their aims. They decided to look for a young woman.

"They are so wrong," insists Hagar. "An older woman would definitely take longer to understand what they want, but she would be an ambassador from them to the town, just as I am. They need bridges of that sort. They want to be part of Beit Shemesh, but there is for all that something isolationist about them."

The Tamuz children go to local schools. The oldest of them are eleven years old, and they are beginning to form their own Society of Children entirely spontaneously. They have circles of friends in Tamuz and beyond. Some of the Beit Shemesh children are joining in with the activities of the Tamuz kids.

"There is no question of educating them to carry on our path," says Yiftah. "They will do what they want to do, maybe with us, maybe not. Tamuz may well be a one-generation phenomenon. I am a bachelor and don't have kids of my own, but I don't mind what our children do. I hope they won't deal on the stock exchange or peddle drugs."

It is clear that, for Yiftah, the two occupations are only marginally different in their undesirability. In their almost casual attitude toward the future, we see a huge difference between Tamuz and the traditional kibbutz. The kibbutz was building for the ages. The members desperately wanted their children to carry on the enterprise and took enormous pains to educate them to this end. The Tamuz members are living in the here and now. They do not worry about the distant future and would not even consider educating their children toward any specific purpose.

The traditional kibbutz saw itself as an educational force, a blueprint for society as a whole. True, they were a minority, but they were the "pioneers going in front of the camp." One day the whole country would be one big kibbutz (Meuhad) or a network of cooperating communes (Artzi).

One of the founders of Tamuz did have that kind of faith. He thought that if they proved how well the new commune worked, neighborhoods all over Israel would form urban kibbutzim. The Tamuz members, however, have long lost any illusions on that score. They have no hope whatever of being a social example for the citizens of Beit Shemesh. They are more than satisfied if they can maintain good relations with the townspeople and make their contribution in the form of education and civic awareness.

In Yiftah Goldman's view, the secret of Tamuz is in its improvisations. Apart from the obvious differences—not owning assets except for homes, living in an urban environment—the main difference between Tamuz and the traditional kibbutz lies in its minimal formal structures. He also points to the concept of flexible membership. Like Hagar and Danny Elbaz, a family can decide the degree of its association with Tamuz.

The "constitution" is only activated if a member leaves the kibbutz. The Tamuz system, as we have seen, is based entirely on trust, and if somebody leaves, it may be a sign that the trust has broken down. In that case you need rules.

Although it is affiliated with the United Kibbutz Movement, Tamuz is much more like the sort of commune that can be found in most countries of the Western world: communities of idealistic people who band together to live a more harmonious life. This is not said in any judgmental way. There is much that is admirable in Tamuz, and its members are making a sincere and genuine effort to live ethically in a society that is becoming increasingly selfish and materialistic. They are also serving people beyond their own front door in a way that the traditional kibbutz is only starting to do.

Possibly the fact that so many of its members grew up on kibbutzim makes it more successful than other town communes have been in the past. They have a better understanding of communal life, more awareness of its opportunities and dangers. It certainly looks as if Tamuz will be a one-generation affair, and that is valid as far as it goes.

12

סמר

SAMAR
TOUCHING UTOPIA

After twenty-three years, Kibbutz Samar still has an open public purse, from which its members take as much as they think they need. It has no work roster, except for the care of children and livestock, and the members please themselves when, where, and for how long they work. The kibbutz has rules, but as few of them as possible. It has officers, but these have been reduced to an absolute minimum. Its few committees are ad hoc. Samar is anarchy, but not chaos. Based on total trust, it is the most daring utopian experiment that has emerged from the kibbutz movement so far. Although very different from Israel's other kibbutzim, Samar is a kibbutz product, the invention of kibbutz children who thought that they could improve on what their parents had created.

If two decades is a comparatively long time for such a radical experiment to survive, it is a short time for myths to be formed, but there is already a legend about Samar's origins: In 1974, with Israel still reeling from the trauma of the Yom Kippur War, Daniella, a kibbutz daughter, wrote a letter that she circulated to fellow children of the left-wing Kibbutz Artzi movement, calling for a new type of kibbutz. The letter was lost, and "Daniella" has never been found. Yossi Avnat, one of the founders of Samar, is not sure that there ever was a letter—or a Daniella. He does not remember what triggered it off, nor does he think it matters.

"It was needed at that time," he says. "I don't know who started it; but very quickly there were fifteen of us who met every week at Givat Haviva and started working it out."

259

Givat Haviva is the educational center and archive of Kibbutz Artzi, and about one hundred youth leaders in their intermediate year between school and army would be called together every week for instruction, enrichment, and social activities. A lot of activity was packed into the weekly get-togethers, but the fifteen managed to find an extra two hours to talk about their new ideas.

"Basically we felt that our parents had got it wrong," recalls Yossi. "We were all from kibbutzim about forty years old, and we were acutely aware of the alienation between the kibbutz member and the kibbutz establishment. We knew all about the tyranny of the work roster and the humiliating dependence on committees. We forged our principles in revolt against the established kibbutz and have held onto them ever since."

Yossi is a balding, gentle man with a soft voice—hardly a fire-eating anarchist rebel, although that is precisely the image that the members had in their early years. Samar was not accepted to membership in Kibbutz Artzi for a decade, and when the matter did come up, Yossi, a son of Mizra, one of the showpieces of that movement, voted against.

We are eating our supper on Mussa and Mazal's terrace. The balmy night is enveloped in black velvet pierced by the incredibly bright stars that shine over Israel's southern desert. Children roll up their salad in homemade pita and stuff it into their mouths or chase each other on the lawn. Jumbo, a huge St. Bernard, jostles a Labrador mongrel for tidbits from my plate.

"One of our first arguments was about admitting dogs to the dining hall," remarks Mussa. His tone combines brashness and humor; his bearded face somehow personifies the place. "We decided against, and the dogs understood, even if some of their owners didn't."

Samar is situated in the Arava valley some fifteen miles north of Eilat on the Red Sea. A green oasis in the desert, with palm trees and reed-covered verandas, between the stark chocolate granite hills of the Negev and the distant mauve mountains of Edom, it is a magical place where anything seems possible.

I had wandered into the kibbutz dining hall three hours earlier and helped myself to orange juice and dates. I could have taken coffee or tea, sour cream, cheese, or bread and jam. None of the cupboards or refrigerators was locked. There was nothing to prevent me making an international call from the dining hall phone, but I just used it to call Mussa in his room. He arrived full of apologies at failing to pick me up from the main road, where the Eilat bus had deposited me.

Figure 12.1.   Samar in 1999.

Source: (Daniel Gavron)

"You mean you walked all that way in the heat?" he asked anxiously. "That's terrible." The walk was less than ten minutes, and the early evening, if not exactly cool, was certainly not hot.

Also getting off the bus was Ruskin, a volunteer from Hull in the north of England. A welfare assessor on an extended vacation, Ruskin had previously worked on a Galilee kibbutz as a volunteer more than a decade earlier. This time he chose Samar because he heard it was "special."

"Was it different from what you expected?" I asked him.

"I think things always are," he replied.

"How is Samar different?"

He thought for a few seconds before replying. "The people are normal."

The name had nothing to do with the founders. It was chosen by the settlement department Names Committee, which decided to call it after the juncus (*samar* in Hebrew), a needlelike plant used for manufacturing paper that was experimentally grown here before the kibbutz was established.

There were a number of locations suggested to the group. One of them was to reinforce Geshur on the Golan Heights. They refused on principle to settle in the Golan that was conquered from Syria in the Six Day War of 1967, notes Yossi with a laugh. Today their decision looks pragmatic and hardheaded, as Geshur might well be compelled to relocate if Israel reaches a peace agreement with Syria.

"We were accused of saying no to everything," recalls Yossi, "but that wasn't fair. We just wanted to do things differently."

The first group, which had increased to twenty-five by then, started at Samar within the framework of the army's Nahal settlement corps. They were joined by a much larger group of sixty members, who were apparently enthused by their ideas, but most left soon after the end of their army service.

There were two basic principles, explains Yossi. The first thing was that the kibbutz member must be autonomous, that the community could not make decisions about an individual's private life. Paradoxically, the second principle was to step up and enhance partnership and cooperation, making the group as tight as possible.

"I think the breakthrough was to stop dealing with equality," he muses. "We believed in equality, but we didn't waste time on it. Not everyone needed three pairs of trousers. One member needed five pairs, another wanted to spend two weeks on the beach in Eilat, a third planned to study for three years in Philadelphia."

There is a distinct echo of Tamuz, also founded by children of the kibbutz; but Samar has taken the whole idea much further. Living in a town, with all the needs of modern life, Tamuz members receive a monthly allowance based on family size. Living miles from the center of the country, Samar members have dared to experiment with the open cash box.

> At first there was a fixed monthly allowance, but we opted for the open box system pretty quickly and have kept it open ever since. Everyone takes what he wants and nothing is written down. We never entirely solved the question of how much money to put in the box. The treasurer put in a certain amount every week, and if a member knew he had to go to Tel Aviv, he would take it early in the week to make sure there was still enough. There is still a box in the kibbutz office for petty cash, but today we all have credit cards.

"Members of Hatzerim also have credit cards," I remark.

"That's different," points out Mussa. "At Hatzerim the treasurer keeps a check on the members to see that they don't go over the limit; here nobody writes down anything."

Yossi remembers that, despite his criticism of the traditional kibbutz, it took him a long time before he truly internalized the idea that the individual superseded the community. The traditional kibbutz assumed that if the community was successful, the individual would be secure. Samar puts it the other way round: if the individual is cared for, the community will be successful. Yossi still regrets that the Jewish festivals are mostly not observed at Samar, as they were in the kibbutz where he grew up. He used to love the celebrations; it turned out that his fellow members of Samar did not. They resented the formal structure of marking Jewish festivals that was imposed on the members. At Samar, if someone wants to do something, he or she assembles an ad hoc committee and does it. If nobody wants to do anything, then that is fine.

It all sounds brilliant, I tell them, but how does it actually *work?*

"I wake up every morning surprised that it is still working!" declares Mussa.

He was one of a group of ten kibbutz-born members in their twenties mobilized by Kibbutz Artzi in 1978 "to knock some sense into the young anarchists of Samar." Mussa was born and brought up in Maanit, a well-established kibbutz in the center of the country. He was told that the members of Samar took drugs, indulged in orgies, and did not work. When he arrived, though, they were all working extremely hard in the intense heat of the Arava valley, picking their tomato crop.

"They were suspicious of us," he recalls. "They looked on us as Kibbutz Artzi informers, but that evening, after work, we joined them in racing an old Vespa motor scooter around the fields. Later they told us that this convinced them that we were okay, that we didn't take ourselves too seriously."

Mussa finds it difficult to describe the process of his "conversion" to the Samar system. He married Mazal, a member of the second Samar group, and the two of them studied at Tel Aviv University: she, psychology; he, Middle East studies. They lived in Tel Aviv during their studies, before returning to Maanit. Back at his home kibbutz, Mussa found himself irritated by what he calls "the small deceits" of life at an established kibbutz. Everything is decided by committees; everything is written down and has to be justified. A member might make a trip to the nearby town, simply to enjoy himself and eat an ice cream. If he picks up a pair of glasses, though, he writes his expenses down to the budget of the Health Committee.

"I realized that they were cheating themselves," he says, "and that Samar was simply better. The Samar system avoided the pettiness and suspicion, the unnecessary rules. We don't tell lies here because there is nobody to tell lies to."

Despite the freedom, there are recognized limits at Samar, notes Mussa. Travel abroad is virtually unlimited, yet the members do not travel very much. At the same time, no member would think of buying a car, although there is nothing to prevent one from doing so. Yossi adds that the members were always cautious and never tried for too much. Another factor is the climate and the location.

"They used to say that the kibbutz was populated by socialists and social cases," he says with a smile "Well, here in Samar it is very hot, and there is not much to do except work. The social cases left us very quickly."

In the early days, recalls Yossi, they would have general meetings at least twice a week. Mazal, Mussa's wife, remembers meetings every night.

"It was dreadfully intense," she says. "At the time we were all tremendously excited by ideology of the first group and keen to join in the new experiment. Looking back, I don't know how we lived like that."

It was partly the pressure that drove her and Mussa to pursue further studies in the United States, where Mazal earned her second degree and doctorate, but they returned to Samar and have remained here ever since.

Today Samar has sixty-six members, with another dozen in various stages of candidacy, but for the first few years there were only about thirty. The small size probably facilitated the informal structure, and various army groups and other visitors helped keep the place going. There is a general consensus that Samar should remain small, not more than a hundred members.

The rate of general meetings has dropped to about one every two weeks. The secretary, who tends to assume his duties rather than be elected, puts up a note and about twenty-five members usually turn up. On the other hand, anybody can turn up to meetings of the general committee; committee meetings on education or the economy are also open. The only formally elected officers are the treasurer and the general manager. The accounts have to be kept; the farming has to be coordinated; everything else can be arranged when and if the members want it.

Personal spending is unregulated, but the purchase of a tractor, the laying of paths, or the installation of outside lighting has to be a communal decision. Unlike Tamuz, the members of Samar have no objection to voting, and only a simple majority is required except in exceptional circumstances. The general meeting does not have statutory powers, and its decisions are only recommendations.

Although a member is not obligated to bring personal plans to the general meeting, whether they concern work, study, or travel, Yossi is a great believer in consultation. The Samar system can only work with maximum communication, he feels. Nine years ago Yossi went to study computer control systems at Ruppin. He was thirty-five and beginning to think about the future, when the members of Samar would be too old to work in farming. For the first year after graduating, he had to work in the north of the country, but after that he found employment at the huge dairy of Kibbutz Yotvata, some five miles to the north. He also set up a computer control unit with two other members of Samar, providing services for regional enterprises, other kibbutzim, and local businesses.

All this was a personal initiative, stresses Yossi, but he felt obliged to bring it to the general meeting at every stage. He did not have to, it was emphasized. Mussa interrupts to make the point that recently Yossi was offered a job at the regional date sorting and storage plant. Although it would have involved a drop in salary of some $30,000 annually, everyone at the general meeting said it was up to Yossi to decide. As it turned out, Yossi decided to remain with the dairy.

I return to the question of how Samar works, and Yossi's wife, Deganit, joins the conversation. Deganit works with Mussa in the date plantation, which she says is a good example because there is a team of seven members who have been working there for about a decade. Dates are Samar's biggest branch and its biggest earner. Although Mussa is the nominal head of the branch, everybody argues all the time.

"It is a positive feature of the system," insists Deganit, in her forties but looking ten years younger in shorts and a sleeveless blouse, her hair tied in a ponytail. "There are arguments all the time, but ten minds are trained on all the problems."

At harvesting time, more hands are needed, so Deganit makes a list of every member of Samar who can be mobilized for the job. This is entirely on her own initiative. Nobody told her to do it. In fact, harvesting time in late summer and early fall is the highlight of the year. Everybody joins the date-picking team after their own work, and the entire membership of Samar works together picking dates until the sun sets. It is also a period when members get to talk to each other more than at any other time.

The following morning, I join the date workforce. We meet in the dining hall (half an hour later than scheduled) and grab a quick snack before being driven to the plantation in a van. Once there, we all clamber on to a "maniscope," a remarkable piece of machinery invented by

Samar for picking the dates and carrying out other operations on the palms. Attached to an imported tractor and built by Ein Gedi, a kibbutz some hundred miles to the north, the maniscope was conceived by the Samar date workforce.

"Because we do not employ laborers from Thailand or anywhere else, and because we have a constant free exchange of ideas, we are always coming up with mechanization projects," explains Mussa.

The maniscope is a platform that wraps itself around the date palm at any required height, enabling us to stand and do whatever has to be done. On this morning we are tying sacks around the date bunches to keep the birds off. Most of Samar's dates are organic, so they cannot use pesticides. Making the date branch mainly organic was an idea that evolved from distaste for chemical fertilizers and pesticides, and later the idea turned out to be a sound economic proposition.

Although still early in the morning, the sun is already hot in the Arava, and we are soon sweating freely. As I work, pushing the bunches into the sacks and tying them up, trying to avoid the savagely sharp spikes of the leaves, my memory goes back to Amiad, a Galilee kibbutz of which I was a member in 1961. Kohner, a kibbutznik with no academic qualifications but an extremely fertile mind, invented the apple-picking platform. Noticing that only one person could stand on a ladder, that the ladders were clumsy, and that the pickers often fell off them, he conceived the idea of an elevated wheelbarrow, a triangular wooden platform, with a wheel and two handles, that could be pushed close against the tree and carry three or four pickers. Kibbutz Amiad patented the device, which sold so well that Kohner was able to open a laboratory workshop and invent many other pieces of equipment, most of them connected with irrigation. His inventions became the basis of a factory that assured the economic future of the kibbutz.

The maniscope on which I now stood, tying sacks around date bunches, was light-years ahead of Kohner's platform, yet the device was clearly its successor, maybe its "great-great-grandson." For all its weaknesses, I reflected, the kibbutz has definitely afforded opportunities for enterprising and imaginative people. Would Kohner have created so much on his own? Possibly he would have, as he was an extremely talented individual, but surely the support he received from the collective was a factor in his success.

Going back to work, even for only a few hours, as well as the conversation of the night before, set me thinking about kibbutz life in a more personal way. Although I was a kibbutznik for only a comparatively short period, the experience was enormously significant. Despite the reservations of most Samar members about the formalized structures of celebrating the Jewish festivals, it is the communal celebrations that most stick in the mind.

Pessah, of course, with several hundred people singing traditional melodies and modern folk songs; the Shavuot festival of the first fruits, with the beautiful flower-garlanded children, dressed in white, dancing among the straw bales; Purim, with everyone dressing up and a bit drunk; Tu Beshvat, the tree-planting ceremony to mark the new year of the trees.

The class bar mitzvah, when the thirteen-year-old children carry out thirteen challenging tasks and perform a show for the whole kibbutz; the kibbutz wedding, in which, after the religious ceremony, bride and groom sit on an improvised stage while their classmates embarrassingly remind them of the key events of their childhoods.

And, of course, the other side of the coin: funerals, where the entire kibbutz sinks into a profound gloom, on this day an enlarged family in every sense of the word, united by sadness at the departure of an elderly member or stunned by the tragic loss of a soldier kibbutznik.

It is at times like these that the kibbutz becomes greater than the sum of its parts. Whirling in a hora circle dance, singing with a hundred other voices, celebrating, laughing, crying, grieving—it all becomes magnified and you feel part of something bigger and more important than yourself. These moments are rare, yet they are an unforgettable part of the kibbutz experience. At Samar, this spirit is particularly strong despite its rejection of many of the traditional kibbutz forms.

We worked steadily until ten o'clock, when we drove back to the dining hall for a substantial breakfast. It was all very relaxed, with none of the pressure to get up and go that I remembered from my own days on the kibbutz. Mussa points out that he can never be sure how many people are going to report for work on a given morning. Maybe ten will show up on a day when only two are needed. Alternatively, only three may be available when there is a load of work to be done.

"Then I have to go and recruit people from other branches," he explains. "If they agree to come, that's fine; but if they don't, there is nothing I can do about it."

After breakfast, the others returned to their sack tying, while Mussa took me to the metal workshop to show me some of the other pieces of equipment invented at Samar. One particularly impressive device shakes the dates from the palms onto nets, and from there they pass onto a moving belt, which carries them to a hopper for sorting and packing.

At the dairy I meet Gigi, an American from New Jersey who came to Samar from the neighboring kibbutz of Lotan (where she was friendly with Ossie Elnatan, whom we met at Tamuz).

Gigi joined Samar because she married one of the members, and he was "even more obstinate than I am." Although she is still only a candidate for membership, Gigi already manages the dairy. This is not so unusual, she notes. Most of the people working in the dairy are either candidates or volunteers.

"The dairy is not really suitable for Samar people because you have to go by the rule book," she explains. "Nothing happens if you turn up two hours late in the dates or if you decide to work one hour one day and twelve the next, but the cows have to be milked at four o'clock—and that means four!"

With 260 milk cows, the enterprise has to be run like clockwork, which is simply alien to the nature of most Samar members. On the other hand, when there is a hitch, Samar is at its best. The other day a cow was sick and the vet came, and Gigi was tied up with him and could not start the milking. She called the metal workshop, and somebody was at the dairy within five minutes, getting on with the work.

Gigi is able to compare Samar with Lotan, where she lived for ten years and which is run in conventional kibbutz style. There are things she loves about Samar, she says, and other things she dislikes. The first thing to say about the kibbutz is that it works. She is responsible for the regional dairy reports, and Samar is as good as anywhere else. Lotan was almost strangled by its committees. The Samar system is much more to her taste. The kibbutz develops according to the wishes and needs of the members. People work hard. They are motivated. The atmosphere is good. There are none of the petty little problems that plague the normal kibbutznik. She gives an everyday example of buying a birthday gift for a fellow member.

"Here I'll just take the money from petty cash," she says. "At Lotan we would apply for the money, provide a receipt, ask to have the amount spent divided between the five friends of the birthday girl and deducted accordingly from the members' personal allowances. Quite honestly, it isn't worth the accountant's time."

"How do you make decisions about the dairy?"

"I have an example ready at hand," she says. "The southern corral badly needs repairing. We need metalwork to rebuild the frames, roofing, and concreting. I am consulting. I'm asking around to find the people who know about these things. There won't be any formal discussion in the general meeting. There won't be an official decision. It will simply get done."

Samar has just opened a tropical fish branch, notes Gigi. There was no discussion in the general meeting, no decision by the management committee, no formal allocation of funds. One of the members decided to take it on, persuaded a couple of her friends to join her, convened an ad hoc committee to discuss the budget with the treasurer, got it approved by the general meeting, and now the branch is up and running. Possibly it will not turn out to be profitable, but, if it gives satisfaction to the members working there, Samar will not hasten to close it down.

"I told you there are things I don't like," says Gigi. "With all its advanced ideas, I am sorry to tell you that Samar is totally sexist. The members are typecast. You will never find men in the children's houses, or the kitchens, or even the dining hall. Never."

Gigi insists that she is not naive. She is not looking for a fifty-fifty division of labor, but surely eighty-twenty is not unrealistic. At Lotan, where a third of the members come from America, there is something akin to that. At Samar, the setup puts enormous pressure on those families who do want to live by the principles of sex equality. Gigi was determined to continue working in the dairy after she gave birth (like Miriam Baratz at Degania ninety years before her), but she also wanted to breast-feed her baby. It was difficult to persuade the women at the baby house to call her whenever her infant wanted to be fed. They were not too understanding about her putting the baby into the house at the age of three months and resented having to maintain continual contact with her.

"What really upsets me," she confesses, "is the educational effect. I see it with my own daughter. I didn't come half across the world to live in a supposedly progressive society to have my daughter tell me that welding is no job for a woman."

The subject had actually come up the previous evening, when Deganit told of her attempts to start a graphic arts office at Yotvata with two other girls.

"If everyone does what she wants," demanded one of the kibbutz veterans at the committee meeting called to discuss the venture, "who will remain to work in the children's houses and the kitchens?"

It wasn't so much what he said that annoyed her, explained Deganit, but the fact that nobody said a word in response, nobody put him in his place. She was appalled by that. At the same time, she admitted that when she and Yossi recently adopted a baby, she was the one to take maternity leave. They had considered the possibility that Yossi would take leave, as there was no question of breast-feeding the infant and Yossi could look after her equally well.

"When it came to it, I just couldn't do it," confessed Deganit. "Yossi and I have always shared the domestic chores, but I simply couldn't accept the idea of his taking the maternity leave."

Mussa admits that the division of work at Samar, like that on most kibbutzim, is on sexist lines, but he maintains that women have a big influence in both the general meeting and the various ad hoc committees. His wife, Mazal, served as treasurer for two years, and it was she who introduced credit cards. Ultimately, he thinks, the women will solve the problem by going outside the kibbutz to work in their own professions, as all over the Western world. Mazal works as a psychologist at the regional mental health clinic in Yotvata, and several of the other women members have jobs outside.

Mussa is worried about the future. He thinks that several of the members have stopped pulling their full weight, and this could reach a critical mass that would endanger Samar's survival. He is also unsure whether members are still exercising sufficient self-control with the public purse. The kibbutz is earning well, and the books are balanced. So far expenses have been modest, but the members have started expanding their houses, which costs money.

Yossi disagrees. The members have on the whole been very responsible about home extensions, building only an extra bedroom or two as their families became larger. No one built on a grandiose scale. Samar can easily afford it. Regarding work, it is simply a question of creating a new branch like his computer control business, something that can give employment to older members and income to the kibbutz.

"You are wrong, Yossi," insists Mussa. "Even if you create your new branch, there will still be people who don't work hard enough. We have always had members like that, but the proportion is growing. We have no sanctions at Samar, beyond personal persuasion, and that doesn't always work. The other thing is that we are more prosperous today and that creates its own problems. In the past only the idealists remained. Today Samar is a comfortable place to live."

"If you are right, we'll stop existing," responds Yossi, "and that's fine with me."

"What if the majority want to go on with Samar?"

"Then we'll survive," insists Yossi. "Look, in the modern world there are two main reasons that people work: money and satisfaction.

Figure 12.2.   Samar in the 1990s.

Source: (Israel Government Press Office)

Here we have always worked because we enjoy it. If we find the right business, the members will work."

Another need is new housing. The kibbutz can afford the home extensions but not new homes. For that they need a new source of income, and that brings Yossi back to the new business. He would like to see another twenty members at Samar, maybe including some of their own children. So far they have only one child who has completed the army, and she is a long way from a decision about her future.

A conversation with Gal, Deganit and Yossi's fifteen year-old son, makes three things abundantly clear: one, he has no idea whether he will live in Samar, although he has enjoyed growing up there; two, he is not at all sure what he wants to do with his life; three, he does not feel under the slightest pressure from his parents to continue living in Samar.

"I have a dream that at least some of our children will continue with a cooperative way of life," says Yossi. "But I am not sure they will live here."

One thing that does not worry them is growing old. In the first years of the kibbutz, when Yossi was the treasurer, he arranged pensions for all the members, and the kibbutz has kept up-to-date with its contributions. Actually, he says, he always thought that "kibbutz was better than pensions." However, the emphasis on the rights of the individual member prompted him to take that extremely prescient action.

Another argument between the two old-timers concerns the terms of admission to Samar. Mussa wants to tighten them up.

"The freer we are, the tougher we must be about admitting new members," he insists. "Our free system can only work with the right type of members, therefore we have to be doubly strict about admitting them."

Yossi does not agree. For him the absence of rules is still a cardinal principle of Samar. If the kibbutz starts making rules for admission, it will not end there.

I leave with regret. It has been a fascinating experience. Samar is not only an oasis in the desert; it is an oasis in the sometimes arid reality of today's Israel. The bus speeds north up the Arava, and the sun sets behind the Negev mountains to the west. It already seems like a dream.

While I was visiting Samar, Mussa and Ofer (Gigi's husband and the current kibbutz treasurer) quizzed me keenly about Kfar Ruppin's conversion to capitalism. Both of them wondered whether the Kfar Ruppin model might eventually suit Samar. It was a surprising submission. Is this indeed the future of Samar? Nobody can be sure, because if there is one thing predictable about Samar, it is its unpredictability. The fiery young anarchists, who have turned into gentle middle-aged idealists, may indeed end their days as elderly capitalists.

Whatever happens, the members of Samar have achieved quite a lot: the building of a prosperous green village in the burning desert wastes, the establishment of a thriving concern based on grindingly hard work in the toughest conditions, the creation of a society with a unique combination of cooperation and freedom, and the achievement of an unprecedented degree of trust among human beings.

Twenty years ago Samar's founders came up with the same critique of the classical kibbutz as that of today's advocates of change. Early on they criticized the lack of personal freedom, the dependence on committees, the *metapelet* complex, the feelings of "us and them." From the outset, all members of Samar were responsible for their own work.

However, the Samar solution was diametrically opposed to the one espoused by today's reformers. Instead of converting to capitalism, Samar went more socialist—or maybe anarchist. Perhaps it is not surprising that others have not followed this route. Samar is unique. It is not a pattern that can be copied on any sort of scale. Mussa says he will be satisfied if it can make it to a quarter of a century. With only another year to go, it almost certainly will. It may not survive very many years past that, at least not in its present form.

Although there have been similar ventures in almost total freedom, both in Israel and abroad, none of them lasted more than a year or two, so Samar already deserves its place in the communal equivalent of the *Guinness Book of Records*. If, as seems likely, Samar is (like Tamuz) a one-generation phenomenon, does that make it a failure? Maybe. But what a brave failure! H. G. Wells called the inhabitants of his imaginary utopia "men like Gods." Although the members of Samar are only men like men, they have dared to aspire to heaven on earth. They have not created Utopia, but they got pretty close.

CONCLUSION

A legend of the Roman siege of Jerusalem in 70 C.E. relates that Rabbi Yohanan Ben-Zakkai was smuggled out of the city in a sealed coffin and taken to the tent of Vespasian, the Roman commander. The venerable rabbi foretold that Vespasian would be emperor of Rome before the year was out. When the prophesy came true, the Roman general asked Ben-Zakkai what he wanted for a reward, and the rabbi requested permission to establish a school of Jewish scholarship. With Vespasian's agreement, Ben-Zakkai founded an academy at Yavne, and it was this center of learning that prevented the Jewish religion from suffering the same fate as the Jewish nation, which was destroyed and exiled after the fall of Jerusalem.

Yavne was therefore an appropriately symbolic venue for the founding conference of the "Communal Trend," an association of kibbutzim dedicated to the preservation of classical kibbutz values. A religious *kvutza* established in the darkest days of World War II, Yavne is named after the ancient academy, where Judaism was preserved. It is a solid, prosperous, successful community, and a kibbutz in every sense of the word. The sponsors of the conference clearly hoped that modern Yavne would achieve for the the kibbutz ideal what the ancient Yavne had done for Judaism.

The conference was convened on on July 6, 1999, by Yaacov Gadish, a former director-general of Israel's finance ministry and a veteran member of Yavne. Representatives of sixteen kibbutzim were officially present, authorized to attend by their general meetings, including Hatzerim and Maagan Michael. The organizers expressed confidence that at least double that figure would eventually join. The leaders of the United Kibbutz Movement and Kibbutz Dati were in attendance, and the leader of Kibbutz Artzi, newly elected to the Knesset, Israel's parliament, sent a supportive message.

A position paper prepared for the conference noted:

> Many kibbutzim are adopting far-reaching changes out of a lack of confidence that they can run their lives according to kibbutz values. In view of this development, it is vital to create an association of kibbutzim that will be a strong foundation for the renewal of the kibbutz on the basis of essential communal values.

The aims of the new association are to guarantee the continuation of the cooperative idea in changing times and to assist kibbutzim to maintain communal lifestyles. The common basis, to which all members of the Communal Trend must adhere, are joint ownership of the productive assets of the kibbutz; avoidance of any differentials in allowances or incomes, unless based on family size, seniority, or special needs; comprehensive mutual assistance among members of the kibbutz; and cooperative and democratic management.

The Communal Trend announced the organization of a series of workshops and seminars to discuss all the problems and pledged it would provide consultancy services for any kibbutzim that needed them. It resolved to create models to solve those problems emerging as the result of changes in the kibbutz and outside it. The new association offered an exchange of views with those kibbutzim that were not ready join but were hesitating over their future path. A small staff, with a budget of some $70,000 a year, intends to lobby aggressively in kibbutzim all over the country to act as a counterweight to the momentum for change.

Opening the conference, Yaacov Gadish said that the leadership of the kibbutz movement lost its way in the 1970s. This led to a loss of confidence on the part of individual kibbutzim, notably to bringing in outside managers. On the other hand, the kibbutz had to solve the members' practical problems. He favored arranging pensions for the kibbutz veterans, as this would remove anxieties about the future and facilitate the maintenance of the cooperative structure. Gadish ended with a call to the younger generation to pick up the torch of kibbutz values.

In the ensuing discussion, many speakers argued that the kibbutz structure is uniquely suitable for the modern world. Communal life answers many of the problems of Western society, with its alienation and lack of human contact. If a kibbutz honestly decided it preferred a different way, this was entirely acceptable, suggested one participant, but if kibbutzim simply drifted away from communal values through inertia, this was a shame, and it was the task of the Communal Trend to prevent this.

The final speaker was a bashful youngster from Sde Eliahu, a religious kibbutz in the Jordan Valley. The only thing unique about his kibbutz was its communal values, he declared. If he was looking for pioneering, quality of life, challenge, satisfaction, good education, Jewish values, religious vitality, and a satisfying culture, he could find them elsewhere.

"What we have to offer is equality, partnership, and cooperation," he declared. "That is what makes us unique. That is our particular contribution. We have to repeat it morning, noon, and night. That is what it's all about!"

He spoke eloquently, but it was probably his youth that prompted the delegates to thunderous applause for the first time that day. It seemed to give them the feeling that there was hope for the future.

For despite the crisis, the doubts, and the radical changes, the kibbutz has much to celebrate in its ninety-first year. Of other similar attempts to create an ethical society, only the communes of the Hutterian Society of Brothers in North America have lasted longer, and they were always on the margins of society. As opposed to the Hutterians, the Shakers, Amana, and others, including the modern American and European communes, the kibbutz always exerted a strong influence on its environment.

Even today, the kibbutz plays an important role in Israeli society and makes a notable contribution to the nation. Less than 3 percent of the population, the kibbutzim still grow and raise 40 percent of the country's agricultural produce, make 10 percent of its industrial output, and produce 7 percent of its exports. Half the volunteers in the army's elite combat units and nearly a third of its air force pilots are children of the kibbutz. Almost a fifth of the army's young officers are kibbutzniks.

The kibbutzim still make important contributions to society. There are drug rehabilitation programs on a number of kibbutzim and prisoner rehabilitation programs on others. In the past decade, several dozen kibutzim hosted thousands of new immigrants from the Soviet Union in a "First Home in Israel" program. Some of these allegedly antisocialist newcomers even remained on their kibbutzim. When an earthquake hit Turkey in August 1999, it was the kibbutzim that took the lead in collecting, processing, storing, and dispatching supplies to the stricken Turks.

It has already been mentioned that, with the opening of kibbutz schools, kindergartens, and day care centers to the general public, the popularity of the kibbutz education system has proved itself. A kibbutz member was recently quoted as claiming that urban wives plan their pregnancies according to prospective vacancies in the day care centers at the nearest kibbutz. So the founders of the Communal Trend had many reasons to feel that their cause might achieve a measure of success.

They were, moreover, reinforced by a meeting that had taken place the day before the Yavne assembly. At the Haifa University conference on the "Search for the Good Society," the kibbutz representatives spoke of their doubts about the survival of the kibbutzim, but the guests from abroad had only good things to say.

"I am very sorry, but I have not come here to mark the funeral of the kibbutz!" declared Seymour Melman, professor of industrial engineering at New York's Columbia University. Melman was not a first-time visitor to Israel. Fourteen years earlier, he had told a Conference on Kibbutzim and Communes organized by the International Communal Studies Association that the kibbutz, with its cooperative democratic structure, was the ideal framework for organizing work in the technological age. Even then, in 1985, the kibbutzim were starting to run their factories like capitalist concerns, with increasingly authoritative managers, and Melman urged them to preserve their cooperative decision making, which he insisted was more appropriate to the modern era.

Although developments in the kibbutzim have, for the most part, been in the opposite direction from that proposed by Melman at the earlier conference, he and others now insisted that even those kibbutzim, which have made radical changes, are still worthwhile cooperative enterprises. In their view, the fact that a measure of inequality has been introduced in many kibbutzim is irrelevant. The kibbutzim are still democratic; they still own their enterprises; the members still live together and help each other. These are the essential features that they applaud.

"What's the big deal about the changes?" demanded one participant. "We are used to much more inequality."

The "big deal" is in the way of thinking, suggests Shlomo Getz, a Haifa University researcher and a member of Kibbutz Gadot in Galilee. The terminology used by the kibbutz reformers is straight out of the neoconservative vocabulary. "Privatization" is a case in point. It has already been explained that privatization on the kibbutz simply means transferring items from specific budgets to a general cash allowance. Although there is no sale of public assets to private owners, Getz sees great significance in the use of the word. It reflects the same social and economic philosophy as "reward for effort" and the "responsibility of the member for earning his living," which (as we have seen) are also popular with the proponents of reform. No less significant is the open talk of "parasites," "mediocrity," and "excellence," terms that kibbutzniks were ashamed to use in the past.

Once money becomes a measurement, everyone starts thinking differently, affirms Getz. He admits that he has become acutely conscious of how much his own research projects earn for his kibbutz. Once a member's work is "evaluated"—and this calculation has been carried out in more than 40 percent of kibbutzim—equality becomes increasingly problematic. Before members knew what they were "earning," they did not think so much about the fact that everyone in the kibbutz got the same. Today, they know what they are "losing."

One of the participants at the Communal Trend conference at Yavne said plainly that it had to be recognized that some kibbutzim would stop being kibbutzim.

"Our job is with the waverers," he asserted. "I am happy to say that all three of my sons have remained at my kibbutz, but I must admit that they do not share my ideals."

Apart from the orator from Sde Eliahu, only one other representative of the young generation spoke at the conference, and very few youngsters were present. Most of the participants at Yavne were middle-aged and older. If any members of the urban kibbutzim were attending, they certainly did not make their presence felt. Yannai Shlomi came all the way from Samar in the Arava, feeling that the distinctive voice of his kibbutz should be heard at the gathering, but in the end he did not ask for the floor.

"They weren't speaking my language," he said later. "I will be very happy if something positive emerges from the Communal Trend. There is a need for new ideas that will preserve our way of life, but I didn't hear anything there relevant to our problems."

It has to be said that the founding conference of the Communal Trend did not project the conviction of a genuine effort to stem the tide of change. It seemed much more like the fulfillment of an ideological obligation, the paying of lip service to a belief in the kibbutz.

And that, sadly, is the bottom line: most kibbutz members no longer believe in their traditional way of life. Even in the case of Hatzerim, a convinced young communard like Ossie Elnatan preferred the tiny urban commune of Tamuz because she sensed a lack of ideological conviction at that enormously successful kibbutz. Although her feeling that Hatzerim will not survive past the next generation can be dismissed as one person's impression, Amir Helman of the Ruppin College, an astute observer of the kibbutz scene, has the same feeling, pointing out that Hatzerim is currently still being run by its founding generation.

"They are my age, but they are equivalent to my father's generation, which founded Kibbutz Afikim in the 1930s," he explains. "My father was prepared to work without personal incentives. I needed the motivation of interesting work. My children quite simply don't see why they should support others."

As we have seen, the generation gap was evident at every kibbutz in our sample. One recalls the opinion of a Givat Brenner youngster that "the kibbutz is suitable for much less than 3 percent of the population." It was not only at Givat Brenner, though, that most of the younger interviewees expressed reservations about kibbutz values. Even at Degania, Maagan Michael, and Kfar Ruppin, where the kibbutz system has proved itself economically, many of the younger generation voiced their doubts. There is a strong resistance to any "ideology." More than once I heard it described as "bullshit," the word angrily enunciated in English.

So what is the face of the future kibbutz—or, rather, what are the faces? Although, as has been stated more than once, each of the 267 kibbutzim is different, the faces are largely represented by the ten kibbutzim that have been described in this book.

Capitalist Kfar Ruppin is one face, probably combined with the Hasolelim model to a greater or lesser degree. Logic suggests that in time differentials will increase rather than remain static. This represents a clear change in the basic ethic of the kibbutz, even if for the time being the lifestyle remains much the same. Neither Kfar Ruppin nor Hasolelim can be defined as a kibbutz as the term has been understood until now. Ein Tzurim is another face: surely a number of religious communities will remain, striving for a Jewish religious way of life. These communities will no doubt be admirable, with a strong sense of mutual responsibility among members, but they also will not be kibbutzim.

The Communal Trend is certainly a third face. Hatzerim, Maagan Michael, and a few dozen like them—estimates vary between thirty and fifty—will continue to be traditional kibbutzim for at least one more generation. Most of them will probably adopt some sort of attribution of assets like that of Maagan Michael, which may permit them to remain kibbutzim a few years longer. Ultimately, though, the fact that only a small minority of the latest generations, even in those kibbutzim, still express a belief in the collective way of life must surely cast doubt on their survival as communal societies for any length of time.

Of the ten kibbutzim depicted, Givat Brenner, with its turmoil, problems, uncertainties, and dissatisfactions, is the most representative. It can be compared to a huge, magnificent, wounded animal, maybe not actually bellowing in pain but clearly asking to be put out of its agony. Its paid manager, who openly proclaims that the traditional kibbutz methods are irrelevant to the modern world, is doing just that, as are more than a dozen consultants in scores of kibbutzim all over Israel.

It is likely then that the majority of Israel's kibbutzim will swiftly evolve into communities, with certain enterprises commonly owned, with a measure of cooperation and mutual assistance, with some Jewish festivals celebrated together, and with an egalitarian tradition that will diminish year by year. The rate at which this happens depends very much on how they manage to cope with their economic situations. The richer communities could maintain cooperative forms longer than the poorer, but even that is not certain. Some of the more successful kibbutzim may resolve to act from a position of relative strength and speed up the process of change while conditions give them freedom of maneuver. The building of nonkibbutz neighborhoods, which will help several kibbutzim economically, is likely to accelerate the "normalization" process, as the boundaries between kibbutz and neighborhood become blurred. Some kibbutzim situated close to large towns will probably become wealthy by building and selling apartments; these are even less likely to remain kibbutzim.

Samar, with its unique blend of obstinate idealism and permissiveness, may not survive very long; others like it will from time to time sprout in Galilee and the Negev Desert. The same can be said of Tamuz and other urban experiments, but Samar and Tamuz are communes of the sort that can be found in any Western country: communities of idealists who reject the ambition and materialism of the majority.

The Israeli kibbutz was something much bigger than that. At its peak in the late 1980s, it was a movement of 270 relatively uniform communal settlements, with a population of some 130,000, based on equality, common ownership, and cooperation. Economically powerful, politically influential, socially self-assured, the kibbutz movement proved that egalitarian communism can work on a large scale over a considerable period of time. It never embraced more than 7 percent of the population—and for most of its existence it was less than half that—but it could lay a legitimate claim to being a trailblazer, a social blueprint, and an educational force. These claims are no longer valid. The

Figure 13.1.   Members of Ein Dor in the 1970s watching a soccer match on the sole kibbutz TV set.

Source: (Yehoshua Zamir)

once-powerful kibbutz federations have become irrelevant, and their recent decision to merge has produced a giant yawn.

In many ways, the kibbutz has simply been left behind. So many of its values have become out-of-date. Working on the land and redeeming the soil have little meaning when mechanization has reduced the number of farmers required in any modern society to a tiny percentage. The idea of reforging a Jewish working class is meaningless in an era where fewer people are needed in basic production and increasing numbers are moving into the information, leisure, and service occupations. In this context, what is one to make of the "inverted pyramid" decried by socialist-Zionist thinker Ber Borochov, who said that too few Jews were workers and too many intellectuals? Were he alive today, Borochov would have to admit that this inverted pyramid is the good fortune of the State of Israel, which is primarily successful as a center of high tech. The values of equality and cooperation are eternal, but they have always needed an extra ingredient, a "glue" to hold them together. In the early communes it was religion; in the case of the kibbutzim it was pioneering and Zionism; today both these ingredients are becoming increasingly rare.

The changes in the kibbutzim reflect the changes in Israeli society. The idealistic, nation-building era when kibbutzim and *moshavim* struggled to earn money to buy land, which they then proceeded to donate to the nation, are long past. Modern Israeli society is much more materialistic and much less idealistic. Even those idealists who remain emphasize the importance of personal fulfillment rather than communal endeavor. Deprived of its sympathetic "sea" of a national pioneering, egalitarian, and cooperative ethos, the kibbutz "fish" cannot survive.

Nor can developments in the world at large be discounted. The kibbutz had its heyday in the 1930s and 1940s, when all over the world idealists were prepared to sacrifice themselves for a "cause." Many a young Jewish intellectual agonized in 1938 about whether to join a kibbutz in Palestine, to go to the Soviet Union, or to enlist in the International Brigade in Spain. The world has changed since then. The collapse of communism and the limitations of the welfare state have also had their effect. If the Israeli environment is no longer "kibbutz-friendly," this is at least partly a reflection of the world environment.

It could be argued that the kibbutz has, as in the past, simply adapted itself to this new environment and reinvented itself in a new format. This is only correct up to a point: the kibbutz is indeed adapting itself to modern reality, but it is doing so by becoming something else. This does not invalidate the tremendous historical achievement of the kibbutz, nor does it negate the choices that the kibbutzim are currently in the process of making, but it does a disservice to the greatness of the kibbutz to fudge the picture. The kibbutzim will continue to exist as settlements; they will still contribute to Israel out of all proportion to their size; they will not be kibbutzim.

Whether this conclusion proves correct or not, this portrait of a moment in time, depicting Israel's kibbutzim as they lose their utopian innocence, is surely instructive for all of us. Along with their other contributions, the kibbutzim have been superlative human laboratories, marvelous environments for the study of individuals and their behavior. Ultimately, then, this has been a book about people: their strengths and weakness, their idealism and ambition, their altruism and selfishness, their honesty and duplicity. The kibbutz saga may be ending; the saga of humankind goes on.

GLOSSARY

aliya	Immigration (or wave of immigration) to Palestine/Israel.
aliya bet	Illegal immigration to Palestine from Nazi-controlled Europe.
asefa	General meeting of kibbutz members.
Gordonia	European Zionist movement inspired by A. D. Gordon of Degania.
Hagana	Prestate Jewish defense organization, which formed basis of the Israel Defense Forces.
Hashomer	Jewish guarding organization of 1909–1920, organized in communes.
Hashomer Hatzair	Left-wing Zionist youth movement of Kibbutz Artzi.
Hever Hakvutzot	Federation of small communes.
Histadrut	Labor federation that served as a union provided social and health services, and owned enterprises of its own; part of the Israeli state-on-the-way.
ICA, later **PICA**	Jewish Colonization Association founded in 1891 by Barons Hirsh and Rothschild to look after Jewish villages in Palestine.
IDF	Israel Defense Forces, Israeli army, formed from the Hagana.
Ihud Hakibbutzim Vehakvutzot (the Ihud)	Federation of small communes and those kibbutzim that split from Kibbutz Meuhad.
Jewish Agency for Palestine	Executive arm of the Zionist Organization.
Jewish Agency Settlement Department	Replaced Zionist Settlement Office (see later entry).
kibbutz (plural kibbutzim)	Communal settlement.

Kibbutz Artzi   Left-wing federation of kibbutzim.

Kibbutz Dati   Federation of religious kibbutzim.

Kibbutz Meuhad   Federation of large kibbutzim.

Kupat Holim   Health fund established by the Histadrat.
  Clallit

kvutza **(plural**   Small commune that preceded the kibbutz.
  kvutzot)

Labor Battalion   Mobile commune of laborers in the 1920s.
(Gedud Avoda)

metapelet   Kibbutz child care worker.

metapelet   Overdependence on the community.
  complex

moshav   Cooperative farming village,
                           more individualistic than a kibbutz.

Nahal   Kibbutz-based unit of the IDF.

Our Community   Influential commune that existed for a few
                           months in 1920.

Palmah   Striking force of the Hagana, based in the kibbutzim.

UKM   United Kibbutz Movement, formed by union of the Ihud
                           and Kibbutz Meuhad.

Yekke   Jews of German origin.

Youth Aliya   Organization of immigration of children from Europe.

Zionist Settlement   Established in 1908 by Dr. Arthut Ruppin to
  Office   look after pioneering settlement in Palestine.

SELECTED BIBLIOGRAPHY

Aner, Zeev, ed. *Stories of Kibbutzim* (in Hebrew). Tel Aviv: Ministry of Defense, 1998.

Avraham, Eli, ed. *The Kibbutz Lexicon* (in Hebrew). Ramat Efal: Yad Tabenkin, 1998.

Badt-Straus, Bertha. *White Fire: Life and Works of Jessie Sampter.* New York: Reconstructionist Press, 1956.

Baratz, Yosef. *A Village by the Jordan.* Tel Aviv: Ihud-Habonim Press, 1956.

Bein, Alex. *The Return to the Soil.* Jerusalem: Jewish Agency Press, 1952.

Ben-Rafael, Eliezer. *Crisis and Transformation: The Kibbutz at the Century's End.* New York: State University of New York Press, 1997.

Bettelheim, Bruno. *Children of the Dream.* New York: Macmillan, 1969.

Bondy, Ruth. *The Emissary: A Life of Enzo Sereni.* Boston: Little, Brown, 1977.

Dar, Yeheskel, ed. *Education in the Changing Kibbutz* (in Hebrew). Jerusalem: Magnes, 1998.

Dayan, Shmuel. *Twenty-Five Years of Degania* (in Hebrew). Tel Aviv: Am Oved, 1935.

Fishman, Aryei, ed. *The Religious Kibbutz Movement.* Jerusalem: Jewish Agency Press, 1957.

Gorni, Yosef, Yaacov Oved, and Idit Paz, eds. *Communal Life.* New Brunswick, N.J.: Transaction Press, 1987.

Greenberg, Harold. *Israeli Social Problems.* Ramat Gan: Dekel Academic Press, 1979.

Harel, Yehuda. *The New Kibbutz* (in Hebrew). Tel Aviv: Keter, 1993.

Keren, Zvi. *Oasis in the Desert* (in Hebrew). Hatzerim: Kibbutz Hatzerim Press, 1975.

Kurland, Samuel. *Cooperative Palestine.* New York: Herzl Press, 1947.

Leichman, David, and Idit Paz, eds. *Kibbutz: An Alternative Lifestyle.* Ramat Efal: Yad Tabenkin, 1994

Leshem, Nurit. *The Song of the Lawn* (in Hebrew). Ramat Efal: Yad Tabenkin, 1991.

Lieblich, Amia. *Kibbutz Makom.* New York: Pantheon Books, 1981.

Maron, Stanley. *Kibbutz in a Market Society.* Ramat Efal: Yad Tabenkin, 1993.

Near, Henry. *The Kibbutz Movement: A History,* vol. 1. Oxford: Oxford University Press, 1992.

Near, Henry. *The Kibbutz Movement: A History,* vol. 2. Oxford: Oxford University Press, 1997.

Ney, George. *To the End of the Process* (in Hebrew). Tel Aviv: Eden, 1998.

Oved, Yaacov. *Two Hundred Years of American Communes.* New Brunswick, N.J.: Transaction Press, 1988.

————. *Distant Brothers: Bruderhoff and the Kibbutz.* Ramat Efal: Yad Tabenkin, 1993.

Pavin, Avraham. *The Kibbutz Movement: Facts and Figures,* 4th ed. (in Hebrew). Ramat Efal: Yad Tabenkin, 1999.

Regev, Eliahu. *The Kibbutz Is Dead, Long Live the Kibbutz* (in Hebrew). Baram: Kibbutz Baram Press, 1996.

Rosner, Menahem, and Shlomo Getz. *The Kibbutz in the Era of Change* (in Hebrew). Haifa: Kibbutz Hamenhad Press, 1996.

Sabar, Naama. *Kibbutz L.A.* (in Hebrew). Tel Aviv: Am Oved, 1996.

Spiro, Melford E. *Children of the Kibbutz.* Cambridge, Mass.: Harvard University Press, 1975.

Tiger, Lionel, and Joseph Shepher. *Women in the Kibbutz.* New York: Harcourt Brace Jovanovich, 1975.

Yambura, Barbara S. *A Change and a Parting: My Story of Amana.* Ames: University of Iowa Press, 1960.

Zamir, Aviva. *Mothers and Daughters.* Cambridge, Mass.: Harvard Institute for Kibbutz Studies, 1991.

In addition to these works, I made extensive use of numerous kibbutz journals and publications in Hebrew, along with the admirable journal *Kibbutz Trends* (formerly *Kibbutz Studies*), published in English by Yad Tabenkin.

INDEX

absorption of new members, 53, 55, 78, 80, 136, 197

agriculture, farming: crisis of, 121–22, 146–56, 212; success of kibbutz in, 2, 5, 6, 24, 28, 123–24, 191, 205, 215, 265–69; as a value, 27, 135, 174; women working in, 24–26, 269–70 (*see also* women)

allocation (attribution) of assets, 11, 152, 156, 193, 196–200, 203–8, 209, 216–21, 228, 236–37, 280

allowances, personal, 127, 251, 262; differentials in, 73, 102, 156, 197, 201, 204, 216–18, 222, 228–29, 235–36, 276; privatization of, 7, 8, 52, 129–30, 221, 223, 234, 278; salaries, 11, 76, 82–84, 90, 94–96, 104–5, 128

anarchism, 260, 263, 272–73

Arabs: Arab Revolt, 55–56, 108; Arab-Jewish confrontation, 27, 29–30, 46, 50, 52, 57–58, 90, 121, 194–95, 214–15, 230–33, 239; relations with kibbutzim, 4–5, 17, 19–20, 22, 25, 49, 109

Balas, David, 143–44, 160

Bank Hapoalim (Workers' Bank), 114, 144, 146, 148

Baratz, Miriam, 20–21, 24–26, 32–34, 134, 269

Baratz, Yosef, 20–21, 25, 32–34, 213

Beit Alpha, kibbutz, 45, 161, 162, 165–66

Beit Midrash, 242, 254–55

Beit Oren Affair, 8–9, 115

Ben-Gurion, David, 5, 48, 58–59, 122, 124, 149

Bettleheim, Bruno, 166

boards of directors for kibbutz concerns, 10–11, 70–72, 97, 115, 125–26, 128, 155, 287

Borochov, Ber, 164–65, 282

bourgeois: family, 7, 162–63; values, 157

Bussel, Yosef, 20–21, 23, 25–26, 28, 31–32, 37, 39, 157–58, 171–72

capitalism, free market: conversion to, 208, 209–10, 216–21, 272, 280; influence on the kibbutz, 10, 61, 70, 137, 159–60, 183, 278

changes in kibbutz structure, values, way of life, 7–8, 10–11, 31–33, 36–37, 41, 68, 70–72, 74–76, 85–86, 107, 114, 153, 156, 171, 186, 188, 202, 207–8, 226–28, changes in kibbutz structure, values, way of life (*continued*) 237–38, 273, 283; opposition to, 35, 68, 73, 74, 76, 80, 101–3, 138, 183, 201, 275–77, 279; process of, 82–84, 89–90, 91–101, 103–5, 151–52, 160–61, 191–93, 196–99, 209–10, 216–23, 229–30, 243–44; Team for Change, 94, 99, 128–30, 135, 203, 234–36

children: children's houses, communal sleeping, 2, 7, 54, 64, 77, 103, 131–32, 152, 155, 163, 165–71, 203–4, 221, 225, 228; education and schools, 9–10, 11, 37, 53–54, 76–77, 79–82, 91, 95–96, 98, 132, 136, 157–58, 159–88, 208, 222–23, 225–26, 228, 240, 277; education to excellence, 37, 164, 221, 279; education to mediocrity, 37, 81, 132, 167, 175, 223, 228, 279; *metapelet* complex, 79, 187, 273; Mossad Hinuchi, 163–66, 173–78; "new human being," 1, 102, 157, 167, 174, 176, 187, 222, 224–25; Society of Children, 7, 53–54, 77, 80, 132, 163–66, 173–74, 222, 225, 227, 255

Communal Trend movement, 275–77, 279–80

communes: early, in Palestine, 19–20, 22, 44, 56; in United States and Europe, 3, 61, 179, 209–10, 229–30, 277, 281–82; urban, 245–57

Communism, 5, 45, 58–59, 138, 283

community: kibbutz, 105; separation of business from, 10, 82–83, 96–97, 125–26, 129, 228, 236–37; settlement, 113–14

cooperative: *moshav,* 5, 28–30, 60, 145–47, 149, 150; Nir Shitufi, 148–49, 198–99; Yam Carmel (Maagan Michael), 193, 197–200, 206, 208

Dar, Yehezkel, 35–37, 164, 171–72

defense role of the kibbutz, 4, 19, 30–31, 46, 50, 59, 200, 214–15, 231–33; Hagana defense force, 56–57, 58, 193–95; Hashomer guards, 22, 56; Nahal, 178, 180–81; Palmah, 56, 180; service in army combat units by kibbutz children, 10, 160, 277

Degania, kibbutz, 9, 11, 15–41, 44, 45, 46, 47, 53–54, 73, 99, 109, 119, 134, 155, 157, 161, 162, 164, 211, 213, 246, 269, 280

democracy in the kibbutz: kibbutz council, 51, 68, 133–34; kibbutz general meeting, 2, 26, 44, 49, 50, 51, 52, 54, 56, 59, 61, 68, 70, 72, 81, 82–83, 84, 85, 90–91, 94–95, 97, 107, 114, 122–23, 131, 133–34, 135, 155, 159, 168, 185, 200, 202, 204, 205, 206, 212, 218–19, 225, 236, 247–48, 249, 250, 255, 264–65, 269, 270, 275; other frameworks, 133–34, 135, 205

dining hall: cost of building and maintaining, 145–46, 152, 155; paying for meals in, 8, 11, 34, 37, 91, 97, 107, 196, 223; as a symbol of kibbutz life, 8, 155, 237. *See also* privatization

egalitarianism: equality, 1, 4, 7–9, 24, 31, 32–33, 36, 38, 44, 61, 84, 96, 102, 104, 107, 119–20, 127–28, 129, 137, 138, 157–58, 159–60, 172, 177, 183, 187, 197–98, 217–18, 220–21, 225,

228, 236, 248, 262, 277, 279, 281–82; "equality to the kibbutz fence," 64; inequality, 6, 7, 10–11, 52, 73, 75, 77, 80, 82–84, 97, 99, 117, 129, 228; sexual equality and inequality (*see* women)

Ein Harod, kibbutz, 47–48, 50, 54, 56, 250

Ein Tzurim, kibbutz, 229–44, 280

Etzion Bloc, 231–33, 239

family: improved status of in the kibbutz, 77, 81, 82–83, 132, 204, 205, 217, 221; the kvutza as, 16, 21, 30, 43, 51, 267; liberation from bourgeois, 7, 162–71

foreign travel, influence on kibbutz children, 6, 65, 180–84, 224

generations: difference in values between, 7–8, 35–36, 53, 79, 157, 159, 164, 172, 187, 203, 222, 237, 243, 277, 279–80, 281; loss of young generation, 6, 36, 65, 76–79, 81, 127, 180–84, 216, 224, 227; generation of sacrifice, 167–71

German reparations, influence on kibbutz, 6, 61–62

Givat Brenner, kibbutz, 43–87, 99, 110, 113, 121, 136, 150, 153, 155, 160–62, 280–81

Gordon, Aharon David, 27, 29, 44, 56, 109, 164–65

Halperin, Ariel, 147–51, 153–57, 228

Harel, Yehuda, 10–11, 153, 228

Hashomer Hatzair youth movement, 44–47, 160–64, 174, 177. *See also* Zionism, youth movement

Hasolelim, kibbutz, 89–105, 113, 153, 173, 217, 228, 280

Hatzerim, kibbutz, 66, 119–39, 143, 151–52, 181, 191, 196, 210, 220, 253–54, 262, 275, 279–80

Helman, Amir, 154–56, 187, 280

hired (outside) workers, 5, 24, 56, 60–61, 124, 153–54, 196, 217, 266

Histadrut labor federation, 6, 46, 48, 49, 52, 55, 144, 148–49, 198

immigrants: absorption of European, North and South American, 17–19, 26, 29–30, 44–46, 49–50, 53, 58, 90, 108–9, 133, 136–37, 176–78, 210–14, 223, 277; failure to attract Middle Eastern, 5, 60–61, 135, 172–73

individual: lack of autonomy of, 1, 10, 38, 51–52, 77, 90, 93, 95–96, 181–84, 187, 243; responsibility of, 3, 31, 73, 95, 151–54, 221–23, 237; rights of, 32, 36, 96, 103, 164, 175–76, 200–203, 207, 246–50, 262–63, 272

inflation, effect on the kibbutz, 7–8, 144–47, 151

interest rates, effect on kibbutz debts, 8, 145, 151

Israel, State of: contribution of kibbutz to, 3–4, 5, 6, 30–31, 58, 60, 120, 133, 138, 152, 160, 178, 180–81, 200, 223, 231–33, 246, 253–56, 277–78, 281–82; effect of Israeli society on the kibbutz, 3–4, 8, 32, 37, 62, 85–86, 149, 159, 172, 183, 186–88, 230, 282–83; support for kibbutzim, 148–50, 154–55, 172

Jewish Agency settlement department, 122, 146, 148–49, 154–56

Jewish festivals, 3, 25, 31, 63, 99, 248, 251, 263, 267, 281

Jewish National Fund (JNF), 28, 90, 149–50, 231

Kfar Ruppin, kibbutz, 209–28, 237, 272, 280
kibbutz: debt, 8–9, 65–67, 92, 113, 117, 138, 143–54, 197; factories, 6, 16, 37, 41, 44, 47, 54, 56, 66, 71–72, 83, 91, 110–12, 119–20, 123–27, 129–32, 137, 152, 159–60, 191, 193–96, 215, 233, 236–37, 266; Hever Hakvutzot movement, 47, 58, 211–13; Ihud Hakibbutzim Vehakvutzot (the Ihud), 59, 143; Kibbutz Arrangement, 66, 114, 147–51, 153; Kibbutz Artzi movement, 45, 47, 59, 145, 149, 160–70, 172, 173–78, 203, 230, 244, 259–64, 275; Kibbutz Dati movement, 229–44, 275; Kibbutz Meuhad movement, 5–6, 47–49, 54–56, 59, 138, 143; neighborhood, 69, 72, 73, 79, 80, 85, 99–100, 113–14, 117, 173, 228, 233–34, 243; "New Kibbutz," 10–11, 125, 153, 199, 228; UKM Fund, 143–45, 149; United Kibbutz Movement (UKM), 9, 91, 138, 143–45, 149, 160–61, 200, 229–30, 236, 244, 257, 275; values, communal, 10–11, 21, 34, 39, 62, 83–84, 89, 99–102, 127–28, 137–39, 157–58, 160–67, 171–78, 180, 182–84, 187–88, 205, 208, 221, 223, 229–30, 237, 275–77, 279–80, 282–83

Labor Battalion (Gedud Avoda), 44, 46–47, 56, 249
Leshem, Nurit, 167–71
Likud political party, 144, 147–49

Los Angeles, kibbutz children living in, 10, 81, 181–84

Maagan Michael, kibbutz, 66, 143, 170, 191–208, 210, 220, 228, 275, 280
Marxism. *See* Communism

Nahalal, *moshav,* 28–29
Neve Yam, kibbutz, 107–17, 191, 195
.
Our Community, Bittania, 44–46, 47, 52, 161, 166
outside society. *See* Israel, State of, effect of Israeli society on the kibbutz
outside workers. *See* hired workers
Oz, Israel, 151–52, 155

pension plans, 11, 83, 96–97, 127, 156, 202, 234, 237, 272, 276
pensioners. *See* veterans
PICA, 109, 195
private property, 1, 11, 52, 73, 127, 229, 234, 237
privatization: of allowances, 7–8, 33, 52, 63–64, 102, 129–30, 156, 234, 236; of dining hall, 37, 91, 196, 223; as a value, 278–79

quality of life, 6, 17, 69, 89, 93, 116, 153, 177, 203, 207–8, 246, 277

Ravid, Shimon, 146–47, 148, 152–53; Ravid Plan, 147
religion, 172, 229–44, 253–55, 275, 282
religious kibbutzim. *See* kibbutz, Kibbutz Dati movement
Rothschild, Baron Edmond, 18–19, 109, 195, 230
Ruppin, Arthur, 19–20, 23, 212;

Ruppin College of Kibbutz Movement, 78, 82, 100, 104, 116, 129, 154–55, 159, 254, 265, 280

Sabar, Naama, 181–82
Samar, kibbutz, 259–73, 279, 281
Sampter, Jessie, 54–55
Sereni, Ada, 52
Sereni, Enzo, 48–49, 51–53, 55, 56–57, 59, 61, 86, 162
sexism, sexual equality. *See* women
shares, 11, 127, 208, 209–10, 216–20
Shepher, Joseph, 185–86
Spiro, Melford E., 166–67
split in kibbutz movement, 5–6, 58–60, 62–63, 110, 138, 210–14
swimming pool, 2, 5, 17, 43, 62, 119, 127, 145, 155, 233, 242
synagogue, 242–43

Tamuz, kibbutz, 245–57, 262, 264, 268, 273, 279, 281
technology, 2, 41, 93, 120, 124, 152, 221, 282
Thai workers, 116, 241, 266
Tiger, Lionel, 185–86
Trumpeldor, Yosef, 26, 46–47, 54

Umm Juni, 17, 19–22, 31, 39, 120

utopia, 1, 84, 165, 185, 220, 259, 273, 283

veterans, 9, 34, 36, 43, 60, 64–65, 67–68, 85–86, 95–97, 101–2, 110, 115–16, 137–38, 174, 193, 197–98, 217–18, 220, 222, 234, 236–37
volunteers from abroad, 116, 178–81, 261, 268

War of Independence, 30–31, 58, 62, 90, 121
women: deprivation of, 163–71; lack of equality, 24–25, 133–35, 184–86, 201, 268–70

Yadlin, Aharon, 138, 143–44, 151–52, 187

Zamir, Aviva, 186, 199–201
Zamir, Eli, 143–44, 199–201
Zionism, 4, 10, 17–19, 29–30, 48, 50, 120–21, 149–52, 155, 162, 230, 238–44, 282; Zionist Settlement Office, 19–20, 23, 47–48, 109; youth movement, 5, 44–45, 47, 100, 108–9, 133, 136–37, 161–65, 177, 180–81, 193, 212–13

ABOUT THE AUTHOR

Born in London in 1935, Daniel Gavron immigrated to Israel in 1961, where he became a member of Kibbutz Amiad in Galilee. After a year there, he and his family lived for another year on a *moshav shitufi* (cooperative village) before joining the first group of citizens founding the new town of Arad in the Judaean desert overlooking the Dead Sea.

After moving to Jerusalem in 1971, Gavron worked as a reporter for Israel Radio, becoming head of English News. Subsequently he joined the *Jerusalem Post*, where he was a senior feature writer. He has written pieces for the *New York Times*, the *Wall Street Journal*, *Commentary*, *National Jewish Monthly*, and *Ariel*. His broadcasts have been heard on the BBC, CBC, National Public Radio, Radio Telefis Eirrean, and others.

The founding editor of *Palestine-Israel Journal*, Gavron also is the author of *The End of Days*, *Walking Through Israel*, *Israel After Begin*, *Peace Pays*, and *Saul Adler, a Biography*. Married with three grown children, he lives near Jerusalem with his wife of forty-two years and his dog.